Essays in Southern African Labour History

Essays in
Southern African
Labour History

Edited by Eddie Webster

RAVAN PRESS
Johannesburg

Published by Ravan Press (Pty) Ltd.
409–416 Dunwell, 35 Jorissen Street
Braamfontein, Johannesburg 2001, South Africa
© Copyright South African Labour Bulletin 1978
First Impression September 1978
Second Impression February 1981
Third Impression February 1983
Cover Design: Jackie Bosman
ISBN 0 86975 085 2
Printed by Creda Press, Cape Town

Acknowledgements: The contributors and the *SALB,* in
association with whom this book is published.

List of Contributors

Dr. Philip Bonner is a senior lecturer in the Department of History at the University of the Witwatersrand.

Rob Davies has recently completed his doctorate at the University of Sussex and is now engaged in research.

Linda Ensor is a research officer at the South African Institute of Race Relations.

Jeff Lever is a lecturer in the Department of Sociology at the University of Stellenbosch.

David Lewis is a lecturer in the School of Economics and the Department of Sociology at the University of Cape Town.

Jon Lewis is a post-graduate student at the University of Cambridge.

John Mawbey is managing editor of the *South African Labour Bulletin*.

Sean Moroney is a research officer at the South African Institute of Race Relations.

Dan O'Meara is a lecturer in the Department of History at the University of Dar es Salaam in Tanzania.

Dr Ian Phimister is a lecturer in the Department of Economic History at the University of Cape Town.

Mark Stein is a post-graduate student at the University of Warwick.

Peter Warwick works for an international publishing firm in England.

Eddie Webster is a senior lecturer in the Department of Sociology at the University of the Witwatersrand.

CONTENTS

SECTION 3

SECTION 4

SECTION 5

LABOUR HISTORY IN SOUTHERN AFRICA

'Labour history,' E. J. Hobsbawm has written, 'is today flourishing in most countries as never before.' South Africa is no exception. In recent years three academic conferences (Oxford in 1974, and the University of the Witwatersrand in 1976 and 1978) have been held on Labour History. Three major books on the history of labour in Southern Africa have been published (Simons and Simons, Johnstone, and van Onselen).[1] In addition at least three seminar collections which include papers on labour history have been published at the University of the Witwatersrand alone (ed. Bonner, ed. Adler and ed. Kallaway.)[2] We hope that the present collection, consisting of articles from the South African Labour Bulletin, will give a further impetus to the debate. All the contributors focus exclusively on labour history, and the five thematic sections locate the main areas of the debate.

While books on the history of labour are not new in South Africa, few have emanated from the universities.[3] What Hobsbawm wrote of Britain is therefore true of South Africa. 'The bulk of the labour historians, whether or not they were or eventually became academics, came from within, from the close proximity of, the labour movements themselves. Initially a great many of them were not academics at all, even when their scholarship and erudition were impeccable, the Webbs in Britain, Bernstein and Meyer in West Germany, Deutsch in Austria, Dolleans in France.'[4] The first attempt to write the history of labour in South Africa was by Eddie Roux, a man active in the labour movement and the communist party in his early years. In fact, the early chapters of the book were written for 'night schools' serving the emerging African trade union movement. Roux was later to leave the labour movement and the communist party to resume his work as a university botanist[5]. Similarly the most comprehensive history of labour to date is that of Ray and Jack Simons, both active in the communist party and the labour movement in the western Cape, although Jack Simons retained his university post throughout his period of involvement[6].

1

Yet the bulk of historical work on the history of labour has come, till recently, 'from within the movement', and thus in the main from outside the universities. Here are some of the better known books: Bill Andrews, *Class Struggles in South Africa* (1941), R. K. Cope, *Comrade Bill* (1943), I. Walker and E. Weinbren, *Two Thousand Casualties* (1961), B. J. Meyer, *Die Stryd van die Afrikaner Werker* (1944), L. Naude, *Dr R. Hertzog, Die Nasionale Party en die Mynwerkers* (1944), E. S. Sachs, *The Garment Workers' Action* (1952), E. Roux, *S. P. Bunting* (1943), Brian Bunting, *Moses Kotane* (1973) and Clements Kadalie, *My Life in the I.C.U.* (1969). It is possible to identify two general characteristics of this type of labour history. In the first place it tends to identify the 'working classes' with the 'labour movement', or even with a specific organization, party and ideology. In the second place, labour history from within tends to be a little antiquarian and preoccupied with giving labour movements the importance which nobody else seems to accord them.

The growing involvement of academics in labour history has corrected some of the biases of traditional labour history. The location of labour historians firmly inside the university has shifted the exclusive focus on formal institutions to informal activities and resistance — an increasing preoccupation with the rank and file as well as with the leaders, the unorganized as well as the organized. Here van Onselen's *Chibaro* stands out: a pioneering attempt to create historically the social world of the compound in the early years of the mining industry in Southern Rhodesia. This has led to a systematic focus on when and under what conditions a labour supply was created, especially since many of the crucial labour institutions date back to the earlier stages of capitalist development. The role of the reserves in limiting the cost of reproduction of labour power for the mining industry, the confinement of African mine workers to the quasi-military institutions of the compound, the emergence of the exploitation colour bar as distinct from the job colour bar, and, of course, the pass laws, predate the emergence of trade unions.

Two forces can be identified as crucial in expanding labour history in South Africa. In the first place there is the entry into the debate in the 1960s and 1970s of a generation of students who were influenced by a systematic critique of the dominant paradigm of liberalism with its emphasis on race rather than on class. Clearly Johnstone's work is important in any intellectual history of the debate. Johnstone rightly rejects as tautological the notion that racism can be explained by racism. He suggests that the answer to the problem of racial dis-

2

crimination is to be found in the structural conditions of South Africa's economy. His book is concerned with establishing that the causes of colour bars on the mines lie in the particular structural conditions of the gold mining industry. He goes on to argue that if class colour bars emerge from the structural demands of the gold mining industry, structural demands which Johnstone calls 'exploitation colour bars', then the 'blame' for racism cannot be laid at the door of white workers. In the final analysis it must be laid at the door of those who create the exploitation colour bars in the interests and demands of their industry, that is the gold mine owners and managers. In the second place the re-emergence of working class action within South Africa in the 1970s coupled with the establishment of 'open African trade unions' has led to a growing need to understand the systematic suppression of independent working class organization and action in South Africa. The *S.A.L.B.* began publication in May 1974 with this as one of its aims. The establishment of the Bulletin was, therefore, both a product of and a service to this renewed worker action of the 1970s.

We conclude on a note of caution. Labour history should never focus exclusively on the social relations generated at the work place or merely cover the social history of the working class. The history of labour, writes Hobsbawm, is part of the history of society. 'Class relationships, whatever the class, are relationships *between* classes or strata, which cannot adequately be described or analysed in isolation, or in terms only of internal divisions or stratification. This implies that underlying a history of labour is a model of what societies are and how they work.'[7]

FOOTNOTES

1. See R. E. Simons and H. J. Simons, *Class and Colour in South Africa;* F. R. Johnstone, *Class, Race and Gold;* C. van Onselen, *Chibaro.*
2. P. L. Bonner, *Working Papers in Southern African Studies;* T. Adler, *Perspectives on South Africa,* P. Kallaway, *Contemporary Southern African Studies,* Vol. I and Vol. II.
3. There are two crucial exceptions, both written in the 1940s, to this generalization. They are: C. W. De Kiewiet, *A History of South Africa: Social and Economic* (London 1941) and S. T. van der Horst, *Native Labour in South Africa* (Cape Town, 1942). However they are both over three decades old and neither deals with labour organization. Nevertheless de Kiewiet remains the best introductory account of the history of capitalist development in South Africa and adds a useful periodization to our essentially thematic account.
4. E. J. Hobsbawm, 'Labour History and Ideology', *Journal of Social History,* Vol. 7, No. 4 (1974).
5. E. Roux, *Time Longer than Rope* (University of Wisconsin Press, 1966). See L. Callinicos. *SALB,* Vol. 2, No. 2, for a review of Roux's work.
6. R. E. Simons and H. J. Simons, ibid.
7. Hobsbawm, ibid.

SECTION 1

CONTROL AND RESISTANCE
ON THE MINES

INTRODUCTION

In order for the capitalist mode of production to be dominant in any social formation you need two conditions. Firstly, you need men and women who do not own the means of production but sell their labour power to the owners of the means of production, i.e. you need a class of men and women who are dependent on wages for their survival. Secondly, the wage the worker receives for the sale of his labour-power must only be a portion of the value created by him. The problem, then, for the capitalist is how to create a class of men and women who do not own the means of production, i.e. who are forced to sell their labour-power for wages. This process of creating a labour supply is called proletarianisation, i.e. the historic process of divorcing the producer from the means of production, the transformation of peasant to worker.

The first article 'opens' the debate with a brief summary of this process of proletarianisation emphasising, in contrast to liberal historiography, the essentially coercive or extra-economic nature of this process. It is argued furthermore that the process of proletarianisation is structured by the continued existence of the pre-capitalist sector, and this sector is perpetuated to provide part of the means of reproduction of labour-power. Thus the process of proletarianisation of the indigenous population has been such that the capitalist sector '. . . feeds off the pre-capitalist sectors through the mechanism of primitive accumulation — with the contradictory results of both perpetuating and destroying at the same time.' (Meillassoux, 1971).[1]

What effect has the incomplete proletarianisation of African workers had on industrial conflict? All four of the contributors in this section are concerned to challenge the view that Africans were simply passive participants in the economy. They are concerned to argue that industrial conflict must be conceived as a continuum of resistance to exploitation, with organized strikes and trade unions at one end and 'desertion' and resistance to recruitment at the other. The absence of formal organizations to articulate worker interests should not be taken as an absence of worker consciousness and resistance. In tightly controlled compound situations resistance must be sought, as van Onselen has aptly put it, 'in the nooks and crannies of the day-to-day situation'.[2]

Furthermore the existence of a pre-capitalist mode of production leads to the emergence of a distinctive form of worker resistance, i.e. 'defensive desertion'. Moroney makes this point clear when he cites the Chairman of Rand Mines in 1907: 'The native method of striking is very simple. It must be remembered that he is not a permanent workman. He is always going home, and if he is not satisfied with the conditions of employment, he simply does not come out again. The conditions of South Africa make it perfectly possible for him to do this.'[3]

FOOTNOTES

1. C. Meillassoux, ed., *The Development of Indigenous Trade and Markets in West Africa*, (Oxford University Press, 1971).
2. 'The analyst who seeks an index of worker consciousness or an outright demonstration of African resistance should not therefore look for dramatic responses. Compound "police", spies, censorship and the sjambok do not produce an environment conducive to the development of public ideologies, organizations, meetings, petitions or strikes. In tightly controlled situations, such as the compound undoubtedly was, the patterns of resistance among black miners should in the first instance be sought in the nooks and crannies of the day-to-day situation', C. van Onselen, *Chibaro*.
3. Moroney.

BACKGROUND TO THE SUPPLY AND CONTROL OF LABOUR IN THE GOLD MINES

EDDIE WEBSTER

Author's Note: The aim of this article, written in 1974, was to summarise the literature on this theme. Since then important work has been done in two areas relevant to this article. Firstly, articles have been written on the transition to commercial agriculture and effects on labour supply. See Michael Morris, 'The Development of Capitalism in South African Agriculture', *Economy and Society*, Vol. 3, No. 4 (1974) and the work of Stanley Trapido at Oxford. Secondly our understanding of the growing supervisory nature of the white mine worker in the labour process has been developed by the work of Rob Davies. (See Author's note, Section 2, Article 1.)

The position of Black labour within the South African economy today, characterised as it is by the institutionalisation of migrant labour, low wages and lack of worker organisation, is mirrored in the development of labour patterns in the gold mining industry since its inception in 1886. Central to an understanding of the gold mines is its extremely sensitive cost structure. Profits are largely dependent on low production costs for two reasons. Firstly because the average gold content of the ore is low. Secondly, the internationally controlled price of gold prevents the mining companies from transferring any increases in working costs to the consumers. Consequently within this narrowly circumscribed cost structure, the usual area of cost minimisation has been wages. The task then for the mine-owners has been to create and contain a vast supply of cheap African labour.

How was this labour supply created and how has it been controlled? The emergence of a wage-earning class through the slow operation of *market forces* — the need to earn enough to purchase a gun, for instance — was clearly inadequate given the needs of the mining industry, and it turned to two 'extra-economic' methods for assistance: the legislative power of the state and the creation of monopolistic recruiting organisations. The central laws in this process of forced proletarianization are threefold:

1) The pass laws which controlled labour on the mines. Introduced under direct pressure from the Chamber in 1896, they stipulated 'that Natives on the Rand must be in the employ of a master and wear a metal plate or "badge" on the arm in token of such employ.' However, the Chamber remained dissatisfied with the allegedly inefficient manner in which it was administered. S. Jennings argues that 'We have a most excellent law, namely the pass law, which should enable us to obtain complete control over the Kaffirs. As at present administered, the pass law gives us no such protection . . . As the matter now stands, we import Kaffirs who sign a contract to serve us for twelve months; many leave after a couple of weeks, and it is impossible to recover them'.[1]

2) The Glen Grey Act: this introduced a labour tax which, in the words of the mine owner and Cape politician Cecil Rhodes, 'removed Natives from that life of sloth and laziness, teaching them the *dignity of labour,* and made them contribute to the prosperity of the state, and made them give some return for our wise and good government.' Lashing out at those who appealed to the missionaries for assistance in inducing Africans to take up work in the mines, the *Standard* (1895) declared '. . . mission work begins at the wrong end — by clothing, feeding and pampering an already lazy animal, and straight away removing hunger, that singular incentive which alone successfully compels a man to labour . . . it is in the direction of taxation that the ultimate solution of the labour question lies.'[2]

3) The Land Act of 1913, which froze African land ownership to a mere 13% of the total land area and so forced Africans into the overcrowded reserves. This Act had the twin effect of suppressing the emerging African peasantry, which was proving an effective counter-class to the White farmer, and creating a pool of cheap labour in the reserves.

By the 1890s, a powerful and well-organised mining capitalist class had emerged with the ownership of both the gold and diamond mines in the hands of a few groups of capitalists. This centralization of control was further consolidated by the formation of the Chamber of Mines in 1887 and two African recruiting agencies. Initially, in 1896, the Chamber formed the Rand Native Labour Association and out of this grew the present recruiting organisations: the Native Recruiting Corporation, which supplies labour from within South Africa and

10

the three ex-Protectorates, and the Witwatersrand Native Labour Association which recruits elsewhere in Africa. The Association had been formed against the background of a growing dissatisfaction among mine-owners. G. H. Stevens, acting on behalf of Rhodes and Rudd, sounded the following warning: 'At present there is no guarantee that tomorrow the Rand will not be boyless. That must be remedied in the interests of the capitalist: there should be some system under which the supply is certain and cannot fail. Such a system would have to be on a colossal scale and administered either by Government or some institution acting under its sanction. There is no use of private individuals and mere amateurs attempting to command a Native labour-supply.' (*Standard*, 21 March 1891).[3]

The Association received an undertaking from its members to abide by its decisions and not to outbid one another in recruiting for labour. The Association formed a Maximum Average wage system for the entire industry, and there was thus no need for individual mines to improve conditions or wages. By 1897, wages had fallen to R58 per year after an average wage of R78 per year in 1889. Looking back at the introduction of the Maximum Average wage system, Percy Fitzpatrick, a leading mine-owner at the time, explained as follows: 'You must understand this, that the necessity for the reduction in the rate of wages arose from the fact that there was competition among ourselves and that little by little one employer bid against another until finally the average became too high and the whole industry took it in hand and tried again to make a fresh start — that was what prompted us to form the Native Labour Association. You see, we could not pool the supply, so we pooled the demand. The employers agreed to divide the supply among themselves, that is, what they could get.' (Evidence before the Transvaal Labour Commission Feb. 1904)

The purpose of these forms of centralisation, then, was to unify the mine-owners through a monopolistic structure of control enabling the mine-owners to pursue best their aim of minimising labour costs. These measures have been labelled the 'wage colour bar' — to distinguish this colour bar from the job colour bars of the White miners. These colour bars of the mine-owners were basically threefold: *the maximum average system* (a collective agreement of the mining companies not to permit the average wages of the African workers to exceed a very low maximum rate); *the recruiting monopoly* (a buyer's monopoly over the recruitment of African labour, to prevent the competitive determination of African wage rates through a free

11

relationship between supply and demand); and *servile labour measures* (such as the closed compound system, pass laws and severe provisions against breach of contract embodied in the Master and Servants Act). Since the essential aim of these discriminatory measures was to secure the cheapness of African labour, they can be referred to as the wage colour bar which constituted the class colour bar of the mining capitalist.[4]

Much has been said about the costs of a system of migrant labour for the employer in terms of high labour turnover. It has been suggested that migrant labour is inconsistent with the notion of economic rationality — a notion which implies a system of free wage labour. Less has been said publicly in mining circles of the benefits of such a system of *institutionalised* migrant labour in ensuring a cheap, rightless, and unorganised labour force.

The benefits can be seen in two broad areas. Firstly, the existence of reserves where Africans allegedly have an alternative source of income to substitute their mine wages has provided the mine-owners with a justification for subsistence wages. It could be said then that this vast army of peasant-workers has subsidized the mining industry for nearly half a century. Secondly, oscillating migration prevents effective class mobilisation. For an effective trade union to arise, there must be a body of lifelong wage-earners, free to sell their labour, wholly dependent on wages without prospects of becoming independent producers and aware of the benefits of collective bargaining. Retaining 97% of the labour force on a yearly contract basis on the mines inhibits the workers from developing skills, both in performance and in control of their work situation, and thus inhibits the emergence of an effective class consciousness. The quasi-military institution of the compound, often structured in a way that encourages inter-ethnic strife, provides an ideal technique for the control of labour. In fact it has been suggested that this system of labour exploitation which enables an employer to control a variety of forms of legitimate violence which he may use against the worker, but which at the same time does not require that he should buy or be responsible for the worker for life as in slavery, is the most theoretically perfect system of labour exploitation yet devised![5]

Industrial Conflict

The basic source of conflict on the mines lies in the fact that what is income for the worker is a cost for the mine-owner — a cost which, we have suggested, the mines have sought to minimise. How the surplus

12

generated by the mine workers is divided between mine-owners and mine workers depends primarily on the power relationship between the two sides. This power relationship is highly unequal as the mine-owners have been able to organise themselves into powerful employer organisations and have had the concrete support of the state. Mine workers, at first White as well as African, were not similarly able to organise themselves collectively to promote their interests through the organisation of trade unions. The primary purpose of a trade union is to maintain and raise wages by limiting competition between workers (preventing undercutting), and applying organised pressure on employers. The trade union is the means whereby the workers can combine to exercise some power over their lives. Through their representations they can bargain with management. By pooling their limited individual funds they can employ full-time organisers and equip themselves with the necessary information. The ultimate weapon the worker has in collective bargaining is the right to withdraw his labour, that is to strike. However, a strike organised by a recognised trade union with pickets to discipline its members, is only one form of industrial conflict. Industrial conflict is better conceived of as a continuum with organised strikes at one end and 'desertion', refusal to be recruited and industrial sabotage at the other end. All these forms of industrial conflict have been seen on the mines.

In the early decades of the mining industry sharp industrial conflict took place between a relatively small artisan and overseer 'labour aristocracy' (20,000) of White workers and the mine-owners over the job-colour bar. In essence, White workers wanted to increase the scarcity of their skills and the mine-owners wanted to decrease this scarcity, creating a more competitive market by employing cheaper, though not necessarily less-skilled, African labour. White workers regarded themselves as a labour aristocracy from the inception of the gold-mining industry. However, the first legal job-colour bar, specifying that only Whites may blast, was passed in 1893.] *

The first White union on the mines was founded in 1892 and the first strike by Whites on the gold mines was successfully organised in 1897 to prevent the Chamber of Mines from reducing wages. In 1907, Whites struck in protest against a proposal by the mine-owners to permit African and Chinese 'indentured' workers to perform skilled work. Immigrant, largely British workers held a jealously preserved monopoly of skilled work at this time and the strike was broken by replacing the strikers with unemployed Afrikaner workers. This was a breakthrough for the emerging Afrikaner working class and within

15 years, three-quarters of the mine workers were Afrikaner.

In 1913 White miners struck (winning recognition for their trade union by the Chamber of Mines), in 1914 and again in 1922, on each occasion advancing their privileged position against the mine-owners' attempts at introducing cheaper African labour. 1922 was the high-water mark in the making of a White labour aristocracy on the mines — a bloody and protracted strike broke out on the Witwatersrand when the mine-owners tried to cut their costs by reducing the number of highly paid (White) workers and replacing some of them with Africans. The White workers resisted this attempt. This was the basic issue of the strike, which began on January 22nd and was only terminated in March after bloody clashes between workers and Smuts's army. Military planes were used to bomb White working class residential areas in Benoni and Germiston; artillery, tanks and armoured cars were brought into action in addition to ground forces employing machine guns and rifles. A Government inquiry reported the casualties as 153 killed and 687 injured, and 4 were executed.

The demands that the White workers had failed to achieve through strike action were won at the polls in the 1924 General Election, when the Smuts Government was defeated by a coalition of the Labour Party and the Afrikaner Nationalist Party under General Hertzog. The Labour Party had been formed in 1909 to promote the interests of the White worker and under the leadership of Creswell was the first political party to articulate a full-blown segregationist policy. The Labour- Nationalist Pact Government secured a virtual monopoly of highly paid, skilled jobs in the mines and, through the Industrial Conciliation Act of 1924, set up a system of collective bargaining which was in effect to exclude the African. Thus if 1922 was the decisive point in the consolidation of the White labour aristocracy, it also marked the terminal point in the parting of ways of White and African mine workers.

Was non-racial class solidarity between African and White mine workers possible in these early years of struggle between capital and labour? In contrast to the successful attempts at class mobilization among White workers and mine-owners, African workers were heavily disadvantaged structurally to organise themselves. However, this is not to imply that Africans were simply responding passively to the process of proletarianization. African mine workers had two avenues open to them for expression of discontent. Firstly, they could refuse to be recruited. It was this refusal on a mass scale after the

14

Anglo-Boer War (with the drop in wages) that precipitated a labour crisis on the mines. It was resolved by undercutting the bargaining power of the African mine worker by importing cheap Chinese labour. Secondly, they could 'desert' — a response which was to lead to the tightening up of the pass laws.

Strikes among African mine workers took place on several mines in 1913 following the success of the White strike. However, as the Commission appointed to investigate the disturbances found, their main grievance was 'the colour bar which blocks practically all opportunities of promotion.' The largest African strike over this period was in 1920 when 71,000 Africans came out on strike for better pay, to lower the prices of the compound store and against the job colour bar. Police were called in immediately and after one violent clash, workers returned to work at the point of police bayonets. Again, in spite of Sidney Bunting's passionate plea to White workers in the strike, they failed to show solidarity and scabbed. As Eddie Roux, an activist at the time, has written, 'the White miners earned ten times as much as the Blacks, many of them employed Black servants in their homes — a victory of Black miners would have increased the desire of the mine-owners to reduce the status of the White miners, since any increase in Black wages would have to be met either by a reduction in White wages or by a reduction in profits. Such was the reality of the situation which the White workers, unconsciously or not, understood very well.'[6]

Five factors seem to me to discourage non-racial trade unions and organisations from emerging during this early period on the mines:

1) The fact that the White worker had access to political power opened the door to economic privilege and this economic privilege gave the White worker a vested interest in the perpetuation of the system.

2) A crucial factor was the relatively easy embourgeoisement of the White artisan who would move out of his class to set up as master on his own and employ his own cheap African labour. The 'caste-like' barrier to upward social mobility blocked a similar process for Africans.

3) The structure of the labour market on the mines was such that White miners could have a gang of African miners contracted to them. These men were under the arbitary control of the White miner, subject to his discipline, and at the mercy of his power to dismiss them.

15

4) The work situation cannot be considered in isolation, as even if interests in friendship did emerge in the workplace (as described by Peter Abraham in his novel *Mineboy*) the battery of racial discriminatory custom and law in the overall structure of society militated against common political action. A good example here would be the fact that African mine workers were housed in compounds which imposed, through the compound policemen, tight control over their lives.

5) Most important of all was the system of migrant labour itself, which as I suggested prevented effective class mobilisation from taking place.

Since 1922, the mine owners' fear of provoking a similar confrontation with White unions has prevented them from making any appreciable dent in the job colour bar. Thus the lot of the African worker has been determined not only by the profit-motive of the mining capitalists, but also by the vested interests of the White mine workers. Hence the White worker's access to political power has enabled him to define his position in antagonistic terms to that of the African worker. The White worker, it is argued by some, produces less value than he receives and is ipso facto, not exploited. Whether he is to be defined as a separate, non-productive class, or whether the White worker is simply to be seen as the privileged stratum of the working class, suffering a rather prolonged bout of 'false consciousness' is a matter of considerable debate (see introduction to Section 4). What in fact has happened is that race has been used in the wider conflict between capital and labour. The White worker, rather than identify himself with a working class overwhelmingly consisting of what he has been taught to believe is an 'inferior' race, has preferred the rather reluctant acceptance he has been given at the lower ranks of the White ruling class.

In South Africa, the state is not simply the instrument of the capitalist class (although it is primarily that); it involves a *coalition* of classes which includes White workers as well as industrial, mining and landed capitalists.

It was this class alliance that set the context for labour relations in the industry for the next 50 years. This structure was challenged by the African mine workers' strike in 1946, which clearly demonstrated the potential power and limits of the African workers. The first effective African Mine Workers' Union had been formed by 1941. Wage demands were made but not met. In 1945 a number of disturbances and strikes took place following the reduction of rations by the mining houses. In the disturbances two men were killed in a police baton charge and a hundred others were seriously wounded.

In 1946, the African Mine Workers' Union (AMWU) called for 'immediate steps to provide adequate and suitable food for the workers and in accordance with the new world principles for an improved standard of living, subscribed to by our Government at the United Nations, an increase in the minimum wage of all African miners at R1,00 a day.' The demand was ignored and the AMWU called a General Strike in August 1946, when 74,000 workers came out on strike for 4 days. Strike leaders were arrested and police surrounded the compounds.

Several violent confrontations developed and on one mine the workers were driven underground at bayonet point. Nine men were killed and more than 1,200 were injured. The strike did not succeed in bringing about an improvement in African working conditions, and General Smuts said of the strike: 'it was not caused by legitimate grievances but by agitators.'

The evidence of the successful organisation of an African mine workers' union is important because it has been consistently argued by the mine-owners that migrant labour and ethnic diversity make unionization impossible. What emerges from this brief look at the AMWU is that it is difficult but not *impossible* to organise, in spite of the fact that both the Government and the Chamber attempted to stifle the AMWU. Giving evidence to the sedition trial following the 1946 strike, the compound manager of the New Kleinfontein Mine admitted Africans 'were not allowed to organise' and that Chamber policy, followed on all mines, was 'to get rid of anybody trying to organise workers.' At the same trial, Senator Basner claimed that the Chamber had initiated a spy system in the AMWU. Despite harassment the union grew steadily, claiming 25,000 members in 1944. In August of that year, following representation from the Chamber, War Measure 1425 was promulgated prohibiting gatherings of more than 20 persons on proclaimed mining ground. With the compounds out of bounds to its officials, meetings now had to be held clandestinely at night under mine dumps.[7]

The second world war was the turning point for the gold mines. It was at this time that the proportion of South African Africans on the mines declined rapidly from a proportion of 80% of the total labour force to less than 25% today. The decline in the proportion of Africans who could draw an alternative income from agriculture in the Reserves coincides with the 'pull' to manufacturing industry, with its 'free' and more competitive wage system. With the decline of the South African peasant-worker, due to accelerating proletarianization, the mines became increasingly dependent on an 'external' proletariat — a factor that has now been brought into sharp focus with the ban on recruitment from Malawi and the change of government imminent in Mozambique. (Even if Mozambique continues to allow recruiting for the mines, they are likely to amend the provision in the Mozambique-South Africa Labour Treaty, which precludes unionisation.)

The increases in African wages on the mines recently is significant only in as much as it is a manifestation of the use of market mechanisms to attract labour to the mines. While clearly this is a tentative step in the right direction, the mining industry will not 'solve' its labour crises unless it turns its attention towards the hazardous nature of the work (reflected in the appalling mortality rate) the lack of job advancement opportunities, the repressive living conditions in the compounds, and, at the core of the reluctance of Africans to work on the mines, the migrant labour system itself. The necessary condition for the achievement and implementation of these reforms is the emergence of a viable and democratic African mine workers' union. While this may sound platitudinous, it relates directly to labour supply.

In a situation in which workers cannot organise or bargain, they tend to react in other ways. One way is simply refusing to be recruited to work on the mines. Another method is that of *industrial sabotage* where individuals tend to destroy or mutilate objects or each other in the work environment. This is done either to reduce tension or frustration or, on the other hand, to assert some form of direct control over one's work or life. Unplanned smashing and spontaneous destruction are signs of a powerless individual or group and it has been suggested that they principally occur in industries which are in an almost 'pre-trade union' state.[8] The current wave of unrest on the mines with its so-called faction fights seems to be, in some instances, a clear case of industrial sabotage.

If the mining industry is to maintain its labour supply, new techniques of control will be necessary, techniques which will inevitably involve the participation of workers in collective bargaining. However, to enable effective bargaining to take place, the mining industry will have to dismantle those aspects of the industry which prevent a system of 'free' wage labour from emerging.

FOOTNOTES

1. Denis Bransky, 'Causes of the Anglo Boer War' (Unpublished paper, Oxford, 1974).
2. Denis Brańsky, ibid.
3. Denis Bransky, ibid.
4. F. A. Johnstone, 'Class Conflict and Colour Bars in the South African mining industry', *Institute of Commonwealth Studies, Collected Seminar Papers* No. 10, (London, 1970).
5. Rex, 'The Compound, Reserve and Urban Location — Essential Institutions of Southern African Labour Exploitation', *SALB*, Vol. 1 No. 5.
6. Eddie Roux, *Time Longer Than Rope.*
7. D. O'Meara, 'The 1946 African Mine Workers Strike and a Political Economy of South Africa', *Journal of Commonwealth and Comparative Politics* (March, 1975).
8. I. Taylor and Walton 'Industrial Sabotage', in *Images of Deviance,* edited by R. Cohen and I. Taylor (Penguin, 1972).

BLACK INDUSTRIAL PROTEST ON THE WITWATERSRAND, 1901-02

PETER WARWICK

A feature of the historiography of industrialisation during its initial stages of development in South Africa has been the acceptance that the role played by the black labour force was largely a passive one. Organised industrial action by black workers, however, can be traced back at least to the turn of the present century, when a series of protests by black workers on the Rand took place. During 1901-2 strikes and mass desertions occurred at the Consolidated Main Reef, Geldenhuis, Langlaagte and Durban Roodepoort Mines, as well as at the Vereeniging Coal Mines and the Brakpan Electric Works. While each dispute can be understood fully only by examining the particular work context in which it took place, the protests happened at a time of transition in the Transvaal from a period of war to one of reconstruction, and in the circumstances of wage reductions and an offensive by the Randlords, in close collaboration with the post-war British administration, to destroy completely the informal bargaining power of the black industrial work force on the gold reef.

The background to the protests will be sketched in as briefly as possible. During the South African War those workers who remained in the industrial region experienced considerable hardship. Shortly after the beginning of the war many of the 20 000 or more workers who remained in the mining area were commandeered by the Boer government either to provide unpaid labour for the commandos, or to work in other occupations related to the war effort. In January 1900 a maximum monthly wage for black workers of only 20 shillings was introduced by the government, a curfew was put into operation, all assemblies of Africans prohibited, and frequent police raids made into the compounds to maintain control over the labour force and to discourage any protests by workers. Africans' expectations were apparently raised by the prospect of a British administration in the Transvaal, since pass books were burned *en masse* by workers when Roberts's columns entered Johannesburg in June 1900. However, afterwards the hardships of those workers in the industrial area were consolidated rather than ameliorated. 8 000 workers were conscripted to build a new railway for transporting coal along the gold reef at the wage rate of only 10*d* a day; 4 000 men were drafted to form an inexpensive labour force for the army; and the remaining workers were retained by the mines for maintenance work at a wage rate of 1 shilling a day. Martial law restrictions were placed on the movement of Africans, so that many workers found it almost impossible to return home and, therefore, were compelled to remain on the mines long after their contracts had expired.

During the war the monthly wages of black workers were reduced by the Chamber of Mines from their pre-war level of 50 shillings to 30-35 shillings. Equally important, however, wage rates outside the gold mining sector were maintained and often increased, and alternative employment opportunities in more congenial occupations were easily available in reparation work, in large-scale public works enterprises, at the ports, and even in other industries on the Rand itself. The gold mining industry was only able to recruit a work force in 1903 which was two-thirds the size of that which it had employed in 1899.

Death rates among workers in the mining compounds before the outbreak of war are not available, but immediately afterwards the number of deaths rose steeply from 92 in May 1902, to 247 in November. Between these months the average monthly death rate per thousand workers was 48,5 and in July 1903, a peak was reached of 112,54. Harsh though conditions may have been on the reef, workers were often in a poor physical condition when they arrived to begin work, having travelled long distances on foot or in closed railway trucks with no sanitary facilities (those transporting workers were classified as goods rather than passenger trains). The problem was exacerbated after the war by the congestion of the railway system, the shortage of rolling stock which caused terrible overcrowding in available trucks, and by further delays in transporting workers from Braamfontein to particular mines. One in eight mining recruits was found physically unfit to begin work immediately.

The post-war British administration also introduced a much more sophisticated system of control over African workers. During the

21

1890s many mining companies systematically recruited workers from each other by employing labour 'touts' to procure newly arrived workers in the industrial area and to encourage desertions from the compounds of neighbouring mines, promising the workers better pay and conditions. In spite of legislative attempts to prevent such practices, especially the pass law of 1895, which compelled Africans to wear a metal arm badge (or later an official pass) numbered as a means of identification, desertions became such a problem because of the inconsistencies and maladministration of the law, which workers were able successfully to exploit, that in November 1898 the number of desertions reported by mining companies exceeded the number of workers legitimately discharged. This system provided black mine workers with the means to exercise selection in their ultimate choice of employer. After the annexation of the Transvaal, however, workers were confronted by a maximum average wage system, the establishment of a monopolistic recruiting agency, the Witwatersrand Native Labour Association, which was created with the intention of 'rendering impossible in the future the indiscriminate touting and traffic in Natives which in the past existed among the mining companies' (Chamber of Mines, Annual Reports for 1900 and 1901, p. 111), and by an administration determined on regulating labour to a greater degree within the industrial area. The Milner regime extended the pass department, developed legal procedures to deal with breaches of contract, introduced a scheme to register the finger-prints of all mining employees to help identify those who deserted, and established regulations to prohibit mining companies recruiting workers in labour districts. The possibility of black workers exchanging employers to find the most congenial working conditions was therefore considerably reduced; the mine workers' former bargaining power, albeit exercised informally and on an individual scale, was largely destroyed by the new rapport which had been established between the mining industry and the state. It was in these circumstances that the protests by black workers took place.

The first endeavours of the W.N.L.A. met with only limited success and some active resistance on the part of workers. In 1901, 192 Venda workers refused on arrival at the mines to begin work, and only after a dispute lasting ten days were they eventually persuaded to do so. 29 Rolong workers also refused to commence work, expressing dissatisfaction with the rates of pay they found to exist on the mines, and the Association prudently returned them to Mafeking.

22

Vereeniging Estate Coal Mine

The first serious protest by workers was in a number of respects untypical of the kind of unrest which followed later, since it did not take place on a gold mine where wage reductions had been enforced. On 7 September 1901, 162 Sotho workers arrived at the Vereeniging Estate Coal Mine from Aliwal North, where many of them had been waiting for up to five weeks for rail permits to enable them to travel to the Transvaal. Two days later the workers held a meeting after which they refused to begin work until they had been paid 1s 6s for each day they had been detained at Aliwal, in accordance with a promise made to them by the recruiting agent. When the Manager, E. M. Goodwin, assured them they would be paid in due course, the workers threatened to return home unless they were paid immediately. The next day 60 of the workers openly deserted, in spite of the warning that by doing so they were breaking the law; the group was detained after crossing the Vaal River and brought back to Viljoen's Drift. When the Sotho refused to re-cross the river, soldiers of the East Lancashire Regiment surrounded the workers, who armed themselves with sticks and stones in a bid to escape. Nine workers were shot dead and fifteen others were wounded.

The most prominent issue in the negotiations between the workers and the management was the deception practised by the recruiting agent who had enlisted their labour; the workers insisted that the agent had promised them that their wages would be paid while they were detained at Aliwal, and that they had been brought to Vereeniging under false pretences, since they had been told they were to work for the government not for a private company. The dispute, however, followed a series of protests by Sotho workers against their maltreatment at the Vereeniging Mine; only a short time before the military had been called in to the estate to quell a disturbance, after which two white workers had been imprisoned for three months for assault. The workers may have known of the reputation of the mine, increasing their determination not to take up employment there. Indeed, conditions on the coal mines at Vereeniging at this time were known to be particularly hazardous; 1 100 desertions took place from the Cornelia Mine between July and December 1902, and when a census of workers was carried out at the end of the year only 850 workers were found out of labour force of 1 150. The spokesman for the Sotho protesters was the headman, Jacob, though it was claimed later that the most militant among them was a worker named Likwala. Although Jacob was officially charged with responsibility for the work party, on the two occasions when he was approached to use his influence with the workers to prevent further conflict, he refused to do so.

Johannesburg Location Riot

On 1 January 1902, a disturbance took place at the Johannesburg location when 6 Zulu policemen and 2 white constables were attacked by 200 (mostly Xhosa) mine workers. The gathering of angry workers was dispersed only after shots had been fired into the crowd, killing 2 Africans and wounding a number of others. Later, 43 participants were sentenced to terms of imprisonment of up to 12 months. The riot provides evidence of the deterioration of relations on the Rand at this time between Xhosa and Zulu workers. Afterwards a meeting was held by the Zulu workers at the location, at which a petition was drawn up to Sir Godfrey Lagden, the Commissioner for Native Affairs, requesting that a separate location be established for them, since the workers wished 'to be removed from immediate contact with other Natives (and more especially the Maxosa element)'. To analyse the riot as one of the earliest examples of 'faction fighting' on the mines, however, would be misleading, unless it is understood that the antagonism between Zulu and Xhosa workers was to a large extent the result of attempts by the mine owners to exercise greater control over the work force by 'divide and rule' tactics. It was reported to the South African Native Affairs Commission in 1905 that the policy of appointing Zulus as gangers over workers from the Transkei was one of the main reasons, in addition to the reduction of wages, why Xhosa workers had shown reluctance to work on the gold fields after the war. Supervision of the compounds and locations increased in intensity during the war and afterwards; many of those recruited for police work were Zulus.

Consolidated Main Reef Mine

Unrest on the reef erupted again at the beginning of April when 116 of the 183 workers at the Consolidated Main Reef Mine went out on strike. In spite of the intervention of the Inspector of Labour the workers refused to go back to work and were all arrested. The origins of the stoppage are not difficult to discover, since a contractor engaged in the construction of a boiler house at the mine was known by the strikers to be paying his employees higher wages than those they themselves received. The workers demanded either equal re-

24

muneration or the right to work instead for the contractor. Indeed, the dispute was aggravated by the intervention of yet another contracting company, Gratton and Stuart of Elandsfontein, which sent a worker into the mining compound to offer the strikers 20 shillings a week if they left the mine and came to work for the company. The Manager of the mine complained that 'if the contractors are allowed to go on they will obtain all the best boys, many of which are as good at certain work as white men, and at the same time unsettle the company's boys'.

Geldenhuis Estate Mine

On 6 January 1902, 536 Pedi workers had been registered for a six month contract to work on the Geldenhuis Mine. At the end of June, 448 workers struck work and demanded to be returned home, claiming that their contract had expired, though it did not run out until 6 July. The Germiston Mounted Police were summoned to the Mine and 16 leaders of the protest arrested and taken to Germiston, where they were charged under the Masters and Servants Act for inciting a breach of contract. The remaining strikers broke out of the compound and marched towards the town threatening to release the detained men by force, and they too were arrested. 432 workers were fined £2 or one month's hard labour, five indunas fined £2 or two months' hard labour, and 11 other leaders £2 or 6 weeks' hard labour. The company offered to pay the workers' fines on condition that they completed the contract though over 100 of the strikers appear to have chosen to go to goal with their leaders instead. The grievances of the workers derived from their dissatisfaction with the nature of their employment. As early as 8 January, Asaph Moruthani, the secretary to the Pedi Chief, Sekukuni II, who had been sent to accompany the work party to the gold fields and report on their conditions of service, complained that the men had been deceived concerning their ultimate destination. Sekukuni had originally refused to supply workers to private industry, but on the assurance of the local administration that the men were required for government work, he had permitted them to leave. It is unclear why the men almost worked out their contracts before resorting to protest action, though it is possible the men may have hoped that the company would turn a blind eye to such an incident so near the completion date of the contract. On 22 May, 164 workers, who had left their employment on the Ginsberg Mine and camped outside Boksburg, had been permitted to return to Pietersburg, together with over 100 workers who had deserted from the East

Rand Mines, rather than be prosecuted and made to complete their contracts. It is possible that this episode set a precedent which other workers attempted to follow. The strike was led by the 5 Pedi indunas, whose task it was to supervise the work force and provide a link between the mining company and the workers' Chief. S. M. Pritchard, the Chief Inspector of Labour, believed the protest was wholly their responsibility: 'the strike was due to the indunas ... That these men were the instigators there would appear to be no doubt'.

Langlaagte Deep Mine

Shortly after midnight on 28 June, 1 100 workers at the Langlaagte Mine broke down the gates of the compound and marched towards the Village Deep Mine from where they had been enlisted earlier. A detachment of the Johannesburg Mounted Police pursued the deserters, who were armed with knobkerries, bottles and stones, and eventually persuaded them to return to the Langlaagte Mine, where they stoned the compound manager's office before going back to their quarters. The 15 leaders of the protest demanded the dismissal of the compound manager, and declared their intention to desert again the following morning unless this was done, though police supervision prevented another mass walk-out. Although the dispute appears quickly to have subsided, the roots of the unrest were deep. Because of the restrictions on the movement of Africans in the Transvaal, many workers at the mine had been prevented from returning home directly their contracts had expired. Moreover, the behaviour of the compound manager, Joseph Woichowsky, turned the workers' discontent into open anger. Woichowsky had been guilty of rejecting almost out of hand applications by workers for temporary passes to leave the compound, which prevented their visiting a store situated within a few hundred yards of the mine. Almost certainly the Langlaagte workers depended on the store to supplement their diet. Protesters interviewed by the police after the walk-out also claimed that Woichowsky had presided over acts of gross cruelty at the mine. Trooper Brickhill of the J.M.P. reported that:

> ... the Compound Manager illtreats them by having them thrashed both in the compound and down the mine with a cat-o-nine tails and thrashed them on the testicles: further ... they were shut up like dogs ... (they) stated they would work and not give any trouble if the Compound Manager treated them as human beings not dogs, and they would not continue to work while he was in charge of the compound and they would kill him if he continued.

Clearly, the relations between the labour force and Woichowsky had deteriorated in the circumstances of renewed mining operations.

Durban Roodepoort Mine

Within a month of the Langlaagte and Geldenhuis protests further unrest was evident at the Durban Roodepoort Mine. On 21 July the black work force of 700 men held a meeting before the morning shift, after which they demanded to speak to the manager and refused to go underground unless they were given an increase in the 30 shillings a month for which they had been contracted. To emphasise their case the workers assembled in the compound with their belongings and threatened to leave the property. Within 2 hours, however, the protesters had been induced to return to work, 'assisted' by the Black mine police, and the threat that if the stoppage continued the strikers would be punished in the same way as the Geldenhuis workers. Afterwards the 3 leaders of the protest, 'Canteen', 'English' and 'Madoda', all from Mozambique, claimed they had been misled by the recruiting agent at their kraals, who had assured them that they would receive wages in excess of those that had prevailed before the war, and that they would be contracted for a period of only 6 months. When they had arrived at the mine they found they were to be paid a mere 30 shillings a month, and that their contract was to extend for 12 months. The leaders, who had agreed to resume work only with the consent of the strikers, emphasised they were underpaid, but that it was only a little more money they demanded.

Brakpan Electric Works

The final eruption of worker protest in 1902 occurred at the Brakpan Electric Works. On 11 September, 61 Xhosa employees under their leader, 'One O'Clock', struck work and marched to Boksburg, following the example of 40 workers who had left the property in June, where they demanded to lay their grievances before the Magistrate. They complained of ill-treatment at the hands of the resident engineer who, they reported, regularly sjambokked workers and had them thrown among burning embers; they protested, too, against the dangerous nature of the work caused by bursting boiler tubes. The Chief Inspector held an enquiry at the works, after which he concluded it had been the intention of the workers to obtain discharges on the pretext of ill-treatment. His verdict was endorsed by the magistrate of the Boksburg Native Court, who sentenced 55 strikers to one month's imprisonment with hard labour since, he believed, 'it was perfectly clear that the desertions took place with the object of getting more remunerative work elsewhere'.

The strikes described above were small in scale; they appear to have involved no more than 2 500 workers. They took place over a period of 12 months, in a variety of districts, and were not confined to one industry. Although the disputes at Geldenhuis and Langlaagte occurred on the same day, there is no evidence to suggest that they were in any way directly related. The only specific link connecting any 2 of the incidents is that the punishments meted out to the Geldenhuis strikers was used by the management of the Durban Roodepoort Mine to threaten their workers to return peacefully to work. (But in view of the 'official' nature of the documentary evidence used for this study it would be unrealistic to conclude, therefore, that the action of one group of workers was necessarily completely unknown to any other group.) None of the protests appear to have been successful in their immediate aims, though the reluctance shown by black workers to migrate to the gold fields induced the Chamber of Mines to re-introduce the 1897 wage schedule at the end of 1902. Any continuing upward movement of wage-levels in the immediate post-war period, however, was prevented by the introduction of indentured Chinese labour to the Rand in 1904. Some improvements took place in the conditions of life in the mining compounds, though it has been argued that this can be related to the fear of censure from the British government on the part of Sir Godfrey Lagden, rather than to pressures for improvements from the mine workers themselves. (Jeeves, p. 17).

Why, then, do the protests merit examination? In the first place they are the earliest organised protests by black workers on the Rand which so far have been analysed. Further research may show other strikes to have taken place before the South African War. Secondly, it is important to understand the way in which what Charles van Onselen has described as the 'individual, informal and largely unorganised' resistance to exploitation on the part of the first generation of black industrial wage-earners in southern Africa evolved into more formal and recognizable expressions of organised protest action. The development of black worker protest is most usefully conceived as a continuum of resistance to exploitation which includes opposition to wage labour on the part of Africans by raising necessary cash requirements in other ways (such as the sale of livestock and argicultural produce); resistance to recruitment by labour agents, who frequently

28

practiced deception concerning wage rates, contracts and working conditions; selectiveness in the labour market to achieve the highest possible remuneration; individual desertions against unsatisfactory working conditions; strikes and walk-outs which though revealing recognizable leadership left behind them no permanent worker organisation; and finally the establishment of black trade unionism. The Industrial and Commercial Workers' Union, formed in 1919, has been interpreted for too long as a movement almost without antecedents. Thirdly, small in numerical terms and unsuccessful though the protests of 1901-02 may have been, it would be surprising if they had been anything else in view of the penalties which faced workers who were brought before the courts, the intensification of police activity on the Rand during the war and immediately afterwards, the swift action of the army and the police against protesters, and the close community of interest between the government and the mining companies, which was attested to by the partisan spirit in which the investigations of the Chief Inspector of Labour were carried out. Finally, the protests took place in a common environment and reveal a number of common features.

The disputes occurred after a period of considerable hardship on the Rand during the South African War, and in the circumstances of a rapidly rising death rate among black mine workers, wage reductions, and a decline in the purchasing power of workers' wages as a result of the inflation of livestock and grain prices, and the prices of other consumption items. They took place, too, in an environment in which the expectations of workers had been raised as a result of the outcome of the war (in this respect the protests might be considered in the context of the industrial ferment in South Africa which followed immediately after the two world wars). Restrictions on the free movement of black workers in the Transvaal, institutional and legislative measures to control more effectively the black labour force, and the more efficient policing of the mining area, implied that it was much more difficult after the annexation of the Transvaal for workers to desert a company either to escape unsatisfactory working and living conditions and repressive supervisors and policemen, or to find alternative better-paid and more congenial work. In these circumstances individual protest action on the part of black workers was made more difficult, and the conditions of life in the mining industry made all the more unbearable.

The deception of black workers by recruiting agents was protested against by workers at the Geldenhuis, Vereeniging and Durban

Roodepoort Mines; at the Brakpan Electric Works and the Vereeniging and Langlaagte Mines workers complained of their ill-treatment by other members of the work force; specific demands for higher wages were made by workers at the Consolidated Main Reef and Durban Roodepoort Mines.

In most of the disputes some form of leadership can be discerned. At the Geldenhuis and Vereeniging Mines negotiations were conducted by headmen in whose charge the workers were placed during their period of employment; at Geldenhuis the induna system provided the cohesive force for the protest, while at Vereeniging the headman, Jacob, appears to have been reluctant to act against the aspirations of the workers, though the *de facto* leadership may have lain elsewhere. In other disputes rank-and-file leaders are cited by name in the reports, though in view of the authorities' desire to prevent further protests, men may have been singled out for salutary punishment; thus, some of the leaders may have been created as much by the management as by the workers, though it is important to recognise that in the subsequent inquiries these men showed themselves willing to represent the grievances of their fellow workers.

The ethnicity of those taking part appears to have been an important binding force in the protests, often stemming from the immediate grievances of the workers. At Geldenhuis the dispute was fundamentally between the management of the mine and the Pedi work force, the unrest at the Durban Roodepoort Mine was apparently confined to workers from Mozambique, and the strike at the Brakpan Electric Works was reported to have been an exclusively Xhosa affair. At Vereeniging the Sotho workers cited the independence of their people as a symbol of protest; when the Provost Marshall attempted to induce the workers to return to the mine he was informed that 'they were Lorethodi's (sic) people and they were going to fight . . . (the British) may beat the Boers but could not beat the Basuto'. Ethnicity appears to have been an important and understandably useful binding element in the earliest protest actions by the first generation of industrial workers in southern Africa (in the Wankie Colliery Strike in 1912, for example). However, it would be premature to conclude, therefore, that class consciousness derived from the labourers' own perception of themselves as 'workers' had not yet begun to transcend ethnic divisions. The impression of ethnic cohesion in the protests may be exaggerated by the inadequacy of the available evidence, since it is possible that the ethnicity of the workers involved in some of the disputes may only have been assumed by the management to have corresponded to that of their leaders. Furthermore, the largest protest, that involving over a thousand workers at the Langlaagte Mine, was not described as having been confined to any one ethnic group.

SOURCES

THE STRIKES: Archive of the Secretary for Native Affairs, Transvaal Archive Depot, Pretoria Public Record Office, London, series C.O. 291.

BACKGROUND: Chamber of Mines, *Annual Reports.*

Alan Jeeves, 'The Control of Migratory Labour on the South African Gold Mines in the Era of Kruger and Milner', *Journal of Southern African Studies* Vol. 2, No. 1 (1975).

D. J. N. Denoon, 'The Transvaal Labour Crisis, 1901-6', *Journal of African History,* Vol. 8, No. 3 (1967).

Charles van Onselen, 'Worker Consciousness in Black Miners: Southern Rhodesia, 1900-1920', *Journal of African History,* Vol. 14, No. 2, (1973); *Chibaro* (Pluto Press, London, 1976).

MINE WORKER PROTEST ON THE WITWATERSRAND : 1901-1912

SEAN MORONEY

Author's Note: I am indebted to Charles van Onselen who read an early draft of this paper and provided some valuable criticisms and suggestions.

The period following the Anglo-Boer War is crucial to the history of labour relations in South Africa. During this period gold mining in the Transvaal was re-established as the most important industrial sector in Southern Africa. This period also saw the consolidation of a monopsonistic labour recruiting system which was to promote extensive labour migrancy throughout the sub-continent. The particular economic and social patterns thus created persist today. Little has been learnt about the people most affected by these social and economic forces, the mass of black unskilled workers, during this and subsequent periods. White worker responses, management's machinations and the State's participation have all been explored to some degree. We know virtually nothing about the processes of proletarianisation experienced by black workers or about their responses to the developing industrial economy.

This neglect has perhaps resulted from a lack of readily available material concerning black workers, in contrast with the relatively well documented activities of management and white workers. These two groups were always assured, as they are at present, of extensive coverage in the contemporary media. Such biases have penetrated South African historiography. The resultant gaps in our history must affect our understanding of present day industrial relations in Southern Africa. The fact that there has been very little evidence of tangible conflict between black workers and management has created the impression of workers as passive participants in the economy. This paper sets out to show that workers, in fact, responded in a variety of effective ways to the manipulative, exploitative and coercive measures adopted by management. These responses and the particular forms they assumed, indicated the formation of a worker rationality encompassing defence, protest and direct confrontation. Usually they did not take the form of strikes, mass walkouts or visible mass organisation. Instead, one needs to identify and interpret a wide range of other more subtle expressions of worker-management conflict.[1] Such expressions developed within, and were thus determined by, a highly repressive economy in which management, in effective alliance with the State, devised and implemented an armoury of measures designed to erode the freedom of mine workers.

Although many of the workers recruited after the Anglo-Boer War would have experienced mine employment before hostilities broke out and caused the closure of the mines, the economic conditions of the rural areas at the start of the century did not make them entirely, or even considerably, dependent on industrial employment for economic survival. As a result, peasants possessed an economic base from which to resist the ravages of the labour recruiting system. The first decade was to see the steady erosion of this base by natural and political forces and the peasant economy was to give way to the predominance of the growing industrial mode. Peasants were to lose control of their means of livelihood and turn increasingly to mine work for subsistence. Their bargaining power in relation to the mine owners who needed their labour was eroded accordingly.

The Randlords emerged from the planning recess afforded by the war with a comprehensive plan to combine in labour recruiting through the Witwatersrand Native Labour Association (WNLA). The scheme was designed to facilitate the systematic recruitment of cheap labour from Portuguese East Africa, the success of which would ensure depression of wages. It also provided for combined recruiting within British South Africa to eliminate competition for labour and the resultant upward pressure on wages. Recruits were to be assigned to member mines on a quota basis. In addition, a maximum average wage schedule was agreed upon which set wages below their pre-war average level. The motivation for these measures derived, in part, from management's irrational quest to work mines of marginal profitability.

Once management experienced initial resistance from potential recruits in rural areas, it embarked, through WNLA and its agents, upon a devastating campaign making use of financial and livestock advances in conjunction with an increasingly effective taxation system, the collaboration of chiefs as well as deception and blatant coercion to obtain labour recruits.[2]

In the actual work situation, management developed a range of measures both to keep unwilling recruits in bondage and to extract most work for least pay, food and accommodation. The compound system and all its accompanying institutions of mine 'police', physical violence and social control, became crucial. In collaboration with the State, a sophisticated 'pass' system was developed to prevent and detect 'desertion'. Laws such as the Masters and Servants Act were effectively used to suppress work stoppages and other forms of worker resistance. On many mines workers were systematically cheated of their wages and forced to stay longer than the periods for which they had contracted.

Despite the fact that worker resistance was progressively weakened, it persisted with considerable effect until the middle of the decade. It is in fact arguable that certain groups of workers during this period had the upper hand in relation to management. The latter, however, through the importation of large quantities of cheap Chinese labour during the period 1904-9, was able to reduce the upward pressure on black wages and destroy much of the basis for black worker bargaining power. Because of the progressive denudation and over-crowding of the rural areas black workers were to remain in a relatively weakened position even after the repatriation of the Chinese workers. Precedents for modes of resistance had however been established.

To summarize, the period under review can be broken into fairly distinct phases. Immediately after the war management made a concerted assault on the freedom of potential workers in order to recruit them not only in sufficiently large numbers but on terms satisfactory to management in the face of the profitability constraints within which it chose to operate. Significant groups of workers at varying stages of proletarianization persistently resisted the machinations of management. They lost this initiative with the importation of Chinese labour although various forms of resistance were to persist.

It is in the context of these countervailing forces that worker resistance during this period should be examined. The patterns delineated above indicate the importance of seeking the roots of migrant labour resistance in the pre-labour situation, as this was the point at which the prospective worker could exercise his greatest measure of resistance. His refusal to be recruited was his most effective lever against the formidable powers of management. Potential recruits in British South Africa reacted strongly against the WNLA system. They were aware that it totally eliminated their freedom of choice as prospective labourers and that the maximum average wage agreement pegged their pay at less than they could bargain for elsewhere. Grant, Native Labour Commissioner to the Chamber of Mines, in evidence before the Transvaal Labour Commission of 1902, stated emphatically that the WNLA system, through prohibiting 'voluntary' labour, was coercive:

> ... a native, before he seeks employment, generally asks a few questions, he satisfies himself as to the character of his employer, the nature of the work and the treatment to be expected. Having selected his employer he offers his service, and under these (WNLA) rules, however eager the boy may be to work, he cannot enter except through one prescribed channel, consequently his voluntary action is distinctly interfered with.

Once a worker had contracted through WNLA, he was processed through a degrading medical examination, usually railed as part of a 'batch' in a cattle truck to the Reef and assigned to whatever mine required him, according to the quota system. It was reported that workers no longer considered themselves to be the free agents they were before the war, and that a worker abhorred nothing more 'than to be compelled to go and work where he does not like to go, even if he is told that he will be fairly paid, that sounds so much like "being commandeered".'

Through an extensive oral reportage system potential workers rapidly developed an awareness, not only of the range of employment and wage rates available, but also of the variety of living and working conditions on each of the mines. Once they were able to secure their freedom from the WNLA system, their subsequent choice of employers was highly selective, being based on this knowledge and revealing a developed worker rationality. In an environment where death rates were sometimes one in ten the choice of mine could be a matter of life or death. One black contractor stated that workers considered bad mines to be 'those which are not very much inspected and some in which ground is left hanging. The boys, when they are engaged, always ask whether a mine is a good one.' There is evidence to show that some groups of workers avoided deep level mines where conditions were known to be difficult and dangerous and management was prone to make immense work demands. Workers also gravitated to the mines where they knew they would find their friends or where they had already been part of an informal network of worker defence. Compound conditions formed a discernible, though somewhat secondary set of criteria.

Workers who wished to enter the Witwatersrand labour market,

35

realising the evils of the WNLA system, would either develop their own routes to the Reef which avoided the WNLA tentacles or would make use of the system to their own advantage. Workers in the Northern Transvaal, for example, were reported to have adopted a definite route to the Reef which avoided the notoriously unscrupulous WNLA agent in the area. Others, in a variety of regions, learnt to 'work' the WNLA system, to take advantage of the facilities and transport provided by labour agents, how to use the complicated pass system and when and how to desert to gain access to other employment opportunities. Many WNLA agents reported during this period that recruits in large numbers were signing on to be transported to the mines and deserting once they neared the Witwatersrand. They would then enter the labour market as free agents, tendering their services where they so desired. Workers, especially those recruited in Northern Transvaal, who wished to rid themselves of obligations to WNLA and enter the Reef labour market independently, used Pretoria as a vital link. Many deserted the WNLA trains at Pretoria and either sought work there, in the military camps or private employ on a relatively permanent basis, or used this employment to gain a pass to travel independently to the Reef. Still others, if they could not detrain in Pretoria or if they had travelled along different routes, deserted in Johannesburg and walked to Pretoria to seek a travelling pass to re-enter the Reef without hindrance. The special labour regulations of the Reef Labour districts did not apply in Pretoria and therefore black workers could not be detained for a period of 6 days for the purpose of identifying deserters. There was evidence of Mozambique workers using the same method. The Secretary of the Association of Mine Managers wrote in November, 1902:

> It appears that particularly in the case of North Basothos and Tsongas they are well informed that on arriving in Pretoria, and making a statement that they wish to go to Johannesburg in order to find employment, passports are freely issued to them without question, and they are fully conversant with the fact that by this means they can obtain work in Johannesburg at higher rates of pay . . . officials assume that natives applying for passports have just arrived from their homes.

In 1906, statements were obtained from three workers who had adopted this method. They were all similar to the following:

> I deserted from the Robinson Deep on or abour 28/10/06 and proceeded to Pretoria on foot. On arriving there I was arrested and when asked by the Pass Officer where I came from, I stated that I had been employed by a Dutch farmer, but had left there and wanted to go to Johannesburg to work on the

36

mines. I was locked up for three days and was then given a travelling pass for which I paid 1/- and went to Johannesburg by train.
(S.N.A. 73/315/07).

In 1902 the WNLA General Manager reported that in April that year, desertions had increased to 1 510 from 899 the previous month. This he attributed to the fact that there was a 'demand for natives by private employers and contractors who pay higher rates than the mines.' He suggested a remedy of offering a higher rate of wages. However the Chamber of Mines persisted with its policy of depressing wages wherever possible and relying on the combined coercive power of its own and the State's institutions to counteract such worker resistance.

Strategies of Worker Defence and Protest in the Work Situation

During the period under review, workers deserted[3] in large numbers. In the first instance workers deserted, as described above, to seek better work opportunities. This category of deserters can be regarded as 'target deserters' who had specific work objectives in mind, perhaps even before they reached the Rand. In the second instance workers would desert when working or compound conditions became unbearable, when they did not receive full pay or when management detained them longer than they had intended. As such it was an active form of protest. This class of desertion I term 'defensive'. In many cases defensive deserters would also set themselves new work targets.

The 'problem' of desertion expended a substantial part of both management's and the State's energy. It drove the Milner Administration, in collaboration with management, to introduce sophisticated methods of prevention and detection. As these methods (such as an expensive finger print system) developed, desertion became more difficult but did not reduce correspondingly. Instead, requiring increased determination and planning, it became a more conscious form of worker protest.

Desertion rates would vary from mine to mine, usually corresponding to the variation of conditions. Pritchard, Director of Government Native Labour Bureau, wrote in 1909:

... generally speaking, the treatment of Natives on the various mines is largely reflected in their several rates of desertion.
(S.N.A. 90/1825/09, Memorandum on Native Labour Supply by Pritchard, 31 March 1909.)

37

An analysis of conditions and desertion rates on the different mines supports this view. The Simmer Deep, for example, had poor feeding, meat rations suspended for 'inefficients', a large rate of cancelled shifts (21,4% per day), and reports of persistent ill-treatment underground. Its desertion rate during 1908 was 618,4 per 1 000. As an example from the other end of the scale, Jumpers Mine had a desertion rate during 1908 of 1,6 per 1 000. Inspectors reported that the standard of feeding in this mine was 'adequate', that very few cases of ill-treatment were reported, that officials had a 'good' attitude towards workers and that few shifts were cancelled.

The procurement of a new pass was essential for a successful desertion, especially if a worker intended to seek new employment. Several instances of pass forgery came to light. The District Controller in Boksburg reported in December 1905 that within 7 months, 1 507 workers had deserted from mines in his districts. During the same period, 18 Africans were convicted of forging passes. White forgers also operated on the Rand and sold passes to deserters at £5 a piece.

A further extension of defensive desertion manifested itself in general labour withdrawal by groups of workers originating from a particular area or tribe or engaged at a particular mine. This form of worker protest is particularly suited to migrant workers who, once they desert, individually or *en masse,* or once their contracts are completed, may refuse to participate in the same labour market until working conditions are improved or home area conditions worsen sufficiently to force them out. This type of action had a strong impact in 1905, when, following the importation of Chinese labour, contract conditions for black workers were made less favourable.[5] Large numbers of black workers from all parts of British South Africa withdrew their labour and management was obliged to improve contract conditions. In 1907, the Chairman of Rand Mines described this form of worker action as follows:

> The native method of striking is very simple. It must be remembered that he is not a permanent workman. He is always going home, and if he is not satisfied with the conditions of employment, he simply does not come out again. The conditions of South Africa make it perfectly possible for him to do this...
> *(Mining Industry Commission, Minutes of Evidence,* S. Reyerbach, Chairman of Rand Mines, 13 June 1907, p.97.)

J. J. Ware of the Trades and Labour Council made a similar evaluation of black worker action:

> There is one thing with the Kaffir in which he is different to the white man. If

things do not suit him he goes home and stays there, he does not go on strike, that is better than any strike.
(Mining Industry Commission, Minutes of Evidence, 28 October 1907, p.1425.)

This type of worker action did have an impact on WNLA and mine management policies. If it had not been for the importation of Chinese labour, commencing in 1904, it is probable that black workers would have won more significant concessions from management through this method.

In the work situation most workers tended to assume defensive forms of resistance as they were denied any initiative within the Witwatersrand's repressive environment. For example, they protected themselves from the high demands made on them through minimum work requirements by keeping their level of efficiency as low as possible. Workers were aware of management's tendency to increase the minimum work requirements of contracts wherever possible. Self-imposed work limits were implemented as a reaction.

Taberer, a Native Affairs Department Inspector, told the 1904 Mining Industry Commission:

I have had natives tell me that they are afraid to put in two holes because their bosses might make that the (required) task.
(Mining Industry Commission 1907, p.1316).

J. H. Johns, a consulting engineer to a mining group, confirmed this type of worker reaction:

I once tried it (piecework) in the Ferreira, and persuaded several boys to drill two holes instead of one. They were paid double for their work and we were all pleased, but they suddenly stopped, and when the mine foreman wanted to know why, they said: "It is all right putting in two holes now, but presently the boss will think that two holes is the day's work . . ." They saw what we were working up to. They saw as well as some of the white men we have had to deal with, only the native was more honest about it. He stuck to it too.
(Mining Industry Commission 1907, p.18448-9)

As another defensive measure, workers made use of the legal system to remedy management's coercive measures. Under British administration, workers would appeal to inspectors from the Native Affairs Department as their 'protectors' if they felt they had a case against management or individual white miners. Workers wanting to lay a charge were faced not only with an unfamiliar legal system but also the inaccessibility of the inspectors.[6] No doubt workers feared retribution from management and this must have also reduced the number of charges actually made. However, in one year alone, 1905, 3 585 complaints were made at pass offices along the Reef regarding shortfalls in wages. Subsequent cases resulted in workers recovering

£10 332 in wages due to them and improperly withheld. Workers also complained although less successfully, about assaults by mine officials and white miners. In 1905, 118 cases of 'ill-usage' were reported and 50 were settled in favour of the plaintiffs. In the same year 609 workers complained of being detained at the mines beyond the length of their contracts. Only 281 cases were settled in favour of the plaintiffs.[7]

As numerous as these cases may seem, it is probable that they represent only a portion of the actionable abuses to which workers were subjected. This type of worker action would have had only piecemeal results and did not directly lead to any reform within the mines. It may also have had a restraining effect on management. However, the action did reveal a capacity for individual resistance which could have formed the basis for group organization and a common worker consciousness.

Home Groups and the Formation of Proto-Voluntary Associations

It is impossible to argue that the type of consciousness displayed by black workers on the gold mines during this period was that of a developed working class. Much worker resistance manifested itself in ethnic identity rather than an overall worker consciousness. However, it is important to view the development of ethnic solidarity in an industrial environment as a particular response to that environment, rather than a simple transferral of tribal values. Workers would form groups, usually tribally based, in their compounds to protect themselves from the compound police, possibly other groups, and most of all, from the coercive measures of management. There is evidence that such groups provided an important measure of security for individual members faced with a daily struggle for survival in the compound and underground.[8]

I have termed these groups proto-voluntary associations. Because of their informal structure and organisation they were difficult to identify by management and were therefore well suited to the mine's systems of control. Management, in fact, fostered tribalism in a variety of ways and this unintentionally added cohesion to these vital groups of worker solidarity, defence and resistance.

There are a few substantial indications of how these groups operated. Many workers insisted on being assigned to the same mine as their 'brothers', usually a group of recruits from a common area and tribe.

40

This was general practice amongst recruits from the Transvaal, Cape Colony, Basutoland and even Portuguese East Africa. In 1903, for example, Angoni chiefs (PEA) told a WNLA agent that they would only send tribesmen to the Reef if, amongst other conditions, 'brothers' were not separated except in fairly large numbers. There is evidence of individual workers who had been separated from their groups requesting permission to be transferred to the same mine as their respective groups. A number of actual disturbances or work stoppages amongst recruits were reported to have resulted from 'home groups' being split up by WNLA. Such disturbances indicated strong determination to remain together with friends in the face of a strange environment.

Cape Colony workers maintained very cohesive groups. Group leaders, often headmen or *indunas,* would represent complaints of the group to management or would write to chiefs or magistrates of their home districts, complaining on behalf of their groups about ill-treatment or bad conditions. This tactic had some definite results as Cape Colony officials would bring pressure to bear on the mines.

The groups provided valuable security for workers in a variety of ways. For example, workers affected by punitive food stoppages could rely on their groups for relief. Pritchard, commenting in 1909 on the use of food as a punitive measure against workers, gave an indication of how workers found support from such informal groups:

> It is well-known that natives share their food and it should therefore have been obvious to those in authority that punishment of this nature would fall as heavily on good workers as it would on malingerers and loafers who it was especially desired should suffer by it.
>
> *(S.N.A. 90/1825/09,* Memorandum by Pritchard, 31 March 1909.)

Many isolated instances of worker action were based on 'home group' organisation. In 1902, for example, 192 'Mapoch' tribesmen arrived in Johannesburg and, dissatisfied with their treatment, they refused to work for 10 days until they were persuaded that treatment would improve. In 1907 a group of Pondo tribesmen refused to work underground on the South Randfontein mine because they claimed they had contracted for surface work only. In May 1907 a group of 60 workers from a common tribe (unnamed) refused to work because their shifts were being cancelled. They decided to return home with their chief's brother.

Many of the work stoppages or strikes on the Reef in the early part of the decade appeared to coalesce along ethnic lines. This Warwick confirms in his account of black industrial protest on the Reef between 1901-2:

The ethnicity of those taking part appears to have been an important binding force in the protests, often stemming from the immediate grievances of the workers. At Geldenhuis (22 May 1902) the dispute was fundamentally between the management of the mine and the Pedi work force, the unrest at the Durban Roodepoort Mine (21 July 1902) was apparently confined to workers from Mozambique, and the strikes at the Brakpan Electric Works (11 September 1902) was reported to have been an exclusively Xhosa affair. At Vereeniging (7th September 1902) the Sotho workers cited the independence of their people as a symbol of protest . . .

It is probable that mass tribal action in the industrial environment, when it did occur, received its main impulse and cohesion via smaller, association-like, home groups. Very often strike leaders would be *indunas* with traditional links and would have had smaller groups under their individual leadership.

It is difficult to estimate what degree of organisation was achieved by these groups. The sophisticated organisation demonstrated by the Ninevite movement over a similar period, as described by Van Onselen,[10] indicated the potential for such groups. Indications are that some 'home groups' did develop into associations with a structure geared towards an industrial environment. In 1907, for example, it was reported that:

At Germiston a new Society has been formed, and so as to escape the stigma of being called Ethiopian, the boys are told that it is not a religious movement but a Benevolent Society, formed to provide a purse for the East Coast Natives working on the Rand, out of which sick boys will be helped, boys dying friendless will be decently buried and boys preaching and teaching in Gazaland will be supported.
(Africa's Golden Harvests, October 1907, p.2.)

This society was organised by an evangelist and is described by a missionary. As such, an emphasis is placed on its religious orientation but it is important that it provided benefits to workers that were meaningful within an industrial environment.

Although one can form only a sketchy impression of these groupings through available evidence, it is clear that they were vital to every worker faced with the vicious environment of the Witwatersrand. It seems that labour organisations have failed to realise their importance and to build on such grass roots structures amongst mine workers. Indications are that they persist today and should receive closer attention.

Work Stoppages and Confrontation

Mass worker action during the first decade of this century was limited in scope and in numbers. Most disturbances were isolated to particular mines and many were mobilised through tribal cohesion. However, the riots and stoppages that did occur indicated the potential that did exist for the articulation of worker grievances and the organisation of effective resistance. Peter Warwick has given a detailed account of the fairly widespread, though piecemeal, instances of black worker protest over the period 1901-2. A substantial proportion of these disturbances were tribally oriented and have been mentioned above. However there is evidence that some confrontations, which usually took the form of work stoppages, demonstrated a definite worker consciousness.

In 1902, for example, workers on the Consolidated Main Reef Mine went on strike because they discovered that their wages were well below those being earned by a contractor's work force engaged in surface construction on the mine. The mine manager complained that:

> ... the contractors, if allowed to go on, will obtain all the best boys, any of which are as good at certain work as white men, and at the same time unsettle the Company's boys.
>
> (*S.N.A.* General Manager, Cons. Main Reef to General Manager WNLA, 2 April 1902.)

The inspector of labour tried to mediate but the workers refused to stand down and were all arrested.

It was competition for their labour, and the realisation that it existed despite the WNLA system, that most stimulated workers to undertake measures of resistance like desertion as well as articulated wage demands. They also were galvanized into action when management transgressed certain rudimentary standards of treatment, as the following example demonstrates.

On Saturday 28 June 1902, 1 000 workers at the Langlaagte Mine broke out of the compound, and marched towards the Village Deep Mine from where they had been transferred. A detachment of police 'persuaded' them to return to the Langlaagte Mine. There they stoned the compound manager's office before going back to their quarters. Leaders of the march demanded the dismissal of the compound manager who had treated them with cruelty and had obstructed their free movement out of the compound. They also complained of being detained at the mine longer than their periods of contract. State officials defused the protest, as they did in many such instances, by promising that 'the matter would be gone into'. It is not clear whether the compound manager was subsequently dismissed. This action seems to indicate that through their experience at the Village Deep

43

Mine, the workers had set certain standards of treatment which their new compound manager did not follow. They reacted forcefully.

Warwick enumerates other instances of management-worker confrontation during the period 1901-2. Other disturbances during the decade, as far as I have ascertained, were not as concentrated as they were over this initial period. Isolated incidents occurred in which workers made limited demands for the improvement of conditions.

A significant strike occurred at the Premier Diamond Mine near Pretoria in 1907. This mine had attracted a labour force of selective workers who were not prepared to sell their labour to the gold mines after conditions worsened in 1905. As a result, it had a high content of Basutoland and Transvaal workers who demonstrated a developed sense of resistance. Although unrelated to the gold mines and the WNL'A system, the Premier, because it received many experienced gold mine workers, indicated the type of resistance that was developing amongst more experienced workers and had the potential to become an important force. In 1907 a major clash developed on this mine which, although it was labelled by management as a tribal conflict, appears to have had an important economic base. Basuto workers had attempted to undercut the rates paid to Transvaal workers for certain prized classes of work. Management had been playing one group off against the other. The inter-tribal fight was reported to have been fierce but the only two deaths that occurred resulted from police action. I judge the fight to have been staged, as a large number of workers immediately demanded to be sent home, possibly hoping that their uncompleted contracts would be waived in the face of unrest. Various reports indicate that living conditions, as a result of chronic overcrowding had become highly undesirable and that there was a high rate of deaths resulting from disease. A detailed examination of the Premier disturbances of 1907 and also of 1913 is beyond the scope of this paper. They do, however, provide a valuable index of worker consciousness during this period.

By the end of the decade, although Chinese labour had been repatriated and WNLA had been abandoned by some mines in favour of independent recruiting, workers still remained in a weak position as a result of the rapid deterioration of the rural areas and serious rinderpest epidemics. Management rapidly developed the manipulative forces at its disposal. In 1912 the Native Recruiting Corporation was established to enforce once again monoposonistic recruiting inside South Africa.[11] This further forestalled any possible improvement in the bargaining position of black workers. Workers from Portuguese East Africa continued to be recruited in large numbers and through their willingness to work for relatively low wages, also undercut the bargaining power of indigenous labour. The methods of resistance previously adopted by workers became less effective. There is evidence that management consciously excluded 'troublesome' workers. Cape Colony recruits were reputed to have been particularly prone to resist management. Labour organisations, such as the I.C.U. that were to develop from the 1920s onwards, mistakenly neglected the power of black mine workers because of the lack of visible organisation displayed in this migrant dominated sector. The preceding analysis shows, however, that potential for organisation did exist. At the earliest stages of proletarianization, workers on the Transvaal Gold Mines were not passive instruments of management. The period examined was unique in some ways but the patterns of resistance that were established persisted throughout the century. Workers were quick to identify the strengths and weaknesses of the exploitative system to which they were exposed, and adjusted their actions accordingly. Within the confines of a highly repressive system, workers did make a positive attempt to minimise the effects of management's power. WNLA for example, had to make some very definite adjustments in policy as a result of worker reaction. This article has shown that workers in a repressive environment turn to a range of alternative methods of varying effectiveness to express their protest and resistance.

FOOTNOTES

1. Kornhauser *et al* have emphasised the importance of looking beyond strike action for evidence of industrial conflict in modern industrial economies: '. . . the general object of study is not the labour dispute, the strike or the lock out, but the total range of behaviour and attitudes that express opposition and divergent orientations between industrial owners and managers on the one hand and working people and their organizations on the other.' Kornhauser, A. Dubin, R. and Ross, A. H. *Industrial Conflict* (New York, McGraw Hill, 1954) p.12. Kerr also describes industrial conflict as expressing itself in a variety of ways which 'are as unlimited as the ingenuity of man.' Kerr, C., *Labour and Management in Industrial Society* (New York, Doubleday, 1964) p.171.

2. For details of these methods see Moroney, S., 'Industrial Conflict in a Labour Repressive Economy: Black Labour on the Transvaal Gold Mines 1901-1912.' Unpublished Honours Dissertation, University of the Witwatersrand, 1976, pp.19-31.

3. I use the term 'desert' which was applied by management to this act, in order to avoid confusion. The word has derogatory overtones. It implies a dereliction of

duty. Withdrawal of labour is more accurate but I have used this to apply to more widespread action (see below). The use of 'deserter', 'desertion', etc. was an important part of management's ideology. Such terms immediately suspended any critical examination of the conditions of employment which caused workers to leave in large numbers and justified the use of every possible pursual and punitive measure.

4. A worker's shift was 'cancelled' and therefore, not paid for, if he did not achieve the required amount of work as set by the mine. Those employed in rock drilling, for example, would be required to drill a certain depth. If they did not achieve this in some mines, they would not be accredited with the work achieved below the requirement. This in fact created a situation where management was able to extract significant quantities of work for no pay at all. For more details see Moroney.

5. Management attempted to introduce a minimum contract length of 12 months. Subsequently, as a result of extensive withdrawal, contracts were reduced to 6 months and eventually, 3 months in duration, a reversion to the original situation. See Moroney, op cit. pp.125-130.

6. Some inspectors were reported to have been unsympathetic to workers and to have worked in close co-operation with compound managers and management generally. If a worker wished to lay a charge through the inspector at a pass office, he would have to apply to the compound manager for a day pass to leave the compound. This would almost certainly be denied if the manager realised the worker's intention. There is evidence that workers consciously obviated this problem by concealing their intent. See Moroney, S. op. cit., p.102.

7. The courts were in fact very lenient towards white miners convicted of assault against blacks. Many were discharged with warnings. Such leniency indicated the State's collaborative role according to which acts of violence against workers were covertly condoned. One inspector of the Native Affairs Department complained in 1906 that in a particular assault case in which the defendant was discharged with a warning, the magistrate made remarks during the case which made it 'appear that he considers flogging of Natives by their employers as justifiable under certain circumstances.'

8. Groups of a similar nature and purpose exist in contemporary mine compound communities. Theology students who were hired as workers on mines during 1976, reported that: 'It appears that there are several informal networks operating . . . A circle of friends emerges out of a particular ethnic group which in turn extends to those working together.' The students also reported that *isibondas* played an important role as elected leaders within each room and facilitated discussion of common problems. This group is closely analogous to the type of leadership that emerged at the earliest stages of migrancy. See Matsobane, P., and Eggenhuizen, T. (eds.) *Another Blanket* (Johannesburg, Agency for Industrial Mission, June 1976) pp.17, 22.

9. P. Warwick, 'Black Industrial Protest on the Witwatersrand 1901-2', *SALB* Vol 2 No 8.

10. C. Van Onselen, 'South Africa's lumpen proletarian Army: "Umkosi Was Ntaba" — "The Regiment of the Hills", 1890-1920' (Unpublished paper, African Studies Institute, University of the Witwatersrand, April 1976).

11. See F. A. Johnstone, *Race, Class and Gold* (Routledge and Kegan Paul, London 1976).

ORIGINS AND ASPECTS OF AFRICAN WORKER CONSCIOUSNESS IN RHODESIA

I. R. PHIMISTER

> We are now, it seems, to have a native newspaper reading community. Such would appear from the practice of the batches of boys assembling outside the Argus Company's premises to read the police news of the daily issue posted up. Amongst the boys is always one who can read sufficient English to interpret the Magistrate's Court, and as he announces the result of "no pass" and "desertion" cases, his audience is highly interested and deeply concerned with their neighbours who are sent gaolwards for a holiday ... it shows boys are susceptible to their surroundings and cognizant of the institutions which exist in their midst. [1]

The generally appalling conditions which were characteristic of Southern Rhodesian mine compounds for over twenty years from at least the late 1890s often literally meant that 'for an African mineworker, the choice of employer or employment centre was ... a life-and-death decision'.[2] For black workers, then, sheer survival was in many cases dependent on an intelligence system concerning labour conditions on the various mines. Associated with this basic 'consciousness of survival' was an equally acute perception of differing wage levels, not only within Southern Rhodesia itself, but throughout the southern African regional economy.

Until recently, however, academic observers of Southern Rhodesian labour history were unanimously of the opinion that African worker consciousness first began to manifest itself primarily in the 1920s.[3] These interpretations, which assumed that the consciousness of African labourers 'should be assessed largely through the presence or absence of associations and organizations which manifestly articulate worker interests',[4] have now been systematically exploded by van Onselen's thorough analysis of black responses and strategies in the Southern Rhodesian mining industry between 1900 and 1933.

Two basic and enduring features gave rise to and shaped the general expression of African worker consciousness: the predominant position of the Rand within the southern African regional economy and the repressive system of labour control and mobilisation operated by mine managements and the state. As regards the first feature van Onselen has explained that

> In the southern African regional economic system there were, for a complex variety of reasons, successive zones of low and high wages. Broadly described, there were zones of low wages in the northern areas of (Southern) Rhodesia and South Africa — i.e. at those points where there was an influx of immigrant labour. To the south of these zones, there were areas of higher wages — i.e. closer to the major employment centres of the respective national economies of Rhodesia and South Africa. Crudely put, the low wages of Mashonaland gave way to the higher wages of Matabeleland while the low wages of the Northern Transvaal gave way to the higher wages of the Witwatersrand. The behaviour of the labour migrant can only be understood against this broad economic background.[5]

Black worker consciousness or concern to maximise wages was therefore expressed in a persistent southwards movement of labour towards the highest-paying employment centres.

Although Southern Rhodesian mines were favourably situated geographically to take advantage of this flow of labour from the northern peripheries of the regional economic system towards the Rand, their limited profitability and concomitant low wages and poor working conditions made them generally unpopular with migrant labourers. These workers, where distances were too great to allow a direct journey to South Africa, sought short-term employment on Southern Rhodesian mines in order to accumulate sufficient savings to continue southwards. They would then desert 'from Mashonaland mines . . . make their way south to the Matabeleland mines, where the process would repeat itself as workers left for the Witwatersrand'.[6] Such desertion, itself an effective form of worker combination,[7] was a device used by Africans, apart from its other functions, to combat the provisions of the Masters and Servants Act of 1901 and the Pass Law of 1902 which together attempted to divert migrants to Southern Rhodesian mines and, once there, to control and hold them for the duration of their contracts.

African mineworkers were confronted not only with coercive legislation, but on the mines themselves were subjected to the harsh discipline of the compound system[8] and to somewhat broader social controls manipulated jointly by the mines and the state.[9] Recognition of this second feature, the repressive control of labour, enabled van Onselen to identify a further major area of worker consciousness, found not in 'direct expression of discontent' but 'in the nooks and crannies of the day-to-day work situation'.[10] It was thus possible to draw an illuminating parallel with the techniques of resistance utilised by slaves in the southern states of North America: 'Side by side with ordinary loafing and mindless labor went deliberate wastefulness, slowdowns, feigned illnesses, self-inflicted injuries, and the well-known abuse of livestock and equipment'.[11]

Details of van Onselen's study of black worker consciousness for the period 1900 to 1933 are not, however, repeated here. Instead, what this paper hopes to demonstrate is that, in most respects, the essential features of African worker consciousness were already well-developed *before* the turn of the twentieth century. In particular, by concentrating on the first formative decade of the capitalist mining industry in Southern Rhodesia, it is possible to trace the origins and early development of that consciousness. Secondly and more briefly, given the fact that the mining industry's central profitability constraints remained essentially unaltered in the years 1934 to 1953, the natural continuation in that period of earlier patterns of worker responses is examined.

The roots of African worker consciousness and responses to the 'modern' mining industry are somewhat diffuse, but three main strands can be identified. The first and most fundamental strand of worker consciousness, in the wide sense of seeking the most lucrative sources of income, was basically an extension and adaptation of past African experiences in precolonial production and trade and appreciation of market opportunities, whether for agricultural produce or labour. Africans in what became Southern Rhodesia assessed employment opportunities on local mines and very largely rejected them in favour of the more financially rewarding occupation of peasant production for the new and expanding markets.[12]

Not all Africans, however, could effectively exercise the option of producing crops for markets. Whether because of remoteness from markets in the early colonial era or because of real limitations within 'traditional' Shona agriculture before that period,[13] Africans also turned to wage labour. But Africans from Southern Zambezia took care, both before and after 1890, to seek out the most remunerative centres of employment. From 1870 and 1886 respectively, these were recognised to be the Kimberley and Rand mines. As early as 1873 at least one Shona was returning from Kimberley[14] and two years later a 'party of Makalakas' were recorded as on their way home from the diamond fields, 'carrying each in great triumph the gun for which he had been working for the past year. They were full of gossip and tales from the Fields'.[15] In 1877, two white travellers described the welcome they received at a Kalanga village when they were 'recognised by one of our Kimberley mining boys, who . . . rushed off to his kraal and told his three companions that their old bosses had arrived. They had been good boys and had been well paid and rewarded for their services'.[16] Ndebele labourers, too, worked at Kimberley, by 1884 as many as one hundred and twenty.[17]

The formal proclamation of colonial rule over Mashonaland in 1890 and over Matabeleland in 1893 did not stop this southwards flow of labour but rather increased it as time went on through the imposition of taxes. Early in 1894, the *Rhodesia Herald* was of the opinion that 'many of the (Matabeleland) natives having worked in the Transvaal and Kimberley mines are practised workmen'[18] and in the Mashonaland district of Victoria most of the tax in 1895 was paid in gold earned on the Rand and at Kimberley.[19] In subsequent years the higher wages of the south continued to attract 'large numbers' of migrant labourers[20] and this factor, together with awareness of the appalling working conditions on local mines, meant that 'Boys who have had years of experience in Johannesburg and Kimberley cannot be induced to go to Selukwe, preferring to go back to Johannesburg rather than risk their lives at Selukwe'.[21] Other government officials testified to a similar awareness on the part of Africans elsewhere; for example, of the Bulalima district in 1898, it was reported that 'large numbers of the young men are away at work, chiefly on the Rand where they are offered higher wages and are better treated on the whole (so they say) than at the Mines in Matabeleland'.[22]

Both in their production of crops for new markets and in the sale of their wage labour, Africans thus displayed considerable acumen from the earliest days of capitalist development north of the Limpopo. Moreover, as the preceding sections have indicated, this strand of consciousness, the well-developed sense of economic self-interest, had lengthy historical roots.

The second strand of consciousness, though, did not draw on the African past in the same direct manner; it was rather a consequence of the imposition and implementation of colonial rule, which, as Rosa Luxemburg has explained, was the struggle against natural economy:

The principal methods in this struggle are political force (revolution, war), oppressive taxation by the state, and cheap goods; they are partly applied simultaneously, and partly they succeed and complement one another. In Europe, force assumed revolutionary forms in the fight against feudalism . . . in the non-European countries . . . it assumed the forms of colonial policy . . . In detail, capital in its struggle against societies with a natural economy pursues (amongst others) the following ends: (1) To gain immediate possession of important sources of productive forces such as land . . . minerals . . . (2) To "liberate" labour power and to coerce it into service.[23]

Although colonial rule was uneven in its impact on Southern Rhodesia during the decade 1890-1900, the speed and crudity of primitive accumulation in this period was sufficient to produce the African risings by 1896-7. Large-scale expropriations of cattle, the exaction of 'fines', the imposition of taxes, the levying of forced labour and the progressive alienation of land were all mechanisms used by white settlers to disrupt the indigenous economy[24] and at the same time induced in Africans what can be termed the 'consciousness of the colonised'.[25] The brutality and 'openness' characteristic of primitive accumulation in Southern Rhodesia left Africans in little doubt as to their new status; in the words of Fanon:

In the (metropolitan) capitalist countries a multitude of moral teachers, counsellors and "bewilderers" separate the exploited from those in power. In the colonial countries, on the contrary, the policeman and the soldier, by their immediate presence and their frequent and direct action maintain contact with the native and advise him by means of rifle-butts and napalm not to budge. It is obvious here that the agents of government speak the language of pure force. The intermediary does not lighten the oppression, nor seek to hide the domination.[26]

As far as the mines were concerned, the 'language of pure force' was employed almost from their inception. Neither wages nor working conditions were sufficiently attractive to bring forth labour in the required numbers[27] and within three months of the arrival of the 'pioneer column' in Mashonaland, the B.S.A. Company Administrator was complaining that 'the mining community both on the Mazoe and Umfuli are suffering from the scarcity and bad quality of the local labour'.[28] The way in which labour power was 'liberated' and 'coerced into service' was candidly explained by a mining commissioner in 1892: 'The natives here seem much more willing to work this year than they were last (year). The chastisement meted out to other kraals of which they are certain to have heard, has no doubt greatly tended to make them better in this respect'.[29] Such measures, of course, could prove counter-productive and a year later it was reported of the same district that 'there is considerable difficulty in getting boys for the small number of prospectors in the district. Some of the

51

Kraals refused either to trade or furnish boys. I think this is in a great measure due to bad treatment received previously'.[30]

The unwillingness of local Africans to work on Mashonaland mines led the *Rhodesia Herald,* in a somewhat confused editorial, to suggest that 'it is quite possible that artificial means will have to be employed to hasten the natural influx of native miners . . . In these days *laissez faire* has to all intents and purposes become an exploded doctrine, and Government regulations and restrictions are found to answer as well or better than the haphazard outcomes of Darwinian struggles.'[31] Insofar as the attempts of isolated mining commissioners and individuals to force Africans to work can be regarded as 'haphazard struggles', the B.S.A. Company heeded the *Herald's* advice and, with the establishment of the Native Department in 1894, forced labour became more widely and systematically practised. But Native Department 'regulation' of the labour market did not entirely supersede the activities of other interested parties. The Tebekwe Mine, for instance, employed a number of Zulu workers who were issued with company rifles and were 'in the habit of raiding the District for Boys and looting on their own account'.[32]

While it is impossible to calculate the number of Africans who were forced to work on Southern Rhodesian mines, it is clear that forced labour was singularly unpopular, was an important cause of the 1896-7 risings and perhaps more than any other single factor, contributed to black consciousness regarding their exploitable and vulnerable colonial status. According to one study of the African risings, the British Army in the Selukwe District in 1896 heard the cry, 'anything is preferable to working in the mines' and Africans themselves later explained that 'the cause of the rebellion was labour recruiting . . . When the white people started the place which they call Selukwe the police used to come to our kraals . . . and when they recruited us they used to beat us.'[33] Certainly Africans seized the opportunity afforded by the risings to destroy mine buildings and property — at one mine damage to machinery alone amounted to about one thousand pounds[34] — and to kill foreign miners.[35]

Forced labour in particular and the mining industry in general were thus perceived as the symbol and the cause of the African's colonised position; indeed, B.S.A. Company officials bluntly informed African leaders that 'they might as well understand once and for all that this is a white man's country and that the white man's object was to get the gold out of the ground'.[36] Conversely, where they were able to exercise the option of choice, Africans were unwilling to assist Europeans in the attainment of their 'object'. At the turn of the century, at least one observer thought that labour scarcity was partly due to this broad 'consciousness of the colonised':

> The grown up people look upon the discovery of gold as the cause of the loss of their country to themselves. They are unwilling to co-operate in the development of what they consider their great misfortune. No doubt this impression tells also on the young men.[37]

Shona insurgents, too, specifically objected to white exploitation of the country's gold. Two European prospectors whose camp was surrounded by followers of the 'rebel' Mapondera, later recalled the demands and remarks flung at them: 'Who gave us permission to come up and wash gold and sink pits? The gold was theirs; the district was theirs; they did not want anyone in the country sinking shafts "Magodi". Curses on the English at Salisbury.'[38]

Finally, these two strands of African consciousness, a sense of economic self-interest and an awareness of their colonised status, were combined and refined as worker consciousness through immediate experiences of labour conditions on Southern Rhodesian mines. This consciousness found expression in desertions, understanding of wage levels and employment opportunities and even in explicit combination where mangement provocation was sufficiently great. The latter manifestations were rare, however, because black workers rapidly experienced harsh discipline on the mines and in an era when co-operation between the state and the mining industry to procure and control labour was brutally clear, workers swiftly appreciated that discontent was best expressed in less obvious ways.

After only one year of capitalist mining development, employers were complaining of three features which both reflected black worker consciousness and which, to greater or lesser degrees, were to remain constant factors in subsequent mine labour history. For example, in the Manica region in 1891, companies complained about the scarcity of labour, the frequency of desertions once Africans were 'induced' to work and the low productivity or 'loafing' of labourers.[39] Although some contemporaries attributed these features to African 'discomfiture of hard work',[40] others realised that 'the majority of the best boys' simply preferred the more remunerative occupation of working as 'bearers to and from the Coast'.[41] Elsewhere, desertion was already a widespread device for registering resistance to forced labour and poor working conditions; in the Umfuli district, 'nearly all' Shona labourers deserted 'after two or three days work'.[42] In the Victoria district, African manipulation of the labour market was so

effective that the local mining commissioner pressed for the introduction of a pass law as early as 1892:

> Numerous complaints have been made to me by diggers and others about the
> difficulty they have in keeping the natives in their employ. They will agree to
> work say for 3 months at £1 per month and their food. They will work for one
> month and then just as they have learnt to strike a drill and are becoming useful,
> will leave without notice and engage themselves to another person, either
> because they get more pay, or because they like the position of the new mining
> (?) camp, or for some other reasons ... (In addition) a Contractor who has
> undertaken to do certain work within a specified time, finds it absolutely
> necessary that he should have good boys who are up to their work, and he will
> have a kaffir in his employ whose duty it is to go from mine to mine and find out
> the boys who are the best (drill) strikers, and the most useful in other ways and
> he will induce them to run away from the master they are working for, by
> promises of increased pay etc.[43]

So widespread was black worker consciousness that it elicited a
degree of grudging recognition from B.S.A. Company officials and
contemporary newspapers, who sometimes abandoned ideology (the
inherently 'lazy native' concept) in favour of pointing to the consequences of poor working conditions. In 1893, an over-enthusiastic
settler who had suggested 'drastic measures to obtain native labour
for the mines', was reminded by an administrative official that 'much
of the difficulty experienced in getting natives to work is due to their
white employers declining to pay the wages due. I cannot consent to
your firing upon any kraal for the purpose of getting labourers.'[44] A
local newspaper was also of the opinion that much of the labour
shortage was due to employers 'who after engaging a boy, let his
period of service nearly expire, and then either cause him to run away,
or drive him off, by trumped up charges, deliberate cruelty, or the
refusal to pay him his money due'. The paper warned that these
methods of treatment were 'rapidly communicated' to other Africans
and concluded that 'ignorant — though willing — and half-clothed
natives cannot be expected to turn out before sunrise on a cold or wet
morning, and work on empty stomachs, getting more kicks than half-
pence, throughout a long weary day. One willing labourer is worth
half a dozen forced ones.'[45]

Where black mineworkers were treated decently, the labour supply
was correspondingly greater,[46] but in general the level of mine wages,
especially in Mashonaland, was too low to attract 'voluntary' labour.
Even during the speculative era of 1894-6 when capital expenditure
and mining development were at their most extravagant, such
largesse as percolated downwards through the system went primarily
into the hands of contractors[47] and did not significantly affect

African conditions of labour. Although the average wages of black labourers did rise noticeably in this period,[48] the increase seems to have come mainly from the richer Matabeleland mines and in any event, mining companies were not prepared to dilute their speculative profits by improving other aspects of African employment conditions.

Management cognizance of African worker consciousness in the form of desertions instead took the cheaper option of improving the control and discipline of workers on the mines themselves. There were few employers who disagreed with the sentiment that 'the only & best means (of preventing African desertions) is to have a proper compound on the mines & appoint a few good boys as police to look after the others'.[49] And as in the forced mobilisation of labour, the state co-operated enthusiastically with the mining industry in this sphere. Before the risings, armed 'Native Policemen' were supplied by the B.S.A. Company to various mines in Matabeleland 'in order to prevent the native labourers deserting'. In 1898, renewed requests for this service were sympathetically considered by the Chief Native Commissioner as a means of halting Africans from utilising a particular mine as 'a sort of half-way house where they can rest and obtain food for a few days, before proceeding to the Transvaal, whither they are tempted by the promise of higher wages than are paid on these fields'.[50] If Africans slipped past these armed guards, only to be caught later, their punishment was severe. A British visitor to the territory was 'told that if a boy will not work, or tries to run away, the usual thing is to take him to the native commissioner, and have him given twenty-five (lashes), and I found that the word "twenty-five" said in English to any of the boys was sufficient to make them grin in a sickly way — they quite understood what it meant'.[51]

Repressive mobilisation and control of black labour was further aggravated by the almost complete absence of effective communication between white employers and African workers. According to one Native Commissioner, 'the "Lingua Franca", between natives and Europeans in those early days consisted of about three words: "Ikona, lo, and voetsak"! I heard Mrs Dr. Forrester ... telling her boy to "voetsak lo kwackwacs" out of her garden (turn the ducks out) and he seemed to understand.' Less amusing and more pertinent to African working conditions on the mines was

on another occasion the Manager of the Bonsor had told ... one of his (work) hands to measure up a lot of cords of mine fuel I had cut for them. This man had a raw boy to carry a very full pot of paint, which he used to mark each stack we measured. The boy could hardly help spilling a little owing to the rough terrain we were measuring in. The official told the boy once or twice not to "spill lo bloody paint" but at last lost his temper and hitting the boy a severe blow with his fist, knocking him over, he asked "Did I not tell ye not to spill lo bloody paint"? and, turning to me he remarked: "The b . . . . does not understand his own bloody language"?[52]

Apart from the often brutal manner in which they were disciplined, black workers also discovered how dangerous it was working on Southern Rhodesian mines and consequently gave 'accident-prone' mines a wide berth. At the Inez Mine in July 1895 an explosion, caused through the carelessness of the white miner in charge of the night shift, killed two Africans and injured two others. As a result, approximately fifty labourers deserted 'and it has had a bad effect on (the) District all round'.[53] The frequency with which accidents occurred at the Tebekwe Mine gave it 'a very bad name (and) Boys from the District would sooner work at any other mine'.[54]

In these circumstances of dangerous working conditions, forced labour and harsh discipline, it would be occasion for comment if black labourers had *not* possessed a well-developed worker consciousness, rather than the converse. The same conditions, however, obliged the majority of African mineworkers to utilise similar techniques of resistance to those discussed by Genovese and van Onselen. Certain techniques were in existence by 1891 and by 1898 were common enough for one government official to summarize the pattern of crime in 'his' district as 'only (those) such as desertion, disobedience, absence without leave, malingering and the like'.[55] Abuse of mining company livestock was also a relatively safe method of registering protest; for example, 'one of 53 oxen belonging to the (Geelong Gold Mining) Company was found dead in the kraal and . . . on the beast being cut open and examination made it was found that a piece of rough stick about six inches long and rather pointed at both ends had been forced up its fundamental orifice and injured the intestines etc. thus causing death'.[56] At the Red and White Rose Mine, where conditions were often appalling, African labourers staged an effective 'go-slow' which drove the mine mangement to frustration.[57]

Occasionally, though, black workers reacted in even more explicit ways against exploitation. In 1895 Shona workers on a small mine refused to work following a management attempt to introduce a night shift, as such labour was not covered by the original terms of their labour agreement.[58] A few years later, Africans at the Sable Hill Mine firmly indicated their opposition to management interference with their private possessions. In the words of the investigating Native

Commissioner, the employer

having noticed that meal etc. was being wasted went through the kit of one lot of
boys and found some candles, matches, and meal which they ought not to have
had in their possession. On going to a second hut, the boys came up brandishing
"Kerries" & speaking very excitedly, saying they had bought the things in
Salisbury. Mr Bennet thinking that he had better not interfere further because
he was unarmed & alone, went away.[59]

Defiance of this nature did not go unchecked. The two 'ringleaders'
were 'punished' and the rest reprimanded by the local Native
Commissioner, after whicn all the workers were 'paid to date and
dismissed'.[60] Desertion, too, was sometimes recognised as open
combination; when reporting the large-scale desertion of Africans
from mines, especially in the Hartley district, the *Rhodesia Herald*
commented that 'in one instance at least . . . it is not a question of the
boys deserting so much as "striking". Some disagreement, we understand, occurred about the terms of payment and the boys are . . .
coming into town in a body in order to lodge certain complaints.'[61]

By the end of the nineteenth century, then, African worker consciousness was already well-established and workers in subsequent
years 'were careful to make inquiries before leaving (their homes) as
to what arrangements would be made regarding medical and general
treatment, also the rate of wages and the number of months they
would be employed'.[62] As the beginning of this paper noted, these
later patterns of African worker responses and initiatives over the
decades up to 1933 have been extensively explored elsewhere. After
that date, black labourers continued to assess employment
opportunities in terms of the regional economic system, and South
Africa in general and the Rand in particular remained the ultimate
target for most migrant workers.[63] The only significant change was
occasioned by the development of the Northern Rhodesian Copper-
belt, the higher wages of which increasingly began to draw labour
from Southern Rhodesian mines.

During the Great Depression, the closure or restricted output of
many concerns and the economic collapse of the African rural areas
released a flood of labourers, many of whom initially sought employment on local mines. The response of the Southern Rhodesian mining
industry was to consistently lower wages, a practice which in turn
ultimately did a great deal to eliminate the labour surplus.[64] Africans
in increasing numbers migrated to South Africa rather than work for
any length of time for local mine wages which averaged between 17*s*.
and 20*s*. per month in 1935. By 1937, a concerned Government
estimated that over twenty-seven thousand Africans, including

migrants who had worked their way through Southern Rhodesia, were 'clandestinely' emigrating to South Africa each year.[65] Officials in the southern part of the colony reported the 'very noticeable' development of labour routes to the Rand mines:

> Gangs of Natives are now to be met all along the border and they do not attempt to conceal the fact that they are going to the Rand, they are very ready to say that they are Portuguese Natives and give one the impression that they think because they say they are Portuguese Natives, they are free to use the road without any interference from the authorities of this Colony. Last year the few gangs I did meet disappeared into the veldt on the sight of a car with a Native Passenger in it.[66]

Migration of this magnitude produced a labour shortage which affected the great majority of Southern Rhodesian mines.[67] The Secretary for Mines warned that the 'labour requirements of the mines on the Rand are almost insatiable, and there appears a danger that, unless attractive conditions of employment are available in Southern Rhodesia, the higher wages paid by the Rand mines will be an irresistible magnet to native labour'.[68] Few local mines were able to respond significantly to the Secretary's warning and as a result the labour shortage continued unabated.

From the Gwanda district, it was reported that 'Hammer boys and those able to operate Oliver Filters are going to the Union for employment'.[69] and at the Antelope Mine further south where 'a slight influx of labour from Gwanda District had occurred ... it (was) suspected that these Natives are merely awaiting an opportunity to cross into the Union territory'.[70] In other parts of the colony, desertions and well-developed labour routes were equally common. One particular route frequently used by Africans from Nyasaland provides a classic example of this aspect of worker consciousness:

> At the Hippo Mine it was stated that numerous Natives from Nyasaland come by train to Umtali and before being registered proceed to this Mine where they obtain work. After a month, having rested and earned a little money, they desert making for Johannesburg. This mine being so far away from Chipinga cannot always have these natives registered before engaging them. Apparently this mine is regarded by some Natives wishing to proceed to Johannesburg as a half way house.[71]

African workers also gravitated towards better-paid jobs within Southern Rhodesia; secondary industry and the large base mineral producers all attracted labour from local gold mines.

This labour shortage, of varying intensity, which persisted in the Southern Rhodesian mining industry between 1936 and 1953 was clearly a result of black worker consciousness. The shortage itself, moreover, resulted in a strengthening or at least made possible a clearer expression of other aspects of African worker strategies. Because their bargaining position was improved by the scarcity of labour, those black workers who remained within the mining industry were able to utilise other techniques of resistance with comparative impunity. Employers in the Umtali district in 1938 complained of 'inefficiency, deliberate slowness, insolence and a changed attitude of lack of respect for the European (on the part of Africans), many of them are not prepared to do a fair month's work for their pay'. But the compound inspector who recorded these management grievances was sufficiently perceptive to note their relationship to employer exploitation: 'there is another side to this question and that is the morality of the employer; the employer who fails to pay wages, unjustly docks tickets, refuses to accept notice, keeps a ticket in hand to prevent desertion, and has little or no interest in housing or feeding conditions'.[72] In the Selukwe area, African workers on a mine which was remote from labour routes took advantage of management reluctance to antagonize the precarious labour supply by malingering. Between ten and fifteen workers reported 'sick' each day in order 'to have a rest'.[73]

The following year, the Chief Native Commissioner criticised the prevalent policy 'of "keeping labour sweet" by complacency towards shiftlessness and absenteeism', but conceded that 'something in the nature of group insistences on the Natives' part . . . is observable'. These ran the full gamut from 'insistence on good food, fair wages and prompt payment' to 'a tendency towards ca'canny and careless work and frequent absentations from duty'.[74] A junior official was even more explicit in his appraisal: 'Employers complain that labourers are very indifferent, irresponsible, and difficult to handle . . . (and) have to put up with impertinence and careless work to keep their employees otherwise their business comes to a stand-still'.[75] Compound inspectors were approached by employers and asked 'to lecture the natives on disobedience. They disregard the instructions of their employers, and for peace and quiet their employers let them have their own way.'[76] Others reported that 'natives are adopting a definitely "go-slow" policy'[77] and concluded that the 'natives remaining in employment are well aware of the labour position and are working in a very perfunctory manner'.[78]

Because of the general nature of Southern Rhodesia's political economy and the particular profitability constraints of the mining industry, both of which rested on cheap, exploitable black labour, explicit African worker combination was not generally tolerated for the greater part of the period under consideration. Although the post-war development of secondary industry with its need for a stable labour force did see a resurgence and expansion of earlier black trade unions like the ICU, no similar movements emerged in the closely-controlled mining industry. In 1953, when anticipating the possibility of such a development in the future, the Chamber of Mines determined the following points:

> If Natives want to start a Trade Union, the Members must have a definite qualification, such as a certain standard of education. If they have Unions, there must be safeguards as they don't account for their funds, they spend them on agitators. A Union where ever Native can join was wrong because they could not think for themselves. They were very good at secret organisations, no one knew what they were up to at all.[79]

This statement by the major mines of the colony, while on the one hand indicative of continuing employer hostility to African labour organisations, on the other was an unintended tribute to black worker consciousness. It was because of their exploitable class position that African mineworkers rapidly became so adept 'at secret organisations (in which) no one knew what they were up to at all'. The combination of state force and management control of compounds was normally sufficient to muffle or suppress explicit worker combination and so ensure that the basis of the mining industry's profitability remained fundamentally unaltered, but African workers, as this paper has demonstrated, from the inception of capitalist mining, developed a variety of often successful techniques of resistance against exploitation.

FOOTNOTES

1. *Rhodesia Herald,* 19.x.1901.
2. C. van Onselen, 'Worker consciousness in black miners: Southern Rhodesia 1900-1920', *Journal of African History,* 1973, 14, 241.
3. Such an interpretation was also uncritically accepted by this writer; see 'The Shamva mine strike of 1927: an emerging African proletariat', *Rhodesian History,* 1971, 2, 65.
4. van Onselen, 'Worker consciousness', 237.
5. van Onselen, 'Black Workers in Central African Industry: a critical essay on the historiography and sociology of Rhodesia', *Journal of Southern African Studies,* 1975, 1, 240.
6. van Onselen, 'Worker consciousness', 248.
7. Ibid., 245.
8. For two examples, see *Rhodesia Herald,* 7.vii.1909, and *Bulawayo Chronicle,* 2.viii.1930. The compound system is exhaustively discussed in van Onselen, *Chibaro,* London, 1974, Chapter five.
9. See, for instance, the discussion concerning control of 'the inducement for attracting native labour, such as women, the sale of beer and the credit system of

stores', contained in N(ational) A(archives of) R(hodesia) S 1175/17, Compound Inspector, Bulawayo, to Medical Director, 16.ii.1931; and van Onselen, ibid., Chapter six.

10. van Onselen, 'Worker consciousness', 249.
11. E. Genovese, *The Political Economy of Slavery* (London, 1966), 74.
12. For details, see Phimister, 'Peasant production and underdevelopment in Southern Rhodesia, 1890-1914', *African Affairs,* 1974, **73**, 217-28.
13. D. N. Beach, 'The Shona economy: branches of production', University of Rhodesia, Henderson Seminar No. 29, 3.xii.1974.
14. ibid., 23.
15. E. C. Tabler (ed.), *To the Victoria Falls via Matabeleland: The Diary of Major Henry Stabb, 1875* (Cape Town, 1967), 234.
16. Tabler (ed.), *Zambezia and Matabeleland in the Seventies* (London, 1960), 73. See also, H. Vaughan-Williams, *A visit to Lobengula in 1889* (Pietermaritzburg, 1947), 88.
17. S. van der Horst, *Native Labour in South Africa* (London, 1942), 84. See also N.A.R. H.Mss. BA 10/2/1, Bailie Diary, 31.v.1876. For Africans working at the Tati mines, see N.A.R. H.Mss. Misc/ED 3, Sam Edwards.
18. *Rhodesia Herald,* 23.ii.1894.
19. Beach, 'The Shona economy', 23.
20. N.A.R. N 1/1/8, NC, Ndanga, to CNC, 24.iii.1897.
21. N.A.R. N 9/1/4, Assistant NC, Gutu, report for year ended 31.iii.1899.
22. N.A.R. NB 6/4/2, NC, Bulalima, report for May, 1898.
23. R. Luxemburg, *The Accumulation of Capital* (London, 1963), 369.
24. For examples of all of these, see T. O. Ranger, *Revolt in Southern Rhodesia 1896-7* (London, 1967), 61, 67-8, 70-81, 86-8, 94, 119.
25. For elaboration, see A. Memmi, *The Colonizer and the Colonized* (Boston, 1967), 81-141.
26. F. Fanon, *The Wretched of the Earth* (Harmondsworth, 1967), 29.
27. Beach has pointed out that the limitations of 'traditional' Shona agriculture obliged some Africans, apart from those who went to South Africa, to voluntarily enter wage employment on local mines, see 'The Shona economy', 23-4.
28. N.A.R. A 2/12/1, A.R. Colquhoun, Administrator's Office, Ft. Salisbury, to Mining Commissioner, Umfuli Gold Fields, 25.xi.1890.
29. N.A.R. ML 2/1/1, Mining Commissioner, Lomagundi, to Mines Office, Fort Salisbury, 'Report on Gold Fields', 25.v.1892.
30. N.A.R. LO 5/2/28, Lo Mogundi District, Report on Gold Fields for month of June, 1893.
31. *Rhodesia Herald,* 22.iv.1893.
32. N.A.R. NB 1/1/3, NC, Selukwe, to CNC, 25.iii.1898. The events referred to occurred before the risings. See also N.A.R. N 1/2/2, NC, Charter, to CNC, telegram, 25.v.1897; 'it is very difficult collecting boys. They wont come voluntarily but have to be forced am sending police out today to collect many as they can'.
33. Beach, 'The Rising in South Western Mashonaland, 1896-7', University of London, unpub. Ph.D. thesis, 1971, 256. See also N.A.R. LO 8/2/1, 'The Matabele Rising' by H. J. Taylor, 30.iv.1896.
34. D. Tyrie Laing, *The Matabele Rebellion* (London, (1897?)), 315.
35. See, for example, N.A.R. N 1/1/5, J. Jameson to Macglashan, 30.v.1896.
36. N.A.R. NB 6/5/1/2, Meeting in Bulalima-Mangwe District between CNC and

61

Indunas, 19.vii.1899.

37. N.A.R. A 11/2/8/17, Prestage to Poulteney, 5.viii.1900.
38. N.A.R. T 2/2/16, 'Parleying held on the Kopje with Rebels and their remarks', 26.ix.1901.
39. *Cape Times,* 10.xii.1891.
40. *Ibid.*
41. N.A.R. LO 5/2/19, Manica District, Report for month of March, 1892, 31.iii.1892.
42. N.A.R. LO 5/2/28, Umfuli District, Report on Gold Fields for month of June, 1893.
43. N.A.R. N 1/4/1, Mining Commissioner, Victoria, to Secretary, B.S.A. Company, 19.iv.1892.
44. N.A.R. A 2/1/5, A. H. Duncan to Heyman, 15.vii.1893.
45. *Matabeleland News and Mining Record,* 21.iv.1894.
46. N.A.R. N 1/1/5, NC, Lomagundi, to CNC, 26.xii.1894.
47. P. Hone, *Southern Rhodesia* (London, 1909), 248.
48. Phimister, 'History of mining in Southern Rhodesia to 1953', University of Rhodesia, unpub. Ph.D. thesis, 1975, 110.
49. N.A.R. N 1/1/5, NC, Lomagundi, to A. Lingard, 21.viii.1895.
50. N.A.R. NB 1/1/6, CNC to Secretary, 30.xi.1898; ibid, A. Wools-Sampson, Managing Director, Consolidated Exploration and Dev. (Rhodesia) Co., to His Honour, the Deputy Administrator of Matabeleland, 27.x.1898.
51. H. C. Thompson, *Rhodesia and its Government* (London, 1898), 82. The same author noted that 'the natives have a marvellous system of communicating with each other . . . (they also) sing a funny little song. It was made by an Englishman, but they have quite adopted it, and, what is more to the purpose, they act in accordance with it — "Ikona mali, piccaninny scoff, Meningy sebenza-this nigger's off", which may be translated thus: "No pay and little scoff, Too much work — this nigger's off"', 164-165.
52. N.A.R. H.Mss. Misc/Dr 2, William Driver reminiscences, 101.
53. N.A.R. N 1/1/3, NC, Hartley Hills, to CNC, 6.viii.1895.
54. N.A.R. NB 1/1/3.
55. N.A.R. NB 6/4/2, Assistant NC, Gwanda, report for May, 1898.
56. N.A.R. NB 6/4/2, Assistant NC, Manzamyama, report for April, 1900.
57. N.A.R. NB 1/1/10, Manager, Red and White Rose Mine, to NC, Umzingwane, 2.xi.1899.
58. N.A.R. N 1/1/9, NC, Salisbury, to (CNC?), 7.i.1895.
59. N.A.R. N 1/1/3, NC, Hartley, to CNC, 10.ix.1898.
60. ibid. For 'cuts' administered to strikers at the North Bonsor Mine in 1900, see N.A.R. NB 1/1/10, NC, Selukwe, to CNC, 26.vi.1900.
61. *Rhodesia Herald,* 5.x.1898. For further examples of African combination, see N.A.R. NB 6/4/3, NC, Bulalima-Mangwe, report for January, 1899; ibid., NC, Belingwe, report for April, 1899.
62. N.A.R. N 9/4/7, NC, Makoni, report for January, 1901.
63. In a very real sense, this was the only 'target' which motivated 'the target worker'.
64. For details, see Phimister, 'Gold mining in Southern Rhodesia, 1919-1953', *Rhodesian Journal of Economics,* 1976, v.10.
65. S 1561/4, Secretary for Native Affairs to Secretary to the Prime Minister (Native Affairs), 15.xi.1937.
66. S 235/438, Assistant NC, Nuanetsi, to NC, Chibi, 7.vii.1936.

67. For discussion of the 'native labour crisis', see *Smallworker,* October 1938, 21-5, and, even earlier, ibid., February 1936, 23-5.

68. *Report of the Secretary, Department of Mines and Public Works, on Mines, for the year 1937,* 8.

69. S 1542/R6A, Compound Inspector, Matabeleland South, report for December, 1937.

70. ibid., Compound Inspector, Matabeleland, No. One Section, report for November, 1937.

71. S 1610, Compound Inspector, Mashonaland, report for September, 1944.

72. S 1542/R6A, Compound Inspector, No. One Area, Umtali, report for June, 1938.

73. ibid., Compound Inspector, Gwelo South, report for May, 1938.

74. *Report of the Secretary for Native Affairs and Chief Native Commissioner for the year 1939,* 7.

75. S 1050, NC, Fort Victoria, report for year ended 31.xii.1940.

76. S 1610, Compound Inspector, Salisbury, report for October, 1940.

77. ibid., Compound Inspector, Bulawayo North and South, report for January, 1941.

78. ibid., Compound Inspector, Matabeleland, report for August, 1943.

79. Chamber of Mines of Rhodesia, private papers, Minutes of Executive Committee Meeting, 20.vii.1953.

SECTION 2

CLASSES, THE STATE AND INDUSTRIAL RELATIONS

INTRODUCTION

It is an obvious, but important consideration that the object of the state is to represent the class relation of capital to labour and of capital in general over particular capitals. In pursuit of this objective the capitalist state (the various apparatuses effecting the interests of the dominant classes) must disorganize the working class. It attempts to achieve this in two ways. Firstly, it may use its repressive apparatus to destroy or prevent the political organization of the working class. Secondly, it may follow an incorporative strategy. Here the state tends to transform working class organization by accentuating the distinction between economic and political class struggle. Thus the institutionalization of class conflict — the narrowing down of conflict to aggressive economism — is the characteristic form in which class conflict expresses itself in advanced capitalist society.

South Africa has followed both strategies simultaneously; incorporating the 'white working class' on one hand, repressing the 'black working class' on the other. In this section both Lever and Davies begin with the period of industrial militancy among white workers which preceded the period of incorporation. They describe the attempts by the state to institutionalize industrial conflict — the 1907 strike being followed by the Transvaal Disputes Act, the 1913 strike by the Industrial Disputes and Trade Union Bill and, of course, the 1922 strike by the Industrial Conciliation Act of 1924. Davies concludes that the 'Industrial Conciliation Variant' is employed by the state when political considerations make the direct repression of some organized section of the wage-earning population impossible or impractical, and that it involves regulation and institutionalization of power won by wage-earners in struggle. It thus represents a practical compromise, in which the owners of the means of production are dominant, and which indeed enables their interest to remain dominant. He goes on to argue that the creation of industrial councils has led to the emergence of a bureaucratic hierarchy of officials, distinct from the rank and file members, whose lifestyle, work and outlook have more in common with employers and state officials than with workers.

Differences between the two contributors are evident. Davies sees the legislation which is passed by parliament as the result of defeat by the working class, and where, as in 1914, it is rejected, this is seen as the result of opposition from white labour. Lever, on the other hand, seems to see a progressive movement towards the Industrial Conciliation Act and explains the failure of the 1914 Bill in the House of Assembly as the result of 'lack of parliamentary time'. Davies, in contrast to Lever, defines the state more specifically as the instrument of the dominant classes and consequently sees industrial legislation as 'the instrument of the classes of property owners dominant in the society'. (See Davies' author's note for his self-critical comment on what he calls his 'simple instrumentalist view of the state' in this article.)

However, they both agree that the Industrial Conciliation Act of 1924 (including its subsequent amendment in 1928 by the Nationalist Labour Pact government) constitutes a convergence of employer interests (with mining capital playing a major role in 1924) and the interests of white workers, who were able to entrench the ground they had won. The South African Labour Party perceived it to be in the interests of their white supporters to exclude Africans from trade union rights. The Industrial Conciliation Act of 1924 thus served to establish a 'joint monopoly' of employers and registered trade unions at the expense of African workers, who were excluded from the industrial conciliation negotiating procedure. Davies has gone on to argue elsewhere that the Pact government represented the achievement of hegemony by national capital, and that the white wage-earners were only in the position of an allied or supportive class to members of the power bloc. The state's policies towards white wage-earners over this period, he argues, have to be seen as interventions which served, in the last analysis, to advance capitalist interests. Economic concessions made to white wage-earners, largely at the expense of Africans, functioned further to divide white from black wage-earners and to ensure that the whites increasingly saw their future within the confines of capitalist society. Furthermore, the industrial relations legislation administered by the Pact disorganized white-wage earners as a militant social force.[1]

FOOTNOTES

1. Davies, R., review of F. R. Johnstone, *Class, Race and Gold, African Perspectives*, No. 5, p.54.

THE CLASS CHARACTER OF SOUTH AFRICA'S INDUSTRIAL CONCILIATION LEGISLATION

ROB DAVIES

Author's Note: In writing this article I had in mind a specific limited objective, namely to focus on the role of the 'industrial conciliation' type of legislation as a means by which the bourgeois state attempts to disorganize wage earners as a political threat to capital (a theme hitherto neglected in virtually all discussions of this question in the South African context). However, while I still agree with this fundamental proposition, I have, since writing the article, substantially developed (and in a number of important respects revised) my views on the making of Industrial Conciliation Legislation in South Africa and its specific effects. In particular I have moved away from the kind of simple instrumentalist view of the capitalist state implicit in the article. The interested reader is referred to Chapters 3-5 of my thesis 'Capital, the State and White Wage Earners. An Analysis of Class Formation and Class Relations in South Africa 1900-1960' (University of Sussex D.Phil thesis, 1977, to be published in a modified form by Harvester Press late In 1978 or early 1979).

South African legislation relating to industrial bargaining procedures is by now well known for its racially discriminatory provisions and for the vastly inferior treatment which it accords to African workers and their organizations. It has also been widely recognized that the provisions currently relating to African workers are designed to impede the development of a vigorous and effective African labour movement which could struggle for an end to the exploitation of African workers. In the forefront of those recognizing these truths are many of the African workers and trade unionists who are themselves most affected. Their practical experience of the works and liaison committees — provided for under the 1973 Bantu Labour Relations Regulations Act — has led numerous spokesmen to repeatedly reject these bodies as a means of continued repression and call instead for trade union rights.

This legitimate, and indeed necessary, demand has been accompanied by calls from a number of powerful voices in the society — among them various employers, white trade union leaders, opposition MPs and academics — which essentially amount to a call for African workers to be given 'fuller rights' within the existing 'industrial relations' legislative structure. The specific form which these proposals have taken has varied quite considerably; from the proposal that Africans be allowed to join registered trade unions, to the proposal that independent African unions be allowed to register under the Industrial Conciliation Act and to participate, to some degree or other, in the various statutory bodies: Industrial Councils, Conciliation Boards, etcetera.[1]

In these circumstances it is becoming increasingly necessary to understand something of the principles which underlie the *totality* of South Africa's industrial bargaining legislation. This paper hopes to illuminate some aspects of these via a study of certain characteristics of the 'most permissive' of the legislation in that totality: that governing industrial bargaining by non-African, particularly white, wage earners.

Origins of the Legislation

In order to understand something of the function and purpose of the legislation in question it is necessary for us first to understand something of the circumstances in which it originated and of the 'problems' it was designed to 'solve'. This necessitates a brief examination of the conditions of class struggle in the society during the first quarter of this century.

By the very early years of the century a distinctly racial division of labour had evolved in the country's most important industry, the goldmining industry. Africans were excluded from skilled and supervisory work, and by 1907/8 the decision had effectively been taken to exclude whites from general unskilled work, thus confining their employment to skilled, supervisory and a small number of clearly defined less skilled categories. However, as Johnstone[2] and others have convincingly shown, the precise limits of this racial division of labour were far from fixed. In their pursuit of profit mineowners sought, especially at times of crisis in the industry, to progressively transfer more and more of the actual production tasks to lower paid African workers: in fact, to attempt to create a structure of production relations in which white employment would ultimately be confined to a limited number of supervisors of African workers. As such proposed modifications involved lay-offs, increases in the intensity of work, and, to a lesser extent, wage cuts, they were resisted by the organized white miners and thus resulted in a number of strikes. The most important of these were in 1907, 1913 and 1922. On each of these occasions the strike in question became general, lasted several weeks, involved considerable violence, and was only ended by being put down with force.

The period immediately following World War 1 was also a period of intense struggle within the newly important secondary manufacturing sector. The proximate causes of the intensified struggle in this sector were the sharp rise in consumer prices during these years, accompanied by a fall in the rate of profit on capital invested in a number of firms as a result of the re-opening of trade routes and enhanced foreign competition.[3] These struggles in the manufacturing sector were however somewhat different in character to those in the mining industry. For though white unemployment, in part the product of the non-employment of unskilled whites in the mining industry, had led the state to intervene in an attempt to secure for whites preferential access to the employment created in manufacturing industry, there was, in this sector at that time, a much less marked racial demarcation of jobs. Furthermore, manufacturing employers, unlike mineowners, themselves lacked the means to procure large numbers of African workers with whom they could replace whites. They therefore responded to the post World War 1 crisis by seeking primarily not modifications to the pattern of production relations, but cuts in real (and sometimes in monetary) wage levels. But despite such differences, the net outcome of these struggles was the same as in the mining industry; they resulted in a number of strikes. These involved white and coloured workers in among others the baking, construction, engineering, clothing, shoemaking, furniture-making and printing industries, with railwaymen, municipal employees and dockers also being involved in important strikes.

At the same time as all of these struggles price rises considerably above wage increases prompted African workers to begin to organize and to strike for the first time on a significant scale. Among the most important strikes by African workers were those by municipal workers in 1918 and 1919, by dockworkers in 1919, by mineworkers in 1920 and by members of the police force in 1918.

Such strikes, which at their high point in the years between 1919 and 1922 involved an annual average of 42 087 workers striking for an average of 16,8 days each compared to an average of only 369 workers per year in the years 1906, 1908 to 1912[4] were viewed with considerable alarm by those in the society who profited from the labour of others. Not only was this because they were regarded as damaging in their own right, but because strikes by white wage earners were seen as providing a catalyst for the potentially far more damaging strikes by black workers. One representative quotation from a Government Commission which reported in 1914 will make this clear:

> Your Commissioners must call attention to the danger in South Africa under existing conditions of industrial unrest, and especially of attempts by strikes and lock-outs to compel either employers or employed to grant concessions. The (evidence heard) . . . show(s) clearly what serious effects such disturbances have upon the native mind. A Government Inspector deposed thus: "Some natives are realising that it is in their interests to form a combination . . ." In answer to the question whether he thought the natives had learnt lessons in combination from the events (of the 1913 strike by white miners), the Inspector replied: "I'm sure of it . . . What they learnt in a week last July might in the ordinary way have taken them 15 years to learn."[5]

Surprising as it may seem to us with hindsight, this was a major concern even where white strikers were involved in acts of hostility against African workers. For example, the Judicial Commission appointed to inquire into the events surrounding the 1922 strike argued that the principal danger posed by the Rand Revolt was that it was led by a conspiracy of Communists who, unbeknown to the rank and file participants, saw 'armed uprisings' as a definite part of an overall strategy to 'induce the coloured as well as the European races in South Africa and elsewhere to adopt Communistic principles, and so prepare the way for the establishment of Soviet republics throughout the universe.'[6] That such interpretations do not stand up as analyses of the causes of African strikes or of the Rand Revolt — being, among other things, dependent upon the dubious notion that there were not sufficient factors internal to their situation to 'stir up' the participants in these struggles without external influence — is not for present purposes directly relevant. The point is that this is the way in which the controlling interests in the society increasingly came to see the situation they confronted in the first quarter of the century.

The Legislation

The role of the state in a society like South Africa is to preserve the coherence of the society as a whole in the interests of those who profit from it. In the circumstances outlined above the state fulfilled this role by regularly intervening in an attempt to offset the dangers as perceived. Immediately this involved direct repression; by means of, inter alia, the declaration of martial law (four times), the use of troops and police to protect strike breakers, the deportation of strike leaders, and the enactment of laws prohibiting 'riotous assemblies'. However, it was increasingly becoming apparent that direct repression alone would not succeed in eliminating strikes, particularly those by well-organized and militant white workers. Furthermore, the inevitable direct conflict which a policy of open repression engendered was, as we have seen, regarded as the means by which white workers fell under the influence of those who saw the long-term solution to these workers' problems in common struggle with African workers. A number of spokesmen — most notably in the first instance those closest to manufacturing employers' interests — accordingly began to suggest as an alternative that the desired result be achieved by the institutionalization and incorporation into suitable structures of the white trade union movement. In these days before the 'art of public relations' spokesmen were remarkably frank about the intention behind such proposals. One Commission for example, reflecting the evidence given to it, argued for the statutory recognition of white unions and the establishment of Conciliation Boards as follows:

> Recognition creates responsibility . . . experience proves that organization in the open, made sober by recognition, is a very different thing from organisation which has to fight against contempt or antagonism . . . (Further) the organisation of labour is an aid to the authority of a conciliation board, because much labour can then be dealt with as a whole. Moreover the (trade union) official is *more likely to take the business point of view* and examine the situation calmly than the workman who has some personal grievance rankling in his mind.[7] (Emphasis added).

Each of the individually most disruptive periods — 1907, 1913/14 and 1922 — was accordingly followed by legislation aimed at giving effect to these proposals. The legislation in question was contained in the 1909 Transvaal Industrial Disputes Prevention Act; the 1914 Industrial Disputes and Trade Unions Bill (which passed through the House of Assembly but was withdrawn in the Senate); and the Industrial Conciliation Act, passed by the Smuts government during the first session of parliament in 1924. Significantly this legislation was passed when the white labour movement had previously suffered its heaviest defeats — in 1907 and 1922 — and it failed, in 1914, where the outcome of the preceding struggle had been less clearcut and the movement remained vigorous and militant. The 1914 Bill was thus withdrawn because of the determined attack mounted against it by the Labour Party and the trade unions.

Both the later instruments of this legislation were designed to 'block loopholes' which had been discovered in the operation of the earlier Act. All three had however sufficient common characteristics for us to recognize a pattern and consider them here as a whole. In broad outline each provided for the establishment of statutory bodies, containing employers' and employees' representatives, for the purpose of discussing industrial disputes. They suspended the right to strike until the procedures laid down had been exhausted. And they contained a definition of 'employee' which excluded 'pass-bearing natives'.

The provisions included under each of these broad headings clearly reflected the dominance of employers' interests; not only over the left wing of the white labour movement, which regarded a worker's right to withdraw his labour as fundamental and was thus wholly against any state intervention of this sort; but also (after compromises) over the right wing leadership which was prepared to 'bargain the right to strike against other benefits' and was thus in favour of the statutory regulation of industrial bargaining procedures in principle.

In supporting statute-regulated bargaining the labour right wingers had in mind at first — when the movement was comparatively weak — a system of 'voluntary arbitration and compulsory awards', and later a system of 'voluntary conciliation'.[8] The first system operated in Australia and New Zealand. Under it either party to an industrial dispute could approach a permanent, supposedly independent and impartial, body — called an arbitration court — which could then make a legally enforceable ruling. The second was based upon the 'Whitely Councils' operating, since 1917, in some industries in Britain. Under the Whitely system a hierarchy of 'standing conciliation boards', containing employers' and employees' representatives, could be established at various levels to negotiate and discuss a wide range of issues. At the top were 'Joint Industrial Councils' which considered wide and general questions relating to the whole industry. Local matters were discussed by 'Area Councils' and below that were 'Works Councils', which could be approached by individual workers with complaints against day-to-day management decisions. The Whitely system was 'voluntary' in the sense that, while the machinery was aimed at preventing strikes, participation did not restrict the workers' *legal right* to strike. But although both systems were, despite their idealisation by labour right wingers, in the last analysis a means of controlling labour in the interests of the employers of the respective countries, neither was acceptable to the dominant interests in South Africa. The first system was unacceptable because the mineowners in particular had at that stage no intention of being bound by an inevitable series of compromise awards e.g. over the precise racial demarcation of jobs, more especially as the Australasian experience had been seen as resulting in a number of 'favourable awards' to workers who had little or no power to extract similar gains in struggle. The second system was unacceptable because it was regarded as ineffective in preventing strikes, and because the range of matters which could be referred for negotiation under the Whitely system was seen as making it 'impossible to maintain discipline in industry'.[9]

Each of the three Bills in question was instead broadly based upon the Canadian principle of 'compulsory conciliation'. Bodies were provided for to serve as a forum for discussion and negotiation of matters considered to constitute 'an industrial dispute'. And while the use of these bodies was not in itself obligatory (which led Ministers to claim that the Bills were in fact based on 'the voluntary principle'), their use was compulsory before any other means could be employed to obtain redress. Under the 1924 Act such bodies could have a permanent existence *at industry level,* in which case they were called Industrial Councils. The choice of the level at which these permanent bodies operated was deliberate and acknowledged: 'the drafter had the mining industry', in which the employers were organized in a powerful and centralised body, 'clearly in mind'.[10] Where no Industrial Councils existed the 1924 Act provided that either party could apply for the establishment of a Conciliation Board to handle a particular dispute. To prevent Conciliation Boards being used by workers (particularly individual workers) as a means of obtaining redress against grievances which were not likely to result in strikes, the Minister was given discretion to judge whether a statutory 'dispute' existed. And, moreover, he was prevented from appointing a Board 'if the dispute (was) in regard to the engagement, suspension, discharge, promotion, transfer or derating of an individual employee or the assessment of contract prices unless in the opinion of the Minister a matter of principle (for a trade union — R.D.) is involved.'[11] Arbitration was provided for but, in the private sector, only as an ad hoc remedy to a particular dispute if *both* parties agreed.

The limitations imposed by these bills on the right to strike were very severe indeed, and in fact went far beyond what even the labour right wingers were prepared to 'bargain' at that time. In the private sector, no strike could be called during the currency of any agreement, nor until a 'cooling off period' of 30 days had elapsed following the breakdown of any negotiations. In the two earlier bills unions were required to ballot members before a strike (a provision very nearly included in the 1924 Act), and to give notice to employers of the intention to strike: a provision which even one generally pro-employer journal described as 'plac(ing) the side of labour at a distinct disadvantage in any struggle, for the success of a strike very largely depends upon taking the other side unawares.'[12] For 'employers' in 'essential public services', similar Acts went even further and totally prohibited strikes under all circumstances. An appeal to a state appointed arbitration board became the final recourse for statutory employees in these sectors.

Finally, on each occasion the clause excluding 'pass-bearing' Africans was opposed by the spokesmen for white labour. Often this was for reasons far less commendable than any desire to forge inter-racial working class solidarity. In the following quotation, for example, it is clear that the need to incorporate more skilled African tradesmen in order to protect the interests of white workers was uppermost in the spokesman's mind:

> Why is the provision (restricting the definition of employee — R.D.) there? The position is this: that more and more of these natives are coming into trades and occupations in this country. Take the case of the goldmines, the native is repeatedly engaged in mechanic's work. He is getting the work today and it is going to *compel* us to organize the natives. There are natives in trades in the Cape and they (the unions) are being *compelled* to organize them here, and if that goes on in the Transvaal we will be *compelled* to organize these men and take them into our unions there ... but you are setting up a new colour bar.[13] (Emphasis added)

Nevertheless the fact remains that these clauses were opposed and their inclusion therefore once again reflects the dominance of employers' interests in this legislation. In fact these clauses were there because the overall intention of these laws was to control and contain the already organized section of labour, not to encourage the organization of then unorganized workers, least of all if they were vital African workers. J. D. Chaplin, for example, a mineowner and a member of the mineowners' Progressive Party was quite explicit on this point when he spoke in support of the inclusion of such a clause in the 1909 Transvaal Act.

> As regards the extension of the scope of the Bill to coloured (i.e. African —

R.D.) labour,' he was reported as saying, 'such a proposal would lead to a nullification of the purposes of the Bill. To think that a number of natives of the class employed in this country could hang up an industrial concern seemed highly absurd (hear, hear)... He was not prepared to see the provisions of the Bill extended to natives. [14]

Effects on White Labour Movement

The practical effects which this legislation had (when fully operational after 1924) on the character of the white labour movement were profound. In the words of one Government Commission reporting on the first ten years of the Act '(statutory) wage regulation made unions less militant.'[15] Immediately and obviously this manifested itself in a sharp reduction in the number of strikes, which were rendered by the Act, in the judgement of one experienced participant, 'almost an impossibility ... in *legal* (form).'[16] Between 1923 and 1929, for example, there were on average only 6 strikes involving white employees each year. But there were other more subtle manifestations as well. Within the union structures power passed more and more into the hands of a bureaucracy of permanent officials who spent most of their time involved in centralised statutory bodies with employers and government officials. More and more decisions were taken 'at the top' and, almost inevitably, as common interests multiplied across the table in the board-room of industrial councils these came to include 'joint participation' in a number of management decisions. For example, unions would often collaborate in working out schemes to undersell competitors in other provinces or industries.[17]

The rank and file membership became, concomitantly, increasingly alienated from 'their' union leaders and apathetic toward unions in general. As the 1935 Commission euphemistically put it: 'As conditions of labour secured through bargaining (procedures regulated by the Act — R.D.) became the standard conditions for a prescribed period, many workers fail(ed) to appreciate the need for continued organization'.[18] In some industries indeed this 'resulted in (an initial) decrease in membership of unions'.[19] Such decreases in membership were, however, shortlived. For employers began to see advantages in the 'new look' unions. In the words of the Commission:

> In these days when the employees of a single workshop often number many hundreds, the arrangement of individual contracts would present many administrative difficulties, and for that reason alone many employers ... (prefer) ... their employees to link up with unions ... The better type of employer also

appreciates the fact that well organized and *well disciplined* trade unions can do much to reduce the evasion of industrial legislation by ... less reputable (competitors).[20]

 Employers therefore began to 'actively assist in the organization of unions,' in the main by entering into closed shop agreements and by providing facilities for the collection of dues.[21] In several cases 'employer participation' extended to collaborating in the bolstering up of union leaderships against internal challengers e.g. by operating the closed shop against dissidents. And in the case of one union, the Typographical Union, employers even became directly involved in 'the maintenance of discipline' within the union, by sitting on a committee of the Industrial Council which heard the final appeals of members in default against union rules — especially ironic in view of the fact that employers had been so insistent that Conciliation Boards should not serve as an appeal against management discipline.

There was of course a price to be paid for all of this. Wage increases and access to better jobs, at the very least not less favourable than the conditions of unregulated class struggle might have determined, had to be conceded to white wage earners. And the state as protector of the interests of the dominant classes *as a whole* ensured that they were; a role which led it into periodic conflict with individual 'rogue employers'. Most employers however considered that price well worth paying, especially as it could be financed at the expense of African wages instead of out of profits, and repeatedly declared themselves broadly satisfied with the functioning of the Act. For example, the 1935 Commission found that the Act was 'judged good in principle ... by employers generally' and that their only complaints related to minor problems arising out of the administration of agreements and inspection procedures.[22]

Since then there have of course been a number of amendments to the Industrial Conciliation Act, reflecting real and important changes in conditions and circumstances. They have not however altered the fundamental character of the Act. Rather, therefore, than attempt to trace these here, this paper will move to draw some conclusions from and assess the contemporary relevance of the preceding study.

Conclusion
The overriding conclusion which emerges is that Industrial Conciliation legislation is, like *all* labour legislation in South Africa, an instrument of the classes of property owners dominant in the society. The 'Industrial Conciliation' variant is employed by the state when

political considerations make the direct repression of some organized section of the wage earning population impossible or impractical and it involves the regulation and institutionalization of power won by wage earners in struggle. It thus represents a practical compromise, but one in which the owners of the means of production are dominant, and which, indeed, enables their interests to remain dominant.

In order to succeed in this, it has been necessary to effect a number of changes in the character of the labour movement concerned. In general this has involved the creation and sustenance of a bureaucratic hierarchy of officials, distinct from the rank and file members, whose lifestyle, work and outlook has more in common with employers and state officials than with workers.

As a compromise solution some concessions have of necessity been part of any such package. In the case of white wage earners, the main group to whom this approach has thus far been applied, these have involved substantial gains in income and job terms. The main reasons here were, we suggested, that white wage earners were and are a comparatively small proportion of the total workforce, that their early militancy was considered likely to influence the majority of the African working class, and that these concessions could be made at the expense of African incomes. (There have however been a number of important economic changes which also partially account for white wage earners' gains e.g. the development of large-scale manufacturing industry created the need for a stratum of supervisors and controllers.)

The suggestion, by sections of the dominant classes, that African unions be accorded some degree of recognition within a similar sort of 'Industrial Conciliation' system, is of course not new. It dates back, in fact, to the late 1920s when the first African industrial unions (as distinct from the I.C.U. general union) began to make their presence felt, and has indeed at several points in time almost been official government policy. When seriously discussed in the 'corridors of state', such a policy has been considered as is all South African labour legislation, on its 'merits' as a means of controlling African workers in the interests of the dominant classes. What distinguishes proposals of this sort relating to African workers however is that, as the granting of concessions even vaguely comparable to those conceded to whites is incompatable with profitability, they have concentrated almost entirely upon the changes which could be brought about in the character of African union leaderships. The following extracts from the report of a Commission[23] appointed by the present Nationalist government but whose proposals were rejected in favour of 'bleeding the African trade unions to death', will illustrate this:

> (Because of, inter alia) the differences in the standards of living of the different races . . . the Commission is unable to recommend the adoption of the proposal that there should be no racial discrimination in industrial legislation . . . (However) notwithstanding (certain) unsatisfactory features characterising the Native trade union movement, the Commission is satisfied that there are a number of unions which are well organized and run on correct lines. The leaders of some of these unions have in the past rendered considerable assistance by advising against, and restraining their members from taking drastic action . . . (The Commission therefore) recommends recognition in separate legislation . . . (which will) bring them into official cognizance . . . rather than leave them to adopt dangerous advice of some unbalanced semi-educated Native or the promptings of disreputable Europeans who batten on Native ignorance and cupidity . . . (However) the Commission recommends strongly against any course which would enable Native workers to hold the balance of power in or dominate the process of collective bargaining; . . . (and an employer should not be compelled to bargain with his Native workers etc. etc.)

The lesson is then clear: should the involvement of African unions in conciliation type procedures become in the future state policy, there may be certain advantages over the present situation which can be utilized, but in the last analysis it will remain a means of continuing the domination over African labour.

FOOTNOTES

1. See, for example, *A Survey of Race Relations in South Africa 1974* (South African Institute of Race Relations) pp. 317-336.
2. F. A. Johnstone: *Class, Race and Gold: A Study of Class Relations and Racial Discrimination in South Africa* (Routledge and Kegan Paul, London, 1976).
3. See the Interim and Final Reports of the 'Cost of Living Commission' (UG 39 1916; UG 1 1919) and the 'Report of the Select Committee on the Cost of Living Commission (Profits) Report' (SC 1 1919).
4. For details of strikes and strike statistics see *Official Yearbooks* (Pretoria, 1910-1930).
5. 'Report of the Economic Commission' (UG 12 1914) p. 50.
6. 'Report of the Economic Commission: op. cit. pp. 47/8.
8. See Second Reading Debates on the 1909 Industrial Disputes Prevention Bill and on the 1923 and 1924 Industrial Conciliation Bills (1909 debates reported in *The Transvaal Leader* 8 June 1909, 9 June 1909, 12 June 1909; 1923 debates reported in *The Cape Times* 6 February 1923, 8 February 1923; 1924 debates reported in *House of Assembly Debates* vol 1 30 January 1924).
9. See *House of Assembly Debates* vol. 1, 8 February 1924.
10. See 'Report, Proceedings and Evidence to Select Committee on the Industrial Conciliation Bill' (SC 5 1923) p. 3.

11. *The Industrial Conciliation Act no. 11 of 1924* ... compiled by M. Schaeffer (Juta, Cape Town, 1934) clause 4 (1) p. 10.

12. 'The State and Industrial Strife' unsigned article in *The South African Quarterly* June-August 1914.

13. 'Report ... Select Committee on the Industrial Conciliation Bill' (SC 5 1923): op. cit., p. 10.

14. *The Transvaal Leader*, 8 June 1909.

15. 'Report of the Industrial Legislation Commission' (UG 37 1935) p. 88.

16. W. H. Andrews, *Class Struggles in South Africa* (Stewart, Cape Town, 1941) p. 37.

17. See H. J. and R. E. Simons: *Class and Colour in South Africa 1850-1950* (Penguin, 1969) p. 333.

18. 'Report of the Industrial Legislation Commission' (UG 37 1935): op. cit., p. 89.

19. idem.

20. ibid., p. 90.

21. idem.

22. idem.

23. 'Report of the Industrial Relations Legislation Commission of Enquiry' (UG 62 1951).

CAPITAL AND LABOUR IN SOUTH AFRICA: THE PASSAGE OF THE INDUSTRIAL CONCILIATION ACT, 1924

JEFF LEVER

In March, 1924, as the crisis of the fourteen-year-old South African Party government reached its height, the Union's first Industrial Conciliation Act passed parliament. The passage of the Act was testimony, in the most immediate sense, to the trauma caused by the great Rand Strike of 1922. But the need for such an act had been recognised years before the white miners had taken up arms against what they saw as a hostile coalition of mine magnates and South African Party government. Shortly after Union the government had promised to introduce Union-wide industrial conciliation legislation.[1] And events thereafter had underlined the need for it. The major strikes in 1913 and 1914 fostered a growing realisation of the critical situation which had been arising on the Witwatersrand gold fields over the years since the mines had started operations. In terms which have subsequently lost their flavour but which are widely used by all parties to the interminable disputes of the time, some effective machinery for the reconciliation of 'labour' and 'capital' was urgently required.

The Industrial Conciliation Act was, thus, to a considerable extent the outcome of the play of forces which had arisen around the gold mining industry, then as later the motor of South African economic development. The labour situation on the gold fields was responsible for much of the shape of South African trade unionism, and, in the first quarter of this century at least, for the linkage of labour with the political system. A study of the events leading up to the Industrial Conciliation Act is of use in examining both the nature of trade unionism at the time, and the configuration of white politics to which

82

it gave rise. Not only the genesis of the Act, but also its consequences are of great importance, for it was to shape later trade union activity and to determine the parameters of collective bargaining in South Africa. Finally, the Act was to be of vital importance in fixing the position of the various races in South Africa within the developing industrial system. For all these themes, a study of the passage of the Act should prove of value.

Conciliation and Control, 1909-1913

In 1909 the elected Het Volk government of the Transvaal introduced the Transvaal Industrial Disputes Bill. The immediate spur to the introduction of the Bill was the 1907 strike of white miners on the gold fields, the first major action of its kind since the gold mines had re-opened after the Anglo-Boer War. The strike had been a watershed for the Het Volk government in general and for Smuts, the Colonial Secretary, in particular. Before 1907 the growing white labour movement on the Rand had looked to Het Volk as a potential ally against the influence of the Progressive Party and its supporters, the Rand mine management class. Both Botha and Smuts had reciprocated to some extent, inveighing against the sinister influence of the Chamber of Mines. Het Volk's handling of the 1907 strike shattered the potential alliance. Government failed to come down on the side of the white miners, and the strike was broken. Smuts, as his sympathetic biographer Hancock has written, 'soon discovered Hoggenheimer to be a fictitious animal', and forged 'frank and cordial relations' with a leading Rand magnate, Lionel Phillips.[2] While it would be over-stating the case to say that Smuts henceforth was the captive representative of the sectional interests of the Chamber of Mines, it is clear that he was impressed by the arguments of the mine management regarding the difficulties in keeping the mines running at a profit. Equally clearly, Smuts and the Het Volk government were alarmed at the potential for unrest contained in the growing militancy of the white miners in particular, but also in the industrial action of any major group of white workers.

The first outcome of this concern was the passage in 1908 of the Railway Regulation Act, establishing the conditions of service of railway workers. The Act contained the first prohibition on strikes by whites in South Africa. Railway employees were henceforth denied the right to strike, under penalty of criminal prosecution. In return, the Act established the principle of compulsory arbitration between the railways administration and employees whenever a dispute between the two arose.[3] This position was to be extended over the whole of South Africa after Union, with the passage of the 1912 Railways and Harbours Service Act. Thus began what might be termed the decomposition of white labour solidarity by statutory means in South Africa. As later events were to prove, the creation of separate statutory machinery for differing sections of labour tended to encourage the compartmentalisation of white labour's industrial activity and outlook. Regulated by a detailed code of management-worker relations, the railway workers remained apart from the labour movement as a whole, and their approach to matters of mutual concern was heavily coloured by their separate institutional position. At this early date, thus, white railway workers were being placed in a position of neutrality relative to the other sections of white labour. There was to be no question of a repetition in South Africa of the powerful British 'Triple Alliance' of miners, railway workers and dockers and transport workers.

By 1909, then, the Het Volk government had indicated that it would not necessarily act as the undiscriminating champion of white workers as political currents prior to 1907 had suggested it might. Smuts' own approach at this time, as later, was to seek compromise between the parties to industrial disputes, but to come down firmly on threats to law and order contained in any major industrial action by workers, It was not, after all, the Rand magnates who gathered in the streets threatening violence. As later events were to prove, this position tended to the advantage of management rather than the workers. When Smuts rose to introduce the Industrial Disputes Bill in the Transvaal Legislative Assembly, it was in the role of the state referee over the contest of conflicting interests.

The major provisions of the Bill were relatively straightforward. Based on the principles of the Industrial Dispute Investigation Act passed in Canada in 1907[4], the Bill aimed, as Smuts emphasised, to 'avoid both the extremes of the "option" on the one hand, and compulsion on the other.'[5] The Bill provided that changes in working conditions proposed by employers or employees had to be preceded by one month's notice. In the event of deadlock, no strike or lock-out could take place until a government-appointed conciliation board had investigated the dispute and a month had elapsed since the publication of its report. Detailed provisions regulated the manner of appointment and operation of these conciliation boards. For example, a dispute involving less than ten workers could not be an occasion for the appointment of a conciliation board. Further, the findings of a conciliation board could only become legally binding if

84

both parties to a dispute agreed to it. The Bill explicitly excluded from its ambit the public service and any person 'who is not a white person.'[6]

Such then in brief outline were the provisions of the first overt measure in South Africa towards a statutorily-defined industrial relations system. The thinking behind the Bill was to be of tremendous influence with regard to later industrial relations legislation. The principle of compromise between compulsory arbitration and completely voluntary industrial relations was itself a key theme underlying the Industrial Conciliation Act of 1924. So too was the exclusion of large sections of the work-force from the ambit of the Act. It is worth looking in some detail at the parliamentary response to the Industrial Disputes Bill, in order to gain some idea of the political and ideological context in which the measure was passed.

The Labour members or sympathisers in the Legislative Assembly levelled a number of criticisms against the measure. One major objection was the limited scope of the Bill: the exclusion of sections of employees such as public servants, railway workers and blacks. Doubt too was expressed regarding the usefulness of the reports of conciliation boards which would not, barring agreement, be binding on parties. But, by and large, the criticisms of labour representatives were relatively moderate. Even Peter Whiteside, member for Siemert and one of the more militant mining unionists, sounded relatively conciliatory when he declared that '. . . compulsory arbitration, a wages board, and compulsory investigation were merely palliatives. So long as the workers had to exist under wage-slavery they had to do the best they could and accept one or other of the palliatives in the meantime.'[7]

For the Progressives, both F. D. Chaplin and George Farrar gave full support to the Bill in terms which indicated their satisfaction with 'the progressive Government, because in the last twelve months the Government has learnt progress is absolutely essential in this country . . .'[8]

It was however the confinement of the provisions of the Bill to white persons which provoked the most spirited debate in the Legislative Assembly. All three labour representatives who spoke in the debate criticised this measure. In the words of H. W. Sampson, member for City and Suburban and the leader of the printers' union: 'It did not seem fair to him that the coloured man should be debarred from the remedies and disabilities which the Bill provided.'[9] Rather different in tone were the remarks of the former Transvaal Commissioner of Mines and staunch champion of white labour, W. J. Wybergh, when he declared:

> He maintained that the more they exempted natives from Acts of that kind the greater was the direct incentive to the employment of natives, because they were being made humble slaves not able to speak for themselves, and therefore were easier to deal with, and more docile and, perhaps, more satisfactory to employers than white people. That was his great reason why he would like to see natives brought under the scope of these Acts in exactly the same way as the white man. [10]

Both Smuts for Het Volk, and the spokesmen of the mining interest such as Farrar and Chaplin, were quick to put their finger on Labour's equivocation in this matter. 'They had got to recognise', said Chaplin, 'that there is a vast difference between the native labour of this country and skilled white labour. I should have thought it to the interests of the Labour Party to see that distinction was kept up . . .'[11] Smuts, in reply to the Second Reading debate on the Bill declared in a statement which gained Progressive Party applause:

> I hope the machinery of this Bill will not apply to natives. (Opposition cheers). I hope that the day is far distant when natives will be guilty of concerted action, so as to take part in a strike. (Oh! Oh!) [12]

The precedent of the 1909 Act regarding the exclusion of Africans was crucial, for it was, in the climate of the times, not one lightly set aside when later industrial legislation was designed. The total exclusion of all Africans from the main industrial relations legislation in South Africa was only accomplished in 1956 with the revised Industrial Conciliation Act of that year. But it was passed in a spirit which hardly differed from that prevailing in 1909.

The Transvaal Act also marks an important step along the road to the present system of industrial relations for the country's White, Coloured and Indian South African workers. The most effective weapon of the industrial worker, the strike, was hedged about with severe restraints. In return, however, there was a potentially important quid pro quo: the extension of official recognition to (white) trade union activity through the apparatus of conciliation boards. But procedural difficulties and the opposition of mine managements to trade union activity negated the effectiveness of this provision and it failed to achieve its goal. Indeed, the new Act seems to have failed completely within four years of its passage. But before considering that development, it is necessary to consider briefly the other leg of what became the Union's industrial relations system, namely, the position of black labour which was excluded from the system adopted for white workers. In short, we must look at the Native

Labour Regulation Act of 1911.

The Native Labour Regulation Act, unlike the Transvaal Industrial Disputes Act, was of application throughout South Africa, having been passed by the Union government in 1911. But, like the Transvaal Act, the occasion for the Native Labour Regulation Act arose largely from the conditions on the Rand gold mines. This time those conditions concerned the recruitment and treatment of the mines' vast black labour force. The numerous provisions of the Act were intended to recognise and regulate the de facto situation of large scale recruitment and employment of blacks by South African industry and in particular the gold mines. Private organisations, most notably the Chamber of Mines, but also smaller labour contractors, controlled the recruitment, housing and feeding of tens of thousands of black workers. A parliamentary Select Committee had taken evidence on this situation in 1911 and revealed the possibilities for abuse and mistreatment.[13] Legislation passed prior to 1902 was still operative, most notably the Master and Servants Act of 1880 and Wet no. 23 of 1895. The 1911 Bill proposed no radical departures from this existing situation. Rather it aimed to tidy up a situation which had got somewhat out of hand. Briefly, the new Bill proposed to standardise the procedure by which black workers entered into contracts to work in white industry. As in the various Masters and Servants laws still in force in the few provinces, criminal sanctions were laid down for the breach of contract by black workers. In addition, government inspectors were given powers to control the treatment and housing of blacks under contract, and minimum standards were laid down. The operations of recruiting agents were made subject to a standard licensing procedure.[14] The Bill, in short, proposed to streamline and, if possible, improve the workings of the contract labour system.

The Bill would in effect confirm a separate and unequal status for the largest section of the black labour force in South Africa. But this was a situation passed over for the most part in silence in parliament. The debates on the measure hardly touched on first premises. Clearly, both government and the spokesmen of the mining industry were in accord in supporting the introduction of the measure. Only the small band of the South African Labour Party MPs attempted to put the measure in global perspective. The leader of the SALP, F. H. Creswell, declared that:

> He was against the bill because it entrenched a system of slavery ... The bill

> took over the worst principles of the Transvaal Act. Blacks were made
> punishable for things which should only have been subject to civil action . . .

The conclusion drawn by Creswell was that

> The white man has less and less of a chance if the mines obtain so much power
> over their blacks. [15]

The self-interest behind the moral denunciation was plain. But however self-interested, it was the merit of the SALP members to have raised issues of first principle; they rightly pointed out the hazards of a separate and inferior status for a large section of the work-force, a status buttressed by the provisions of the Bill. Other MPs were more concerned to declare, in the words of Henry Burton, Minister of Native Affairs, that the Act 'was necessary especially in the interest of the native.'[16] The measure was in fact congenial to the interests of the dominant groups in parliament at the time: the mining industry spokesmen, the rural members eager to reinforce the question of penal sactions for black employees, and the leaders of the government, themselves favourable to a measure which would both please the mines and improve their control over large numbers of transient black miners scattered throughout the Rand.

* * * * *

By 1912, thus, labour relations on the gold fields had received the close attention of two elected governments, and two major measures had been enacted. By accepting the force of precedent, and by a near ideological unanimity which took for granted the separate and subordinate status of the Black workers, South African politicians had laid the groundwork for two discrete systems of industrial relations. Notable among all this had been the firm agreement among organised industry, the white agricultural interest, and the government. Within the closed circle of white politics, the only dissenting voice had been that of white labour, but it was opposition that was not strongly pressed, and which, in any case, could be dismissed as special pleading of a sectional interest. But the SALP and the spokesmen of white labour were quite correct in arguing that industrial conciliation for the white man and contract labour under penal sanctions for the black man was a situation which deserved deeper reflection from the country's politicians than it received. It will be seen below how these same labour spokesmen met the challenge posed by their accession to power thirteen years later.

The Failure of Conciliation, 1913-1922

Sporadic strikes had occurred on the Rand after the passage of the 1909 Industrial Disputes Act. But these were no more than a prelude to the major outbursts in mid-1913 and at the beginning of 1914, involving thousands of white workers, the imposition of martial law and the deportation of nine leading strikers. The details of these strikes have been recorded elsewhere.[17] For present purposes, it is sufficient to note that these strikes pushed the Union government into attempting to carry out its promise of 1911 to legislate a Union-wide code of industrial conciliation (thereby also revising the unsatisfactory aspects of the Transvaal Industrial Disputes Act.) In fact, the strikes provoked far more. In early 1914 the government published six bills with important implications for labour. Two of these bills directly related to industrial conciliation and trade union activity: a third, the Riotous Assemblies bill, made clear the government's intention to ensure that conciliation would be accompanied by statutory provisions to strengthen the state's police power. It is of significance that of these latter three bills only one, the Riotous Assemblies bill, was finally enacted the same session.

In April 1914 the government introduced into parliament a combined measure, the Industrial Disputes and Trade Unions Bill. The Bill, declared F. S. Malan, the Minister of Mines and Industries, 'approached the question of the relations of capital and labour' from the point of view of the 'reformer' and not the 'revolutionary.' The Bill largely followed the existing Transvaal Act in its conciliation provisions, but proposed to amend certain details of its operation which had hindered the appointment, operation and effectiveness of conciliation boards in the Transvaal in the past four years. Further, the Bill contained provisions for the establishment of labour bureaux and for the registration of trade unions. The Bill proposed to exclude 'Government services, natives falling under the Natives Regulation Act (sic), and the indentured Indians of Natal.'[18]

In the flush of the militancy produced by the strikes and the triumph of Labour in the 1914 Transvaal Provincial elections, the SALP displayed considerably more opposition to the Bill than their predecessors had done in 1909 in the Transvaal Legislative Assembly. Creswell declared that the idea of the Bill:

> ... was to bring the Trade Unions under the law for the purpose of getting them in such a position that they could be brought under the grip of the law and prevented from expanding.[19]

The SALP member for Roodepoort, C. H. Haggar, went so far as to declare that:

> In this country today the class war exists, and the class war is going to be waged until one class is wiped out.[20]

W. H. Andrews, shortly to be one of the leading figured in the leftwing breakaway from the SALP, said that his party 'disapproved of the whole spirit of the Bill.'[21] It was left to J. X. Merriman to puncture the wilder pretensions of the representatives of white labour: 'When he heard the hon. member for Jeppe . . . talking some balderdash about shifting the basis of society — Good Heavens! a small minority of this country was going to shift the basis of society (Laughter) . . . The workers who the hon. member said secured the great resources of this country, what were they compared to 200 000 men who did labour at the resources in this country and got precious little consideration?'[22]

The Industrial Disputes and Trade Unions Bill passed the House of Assembly, but failed through lack of parliamentary time to pass the Senate. The advent of the World War, and the patriotic upsurge among English-speaking workers, relieved the government of immediate pressure on this score. Nine years were to pass before a similar measure came again before the South African parliament. A considerable amount of less contentious industrial legislation did, however, receive enactment in this period. A Factory Act was passed in 1918, as was the Regulation of Wages, Apprentices and Improvers Act. The latter was the first step along the road to a system of wage determination, but its scope was very limited. A further wage determination measure was considered by the government in 1921, but was not put through parliament. In 1922 the Apprenticeship Act was passed, providing for the standardisation and control by the state, employers and trade unions of the conditions of employment of apprentices and the scheduling of specific artisan trades. With F. S. Malan in the lead, it was clear that the SAP government was giving serious attention to the problems of the industrialisation of the urban areas and their concomitant social and economic pressures.

But while these actions represented progress of a sort in the industrial field, the prize of a workable industrial relations system, and of industrial stability on the gold mines, remained beyond the grasp of the SAP government. Once again it was the gold mining industry which proved to be the spur to further, and this time relatively effective, measures. The acceptance of the Status Quo Agreement on the mines in 1918, after the industrial truce of the war years, provided a breathing space of sorts. The agreement gave the white miners the job security which they desired. But the agreement soon came to be seen by management as an obstacle to the efficient and profitable working of the mines. The steps, leading from the abrogation of the Agreement in December 1921 by the mines, to the Rand Strike and later Rebellion of March 1922, need not be recapitulated here.[23] The precipitating cause of the Rand Strike was the declared intention of the mine managements to dismiss semi-skilled white miners in order to cut the wage bill. These dismissals in turn were linked to the functioning of the colour bar on the mines.

But other issues were also involved. The Mining Industry Board (the Brace Commission) which investigated the events which led up to the strike, and produced a report in 1922, made it clear that behind the question of the colour bar lay grievances regarding the industrial relations of the mines. The Operation of the Status Quo Agreement, for example, had been used not only to keep the jobs 'white', but was also interpreted by the white miners in a way that posed problems of worker control versus managerial prerogative.[24] The Board phrased the matter as one of 'interference' in the 'authority of the Manager' which was carried out 'to a deplorable extent.'[25] Nevertheless, the Board realistically discerned the need for a standing conciliation and grievance machinery on the mines. A recommendation was accordingly made to institutionalise the operation of the previously unofficial conciliation boards on the mines, entailing among other things amendments to the existing Transvaal Industrial Disputes Act.[26] Such amendments had been promised by the Union government, should the Mining Industry Board report along those lines.[27]

The road was now open to the introduction of a new industrial conciliation bill in the Union parliament. The occasion, a pressing one of near civil war, proved sufficient this time to spur the central government, and F. S. Malan in particular, to energetic action in this regard. And no international hostilities arose to divert the interest of General Smuts and his Cabinet.

The Passage of the Industrial Conciliation Act, 1923-1924
Some eleven months after the Rand Strike and the subsequent armed unrest had been smashed, F. S. Malan, Minister of Mines and Industries, introduced the Industrial Conciliation Bill into the House of Assembly. The Bill passed its second reading, was referred to a select

committee which took evidence on the Bill, and returned it to the House for its third reading. Lack of time prevented its further progress through the Senate in the same year, 1923. A similar fate had overtaken the 1914 Industrial Disputes and Trade Unions Bill; but unlike the earlier Bill, the present one was not allowed to drop. The Industrial Conciliation Bill was re-introduced in 1924, and became law shortly before the prorogation of parliament for the general election of that year.

While maintaining the basic principle behind the 1909 Transvaal Act, the new measure went considerably further. In particular, in addition to statutory recognition for special ad hoc conciliation boards in cases of industrial dispute, the Bill allowed for the creation of standing employer-employee councils with wide powers of negotiation and wage determination. In a provision ultimately embodied in the Act, these boards, or industrial councils as they were finally termed, could obtain legal enforcement for the agreement reached in the councils. And these agreements, once the Minister was satisfied of the representative character of the parties to the council, could be made binding on all employers and employees in the specified industry, whether or not they were parties to the agreement. While the machinery of industrial council agreements or conciliation boards was still in operation, no strike or lock-out was permitted to take place. Provision was made for the registration of trade unions — a measure which entitled recognised unions full recourse to the conciliation machinery laid down by the Bill. Finally, government servants, agricultural and domestic workers, contract Africans and indentured Indians (but not other Africans, Indians and Coloureds) were excluded from the provisions of the Bill by not being included in the definition of 'employee'.[28]

Malan's second reading speech on the measure was mild and conciliatory. It was clear that the combined ranks of the NP and the SALP, although still smarting from the debacle of 1922, were also hard put to it to offer vigorous opposition to the measure. Their dilemma was to reconcile their generalised suspicion of and hostility to the Smuts government — emotions shortly to give rise to the formal Pact agreement, and at this time expressed in an informal, but manifest alliance — with the appeal of the Bill to the interests in particular of the most established trade unions. Symptomatic of this half-hearted opposition were the arguments of H. W. Sampson, MP for Jeppe and spokesmen for the South African Typographical Union. The SATU had, in 1919, established with their employers a most successful joint board, and had refused to join the 1922 Strike on the grounds that it would have meant a breach of contract. Sampson himself could not but welcome the broad direction of the new Bill, and in fact was to co-operate whole-heartedly in committee in suggesting useful amendments. In reply to Malan's second reading speech, Sampson moved the SALP's amendment that the Bill be referred to a select committee before the conclusion of the second reading, thus enabling the committee to consider measures of principle as well as detail. But this standard parliamentary ploy did not in fact represent a deep disagreement over principles, as Samson's arguments showed. He gave cautious endorsement to the main principles of the Bill, while objecting to its 'onesidedness.'[29]

Other SALP MPs were more vigorous in attacking the measure, but it was left to the NP MP for Vredefort, J. H. Munnik, to express in harshest language the smouldering resentment of the defeated miners:

> Trade unionism today was lying bleeding, and for this the government was largely responsible . . . if the Minister was under the impression that there was industrial peace in South Africa, as far as the mine workers were concerned, he was labouring under a delusion.[30]

But despite such high generalities, little of substance was brought against the Bill. Perhaps the major complaint on which opposition members harped was the exclusion of employer bodies from the requirements for registration which the government proposed for the trade unions. This was eagerly seized upon by the SALP as evidence of the government's bias in favour of employers. The final Act applied this requirement equally to both employer and employee organisations.

Matters of detail received a thorough airing (with however a significant exception, to be dealt with later) in the select committee and the committee stage of the Bill in 1923 in the House of Assembly.[31] The evidence before the Select Committee is of particular interest in that it revealed cleavages within both labour and capital as well as the cleavages between them. The cleavage was in both cases a two-fold one: established artisan unions versus the semi-skilled white mine unions on the one hand; representatives of secondary industry versus the Chamber of Mines on the other. These divisions, while perhaps not giving due weight to very definite individual differences of opinion, seem essential to an understanding of the often blurred and confusing empirical evidence.

In broad outline, the line-up can be summarised as follows: the established artisan unions and those representing public sector and white-collar employees welcomed the provisions on industrial conciliation while objecting to the exclusion of some categories (for example, government servants) from the provisions of the measure, to the lack of enforceablility of agreements (subsequently conceded), and to the possibility of state interference in internal trade union affairs. Spokesmen for the shattered miners' unions (then, as now, basically unions of the semi-skilled, with no apprenticeship requirements) were more militant in expressing opposition to the potential stifling effect of any statutory restraint on union activity. Archie Crawford, leader of the previously influential S.A. Industrial Federation, and of the engine drivers on the mines, declared that:

> I do not approve much of standing conciliation boards. I do not think the workers should be compelled to do anything. I think the relationship should be very free[32] . . . There are times when it is desirable that the dispute should be fought out, and when nothing else will bring about a lasting peace but a fight to the finish.[33]

Central to the arguments in the Select Committee was the frank recognition by several employer and union representatives of the crucial importance of the 'joint monopoly' implications of the proposed measure. It is significant that the main employers' evidence came from representatives of the building industry, who had also supported the proposed wage determination measures in 1921. Established employers in building, printing and other industries were eager to take out wages as a factor in competition, and found common cause with their union counterparts in this matter. On the other hand, both employers and many employees in the gold mining industry were able to avail themselves of this possibility. Semi-skilled white workers on the mines suffered a double disability compared with their more favoured artisan colleagues in industries other than the mines: they commanded no great scarcity value in an industry unable to pass on a higher wage bill in terms of a higher price for their product. As Crawford quite validly put the matter:

> A standing conciliation board may be a menace to the community. I do not know but what they are in many cases. If standing conciliation boards were created the interest of the rest of the public would have to be very jealously guarded. You would find a danger of conspiracy between employer and employee in the interest of higher prices and those would finally land on the primary producers, and the farmer and the coal and gold producers, etc., would be impoverished.[34]

Completely absent from the proceedings of the Select Committee were any spokesmen from the Chamber of Mines. But it is clear that

Chamber absence did not mean lack of Chamber interest in the measure. In fact, as F. S. Malan made clear, he had been kept very well informed of the Chamber's feelings about the Bill, and may even have accepted Chamber objections to details in the measure, as shall be seen later.[35]

Despite the cross-currents of opposition to details of the Bill, the underlying consensus over the even-handedness of the measure was indicated by a unanimous report of the select committee of 1923. In his second reading speech on the re-introduction of the bill in January 1924, F. S. Malan was able to say, with reasonable accuracy, that 'perhaps with (the exception of) a few minor details, the parties concerned are satisfied with the provisions of this bill.'[36] The major changes in the bill between 1923 and 1924 included the following. The agreements reached in industrial councils judged to be 'representative' or the agreements of conciliation boards could be extended to the whole of a specified industry; workers in 'essential' municipal services were prohibited from striking; a clause making strike ballots mandatory was deleted. Further changes, which were opposed by Sampson for the SALP, included: first, the inclusion of a provision allowing 'any' group of employees (and thus possibly non-union workers) to call a conciliation board; second, the dropping of the clause which made illegal any stipulation by an employer that his workers should not belong to a trade union; third, the inclusion of a provision that no conciliation board could be called on behalf of individual workers objecting to changes in wages, working conditions, status or piece rates, 'unless a matter of principle was involved.'[37]

It was this last provision, Clause 4, which sparked the most heated and prolonged exchanges in the 1924 debates on the Industrial Conciliation Bill. Behind this seemingly minor detail lay wider issues and wider interests. Rand members of the South African Party — representatives of the mining industry and of the English-speaking urban middle class — argued strongly that the exclusion of such a clause would allow workers to call conciliation boards over any petty grievance about wages, promotion and working conditions. Sir Abe Bailey, MP for Krugersdorp, said that: 'If you strike out this proviso where these disagreements have to go before a board of conciliation, then you strike at the very root of discipline. My hon. friend must remember that before the strike in 1921, if there was any dispute on promotion or salaries or anything else, it was at once rushed to a board of reference . . . Disputes, differences and so forth must be left in the management's hands.'[38] The spectre of worker control and the dissipation of managerial authority raised by the Brace Commission was alive and walking again. It did not require much percipience from SALP members to divine the source of inspiration for this particular clause. As R. B. Waterson, SALP MP for Brakpan, claimed:

> The position is that the Chamber of Mines is behind the proviso. Why are they behind the proviso? It is because the Chamber of Mines is top dog in South Africa.[39]

Whatever the origin of the clause — and F. S. Malan admitted later in the debate that he had indeed consulted the Chamber of Mines[40] — other SAP members were able to show that the Clause had the backing of other employer organisations such as the builders', who were on the whole staunch supporters of the Bill. The controversial clause was pushed through by the government on a division — one of only five divisions in the committee stage of the Bill on which government and opposition confronted one another on strict party lines. Otherwise the debates were noted for the reservations uttered by a number of South African Party backbenchers about various provisions in the measure.

Some former Unionist MPs in the S.A.P. urged stricter controls over strikes, and asked for a prohibition on the use of union funds for political parties without the express consent of the majority of union members. It was 'very half-heartedly' that Malan's back-benchers supported him, claimed W. Rockey, MP for Parktown, and 'when a Minister wishes to put more power into the hands of trade unionists, no matter how good they may be, we believe the Minister is doing the wrong thing.'[41] The uneasiness of a number of English-speaking SAP MPs found little response in the House. And on the left Walter Madeley later the parliamentary leader of the non-governmental faction of the divided SALP after 1928, was very much alone when he stated the standard radical objection to industrial conciliation:

> . . . the more you kick them, the more you oppress them, the more determined you make them to organise themselves into a strong entity likely to put up a strong fight against their employers.

He supported the Bill, said Madeley, but 'I look upon this Conciliation Bill as going to have a weakening effect on trade unionism . . .'[42]

The Industrial Conciliation Bill passed the House of Assembly on 3rd March, 1924 after a last barb from Sampson on the iniquity of the Chamber of Mines in declining to give evidence to the select committee, and then consulting privately with the Minister. Sampson, on behalf of the SALP, declared that they had 'not quite succeeded' in securing a bill which would 'work automatically'. The Minister, at the behest of the Chamber of Mines, had allowed himself too much discretion, especially over the appointment of conciliation boards. The Minister would have to be 'very careful', said Sampson, 'or the Bill will be useless.'[43] The implication — that a careful Minister could make for a useful Act — was clear enough.

* * * * *

One issue which has so far received no mention in this discussion of the 1923-1924 debates on the Industrial Conciliation Bill is the question of the exclusion of African contract workers from the ambit of the Bill. Since this question soon became one of the major trade union issues, the importance of the omission is evident. What then was made of this highly consequential decision at the time? The short answer is: nothing, or at any rate, very little. The issue does not seem to have been mentioned, let alone ventilated, in the debates over the Bill in the House of Assembly and Senate. (Admittedly, the parliamentary records for 1923 are very incomplete.) The only record of the issue being raised in parliament was in the evidence of the 1923 Select Committee on the Bill. Here it was done twice, first by an artisan trade union spokesman, second by the employer representative K. B. Quinan of a Somerset West explosives factory.[44] The former deplored, in passing, the exclusion of contract Africans, the latter dismissed the idea that the inclusion of blacks was desirable. The Committee quickly passed on to other matters. As shall be seen, it was only in 1928, four years after the passing of the Act, that the issue received the attention of parliamentarians at any great length. Why was this so? A number of reasons suggest themselves. First, there was the precedent of the 1909 Transvaal Act. Second, the Native Labour Regulation Act had been in force for twelve years. To include all workers under the provisions of the Industrial Conciliation Act would have been in effect to have made the former Act null and void, to have removed the whole basis of contract labour. And for that no white political party — not even, despite its protestations against 'slave labour', the SALP — was prepared. The SALP itself scented electoral victory in the air: it looked forward to administering the SAP Industrial Conciliation Act along Labour lines. Time enough later to get to grips with the problems of a docile black labour force and of the factors which kept it so.

The passage of the Industrial Conciliation Act was a matter which involved, in the main, two industrial groups: organised employers on the one hand, organised white labour on the other. Neither, despite the confrontation of 1922, was completely homogeneous. Important special conditions qualified the solidarity of both blocs. Each group found its political centre of gravity in two opposed political parties, and at this time the conditions were relatively ripe for an articulation of pure class interests in the political process.

Highly important too was a third party to the issue: the SAP government. It too was not homogeneous, and in addition stood prima facie an accomplice of one of the other contending interests, 'capital'. But it seems clear that the SAP Cabinet, and especially F. S. Malan, did not wholly represent business in politics, while conceding points to that influential party within a party, the Chamber of Mines. Malan's guiding principle in the establishment of the Industrial Conciliation Act had been to do unto employers what he did unto employees, and the grudging acceptance of the SALP reflected his success. The Industrial Conciliation Act was not to any extent an issue in the crucial general election of 1924, as Taft-Hartley was in the U.S.A. in 1948, and the Taff Vale Judgement was to Labour in Britain in 1906. In the debates over the Industrial Conciliation Bill the National Party had remained largely a sleeping partner, rousing itself now and again to make the token speeches which proved its common opposition to the SAP government. Whatever else kept the pot of white politics boiling over at this time, it was no fundamental, irreconcilable clash over a workable framework of industrial relations.

The Aftermath

In passing the Industrial Conciliation Act, the S.A.P. government had in a very real sense pre-empted the actions of an NP — SALP governing coalition. The Pact government thus came to power with part of its industrial programme already in existence. Significantly, the new government only attempted to amend the Industrial Conciliation Act in 1928, and the provisions of the proposed amendment were wholly in line with the spirit of the Act of 1924. Due to the lateness of the session, that amendment failed to gain enactment. It was only in 1930 that the Industrial Conciliation Act was first amended, along the lines of the 1928 proposals, which will be discussed below.

With industrial and conciliation wage determination machinery already in operation under the Industrial Conciliation Act, the SALP pressed ahead with two further measures: a wage determination measure for non-unionised or weakly-organised workers, and the legalisation of the job colour bar on the mines which had been declared ultra vires in the 1923 court case Attorney-General vs G. H. Smith.[45] The latter lies outside the scope of this chapter. The former, the Wage Bill, does however deserve consideration, for it was clearly seen as the complement to the machinery of the Industrial Conciliation Act in the determination of wages. The main provision of the Wage Bill was the creation of a state Wage Board with power to investigate conditions in particular industries (excluding agriculture and domestic service), and to issue minimum wage determinations for the job categories involved, no discrimination on ground of race being allowed. It was this last part around which major political interest in the Bill revolved. Simply stated, the issue was: was it intended that the non-discriminatory wage determinations of the Wage Board would·act as a wage colour bar pricing blacks out of jobs and whites into them? The participants in the debates on the Bill were well aware of the discriminatory potential inherent in this overtly colourblind provision. For the many labour spokesmen involved, it was after all nothing more than the statutory enactment of 'equal pay for equal work', or the 'rate for the job', and all were aware how advantageous that could be to white workers in Southern Africa. It was, nevertheless, often politically prudent to obfuscate the issue — and for none more so than the SALP, junior partner in the Pact.

Their official ideology, and those left-wing activists who took the ideology seriously, pulled them one way; their perception of the self-interest of white workers and voters another. Thus even such an experienced veteran of the labour movement as W. H. Andrews persisted in trying to square the circle: socialist non-discrimination and brotherhood on the one hand, measures to encourage the interests of white workers on the other.[46] By obscuring this dilemma, the 'left' and the 'right' in the SALP were able to support the Bill, each seeing in the measure what it wanted.

More revealing, since the schizophrenia of the SALP had long been public knowledge for those with eyes to see, was the attitude of the major capitalists to the measure. Again the division between the secondary industry and the Chamber of Mines was quite evident. In fact more so. For the new government was the Pact with men behind it who had lost the industrial battle of 1922 only to win the electoral struggle of 1924. There was thus no question of a repetition of the events of 1923, when the Chamber of Mines had been able to press its point of view directly with the Minister in private, without making public possibly embarassing representations through the medium of a parliamentary select committee cross-examination. The Chamber of Mines, through its chairman P. M. Anderson, gave extensive evidence before the select committee on the Wage Bill in 1925. Before him, the SA Federated Chamber of Industries had made it clear that it had no fundamental objections to the measure: it was after all merely an extension of the principle of joint monopoly by other means.[47] The situation of the Chamber of Mines was quite different. It had fallen from its privileged position of confidant of government Ministers and was now the butt of politicians to whom it had, in their public rhetoric, represented the epitome of sinister elite manipulation. Was the Pact proposing radical intervention into the affairs of an industry which had previously managed to accomodate itself relatively comfortably to the revenue-seeking propensity of the Union government? Were white workers here to find their final victory over an oppressive management? The note of something approaching panic-stricken uncertainty seems evident from the testimony of Anderson.

Rather ingenuously, since the bill gave no warrant for it, Anderson first argued that the measure would not apply to the gold mining industry, since it was highly organised and paid high wages, and, Anderson claimed, the Bill was only intended to apply to 'sweated' industries.[48] Coldly rebutted by the Minister of Labour, F. P. Creswell, on this score, Anderson suggested that the measure, if applied to the mines, would apply only to whites.[49] He was told that there was no such provision in the Bill. With some justification, Anderson argues that:

> The Bill puts into the hands of the Minister the determination as to which occupations shall be carried on by whites, blacks or coloured men: and it affects us seriously in connection with certain of our occupations which are on the borderline ... I think that there is that danger that the Board has power to change a class of labour in a particular trade ...[50]

Anderson was unable to obtain reassurances from the government members of the select committee on this point. It is however of interest to note that no wage determination was enacted for mine labour under the Pact government — although an award was made in 1927 by the Mining Industry Arbitration Board, consisting of members of the Wage Board, but appointed under the Industrial Conciliation Act. The Award in general appears to have accepted the Chamber of Mines' argument that white mine wages were reasonable, and no large increases were granted.)[51] As far as white miners were concerned, the new government was able to redeem its electoral promises by the passage of the colour bar clauses of the Mines and Works Act of 1926, reserving a wide range of mine jobs for whites and Coloureds. Despite pointed remarks by otherwise sympathetic members of the select committee such as C. Stuttaford, who exposed the bareness of Anderson's claims that the industry was 'organised' when eighty per cent of the mine workers, black Africans, were not,[52] Anderson's basic position was to prove not incompatible with that of the most influential SALP members of the Pact. A concerted programme of wage regulation for the majority of miners, the blacks, was simply not on the programme of the new government.

* * * * *

In March 1928 the Minister of Labour, now Thomas Boydell, introduced a bill to amend the 1924 Industrial Conciliation Act. The main proposals were as follows.[53] First, industrial council agreements were to remain in force until such time as they expired, or that a new agreement was reached by the parties to the council. Second, industrial councils were to be competent to hear all disputes in the industry concerned, whether or not the matter was covered by the relevant industrial agreement. What in fact this amounted to was a reversal of the 1924 decision to bar an appeal over matters regarding individual grievances such as pay, promotion and so forth. Next, conciliation boards were to be allowed to include among their members persons not employers or employees in the particular industry concerned. Fourth, an anomaly concerning strikes was to be amended: strikes had previously only been officially recognised as such when the parties to it had 'declared' it. Fifth, a provision was included regarding wages which had been underpaid. Sixth, an industrial council agreement could be suspended from operation in 'native areas.' This provision, foreshadowing the major post-Second World War dispute over black African housing, was aimed at expediting the building of housing in black areas on a lower cost basis than prevailed outside black areas. Finally, the operation of industrial council agreements was to be extended, with the Minister's permission, to Africans who had previously been excluded from the operation of the Act, owing to the definition of 'employee' in the

101

original Act. This measure was aimed at preventing employers from substituting lower-paid African workers for non-Africans paid at the stipulated industrial council rate. To this end, the definition of 'employee' in the appropriate clause was to be amended to include contract Africans. The clause defining 'employee' for the purpose of registered trade union membership was however to exclude Africans registered under the Native Labour Regulation Act and 'pass-bearing' Africans.

It was this last provision which gained the greatest response from MPs and the debate which would have been appropriate in 1924 only now took place. The occasion was in the same year as, but before, the open 1928 split in the SALP between 'Creswellite' and 'National Councillite' labour supporters. It revealed quite clearly the essential equivocation and contradiction in the SALP's position. Boydell, a future 'Creswellite', argued that the operation of the Wage Board took care of the interests of the African workers, and went to say:

> ... What we are not prepared at the moment to do, is to allow the natives to organise and function under the Industrial Conciliation Act, the same as carpenters, joiners and other organised trades which have had many years experience in trade unionism, and which can be calculated to hold their own with the employers. The time will come, possibly, when the Natives will reach that stage of advancement, and something on these lines will have to be done; but that time has not yet arrived.[54]

W. H. Sampson, also a later Creswellite, in an unusually confused speech, followed several lines of argument at once, not always in harmony with Boydell's statement. The SALP, argued Sampson, had never been in favour of excluding Africans from the provisions of the Industrial Conciliation Act, but it had been a SAP condition for the passing of the measure that they should be excluded. (The first half of this claim, at any rate, was of dubious validity.) Anyway, argued Sampson, there was nothing preventing the formation of African trade unions. They were just not recognised under the act. It was true that the Native Labour Regulation Act and other measures prohibited many Africans from striking. The SALP had always favoured doing away with these Acts for this reason. But, said the trade unionist, Sampson,

> We are not going to create problems by admitting to our unions a class of people who are backward, people who are just emerging from barbarism, and do not understand trade unions. They will have to go through the mill, the same as others have had to do. You cannot bring these people all at once into the system under which the white people live ...

Sampson then evidenced the activities of the Industrial and Commercial Workers of Clements Kadalie as proof of the inability of Africans to operate trade unions at the present time.[55]

The intellectual disarray of the SALP over this same issue was plain. But it was equally clear that no one inside parliament at least had a consuming interest to take advantage of the fact. Boydell received support for his position from both English-speaking urban representatives of the white middle class, and from rural members horror-striken at the idea that any tampering with the principle of criminal sanctions for breach of work contracts could be contemplated. As O. R. Nel, MP for Newcastle stated:

> ... If there is one thing we on the Platteland must fight against, it is the whittling down of the Masters and Servants Act. It is the only means we have of controlling natives.[56]

It was left to F. D. Chaplin, however, while supporting this provision in the Bill, to get in the cruellest cut of all, and incidentally to reveal a basic community of interest among the parties in the legislature:

> The Government agreed before that the natives must be left out, because it is common cause that it is impossible to face conditions which would raise to a large extent the standard of native wages on the mines. The Minister of Defence (Creswell, SALP leader) has talked for twenty years or more as to the necessity for doing away with what he calls servile labour, and for stopping the importation of natives from Portuguese East Africa. The Minister, however, is sitting in a Cabinet, which is sending one of its members to Lisbon to make sure that this labour is maintained. I am glad it is so ... The Minister does not go further by making this applicable to the natives, because he knows he dare not do so, for if he did do it, wages would go up to such an extent that a large proportion of the gold mines would be unpayable, and the country cannot do without the revenue it derives from the mines; the only possible remedy would be a reduction in European wages ...[57]

Conclusion

The passage of the Industrial Conciliation Act in 1924 involved a government-imposed compromise between eventually two groups: organised business and organised labour, both of whom could count on the support of political representatives to articulate their interests. It was, in a very real sense, a conflict between two sections of urban English-speaking society in which a largely Afrikaner government acted as arbitrator and guide. On this level the contest was strikingly lacking in the kind of ethnic polarisation that made for the least soluble of white party political issues in South Africa. Instead, the creation of the new industrial relations framework was a case-study in economic politics; and the solution was largely an economic one:

the encouragement of joint monopolies of employers and employees to regulate wage competition and to institutionalise collective bargaining.

But on another level — one which, as we have seen, was scarcely raised in the course of the debates on the proposed measure in 1923-1924 — the Act rested on a basic ethnic foundation — the virtual exclusion of the black African worker. The Act thus gave major impetus to the tendency towards the separationist or exclusionist tendencies in white labour's activities and must therefore be accounted one of the major factors giving rise to South Africa's partial labour movement. The causal chain is of course less than simple. The Act was influenced by exclusionist practices already in existence; in turn, it strengthened and elaborated these practices.

The long-term effect of the Act was however not just to reinforce a trade unionism of differential incorporation: it also undermined the distinctiveness, and the potential militancy, of the white (and Coloured and Indian South African) Labour movement. By providing a framework for particular categories of employees only (basically those in the private sector) the Act furthered a continuing 'decomposition of labour'[58] by hiving off workers into separate institutional cocoons. Thus while unions in the private sector had a major commonality of interest in the workings of the Industrial Conciliation Act, workers on the state-owned railways in particular were more concerned about their status under the separate Railways and Harbours Service Act.

Finally, along with sectionalisation went bureaucratisation. The Act gave a powerful thrust to the formation of unions able to operate within, and take advantage of the new network of regulations and institutions. Increasingly what was needed was less the militant union organiser than the adroit negotiator and adept office manager. The strike weapon was watered down so that it became almost obsolete as a weapon in the armoury of many unions.[59] The Act, said one unionist two years after its passage, 'has created confusion in the labour ranks, and has destroyed that clarity of thought and action which is essential to progress, as one seldom knows where the function of an Industrial Council ends and that of the Union begins.'[60] But for many other unionists this institutionalisation of the role of the union, and its consequent acceptance by employees, was precisely its advantage. Root-and-branch opposition to the Act was in fact confined (then as later) to a small minority of left-wing activists. Most unionists were keen to see an extension, rather than limitation, of the scope of the Act. In particular they desired the deletion of the clause barring resort to a Conciliation Board 'unless the matter of principle is involved' — the issue on which so much time has been spent in debate in 1924.[61]

Later white participants in the South African industrial relations system have, for the most part, praised the structure and practices which were a product of the Industrial Conciliation Act of 1924. It has been widely acclaimed as the source of South Africa's relative industrial peace. While this argument can be overemphasised (since the Act must be seen in the wider context of a generally upward rise in the rate of economic development in South Africa), the Act has been effective in its own terms. For such a complex piece of legislation, that is perhaps to say a lot. But in accommodating one set of problems, the Act bequeathed another to succeeding industrial actors. Of those, the foremost one was undoubtedly the status of the black African worker; it is a problem whose resolution remains uncertain half a century later.

FOOTNOTES

1. House of Assembly Debates, 14th February 1911, col. 1139.
2. W. K. Hancock, Smuts; *The Sanguine Years*, (Cambridge, C.U.P., 1962) p.237.
3. Debates of the Tvl. Legis. Assembly, 1908, pp. 947 ff.
4. Debates of the Tvl. Legis. Assembly, 1909, col. 66, see also R. U. Millar and F. Isbester (eds) *Canadian Labour in Transition*, (Scarborough, Ontario, Prentice Hall, 1971) p. 184.
5. Debates of the Tvl. Legis. Council, 1909, col, 127.
6. Debates of the Tvl. Legis. Assembly, 1909, col, 70.
7. ibid., col. 78.
8. ibid., col. 90.
9. ibid., col. 86.
10. ibid., col. 93.
11. ibid., col. 82.
12. ibid., col. 98.
13. S.C. — 3 — 1911.
14. House of Assembly Debates, 1911, cols. 1083-1087.
15. ibid., col. 1089. (Dutch language edition of Hansard. These words do not appear in the English version, though its general drift is similar.)
16. ibid., col. 1083.
17. R. E. and H. J. Simons, *Class and Colour in South Africa 1850-1950*. E. Gitsham and J. Trembath *A First Account of Labour Organisations in South Africa*, and I. Walker and B. Weinbren, *2000 Casualties*.
18. House of Assembly Debates, 1914, vols. 1945-1949.
19. ibid., col. 1974.
20. ibid., col. 1978.
21. ibid., col. 1974.
22. ibid., cols. 1990-1991.

23. See R. E. and H. J. Simons, *Class and Colour in South Africa*, and F. A. Johnstone, *Class, Race and Gold*, especially part 2.
24. U.G. 39 — '22, p.7.
25. ibid., p.21.
26. ibid., p.43.
27. Cape Times House of Assembly Debates, 1923, p.47.
28. ibid., p.47, 48. See also *Statutes of the Union of South Africa, 1924*, p.556, for precisely which Africans were excluded. These were any worker 'whose contract of service or labour is regulated by any Native Pass Laws and Regulations, or by Act No. 15 of 1911 or any amendment thereof or any regulations made thereunder, or by Law No. 25 of 1891 of Natal or any amendment thereof, or any regulations made thereunder, or Act No. 40 of 1894 of Natal or any amendment thereof . . .' The 1937 Industrial Conciliation Act broadened this definition further to include persons whose labour contract was regulated by the above Acts and by section two of the Masters and Servants Law (Transvaal and Natal) Amendment Act, 1926, and by the Natives (Urban Areas) act, 1923, and amendments to, and regulations issued in terms of, these Acts. *Statutes of the Union of South Africa*, 1937, p.428.
29. ibid., p.43.
30. ibid., p.56.
31. S.C. 5 — '23.
32. ibid., p.66.
33. ibid., p.68.
34. ibid., p.66-67.
35. See Malan's Second reading speech on the Bill in 1924.
36. ibid., p.16.
37. ibid., pp.17-18.
38. ibid., p.163.
39. ibid., p.171.
40. ibid., p.571.
41. ibid., p.211.
42. ibid., p.518.
43. ibid., p.570.
44. S.C. 5 — '23, pp.10, 101.
45. See 'South African Correspondent', 'The Colour Bar Decision in the Transvaal', *Journal of Comparative Legislation and International Law*, Series III, vol. 6, 1924.
46. See the evidence of W. H. Andrews in S.C. 14-25, pp.1-9.
47. ibid., pp.45-65.
48. ibid., p.68.
49. ibid., p.87.
50. ibid., p.89.
51. Tvl. Chamber of Mines 38th Annual Report 1927, pp.42-43.
52. ibid., p.87.
53. House of Assembly Debates, 1928, cols. 2292-2300.
54. ibid., 2299.
55. ibid., cols. 2771-2776.
56. ibid., col. 2888.
57. ibid., col. 2781.

58. The phrase is R. Dahrendorff's, *Class and Conflict in Industrial Society,* p.60.
59. See the complaints on this score by an active unionist, C. F. Glass, in *Forward,* 26th February 1926.
60. ibid.
61. See in this connection a report on I.C. Act amendments in *Forward,* 30th March, 1928.

SECTION 3

EARLY AFRICAN TRADE UNIONISM

INTRODUCTION

African trade unions go back to the period of protest during and after the First World War. Faced with rapid inflation and accelerating labour migration, African workers began to act spontaneously in defence of their interests. In 1918, 152 'bucket boy' sanitation workers struck for a small rise in pay. In 1920, 70 000 mineworkers went on strike. An abortive attempt at organizing African workers into the Industrial Workers of Africa (IWA) was made by a group of syndicalists after the First World War.[1] However the most successful attempt at organizing African workers during this period was the Industrial and Commercial Workers Union (ICU).

There have been three major thrusts towards African unionization in South Africa's labour history — the ICU and FNETU in the 1920s; the Joint Committee of African Trade Unions and the Council of Non-European Trade Unions (CNETU) during the Second World War; and SACTU and FOFATUSA in the '50s and early '60s. Each wave of unionization was followed by repressive legislation — the state's response to the ICU was the Industrial Conciliation Act, excluding Africans from formal collective bargaining, and the Native Administration Act with its 'racial hostility' clause; the unions of the 1940s were countered by the Suppression of Communism Act, the Amendment to the Industrial Conciliation Act (1956) and the Bantu (Settlement of Disputes) Act; and SACTU and FOFATUSA were hit by the repressive legislation of the 1960s. What seems to have happened in South Africa is that at each stage in the emergence of embryonic African trade unions, the process of maturation has been ruptured at a crucial point as the unions have been unable to convert from temporary movement into permanent organization. The state, faced by this successful organization of African workers, chose repression rather than incorporation.

From where did these early unions draw their support? Bonner has argued that the only section of the ICU's membership which could be effectively organized was the African urban working class, and it is in their 'failure to organize this group that the ICU can chiefly be

111

criticized'. However, this, as Bonner has since argued, seems to stress its failure as a trade union, at the expense of the ICU's success as a populist movement articulating the aspirations of farm tenants experiencing the dislocating effects of capitalist relations of production. Yet for an effective trade union to arise, there must be a body of life-long wage-earners, free to sell their labour, wholly dependent on wages without prospects of becoming independent producers, and aware of the benefits of collective bargaining. These conditions were to develop in the rising manufacturing industry which employed a growing number of permanent industrial African workers. As the 1935 Industrial Legislation Commission noted, 'the trend of industrial development during the past few decades has been such that it is much more convenient for employers to negotiate with one large union representing all classes of workers in the industry, rather than with a number of separate crafts representing only sections of their workers.'[2] Both Lewis and Stein focus on this new 'industrial unionism' and show how, by emphasizing economic issues and using 'lightning strikes', these unions were able to achieve a certain amount of success.

One of the central problems of African unions, it is often said, is their explicit exclusion from the cornerstone of the South African industrial relations system — the Industrial Conciliation Act. This means they cannot oblige employers, the Department of Labour, Industrial Councils or registered trade unions to co-operate. They have to rely on their goodwill. What is of particular interest during this period is that both FNETU and the Joint Committee of African Trade Unions were able to depend on the goodwill of at least two of these bodies. The African trade unions which emerged in 1928 — clothing, furniture, bakery and laundry workers — were all parallel unions, that is, they were set up by registered unions on racial lines because Africans were excluded from the Industrial Conciliation Act. They were able to attain a degree of independence by forming the Federation of Non-European Trade Unions (FNETU). However, this is an exception and in most cases in South Africa skilled workers (white workers) have not helped the unskilled (black workers) to organize, but have chosen on the contrary to use race as a mechanism for excluding them. This tendency contrasts with the 'normal' pattern of trade union development where, after an initial period of exclusion by craft unions, trade unions were to help the unskilled workers within their industry to organize. For example, according to H. A. Turner, 'An important motive in the expansion of the British

Amalgamated Engineering Union (AEU) from skilled mechanics, to recruit lower skilled operatives, was that the standards of the former were threatened by the lower wages of the latter and by the increasing technical possibility of replacing skilled by less skilled labour.' The consequence was that the differential between skilled and unskilled wages was lowered, which was done by raising the wage of the unskilled workers, without harming the position of the skilled.[3] The Joint Committee of African Trade Unions, on the other hand, was able to achieve a close working relationship with the Department of Labour. The public statement from the Chairman of the Wage Board paying tribute to the valuable role played by African unions, quoted by Stein, is evidence of this.[4] This is in sharp contrast to the attitude of the Department of Labour in more recent times.[5]

In was during this earlier period that the fragmentation of skilled work and the reorganisation of the labour process on the basis of 'semi-skilled' operative labour was taking place. Industrial capitalism involves a double relation: a specific form of *ownership* of the means of production and a specific form of *control* over the labour process. Through 'deskilling' craft workers, capital was taking direct control over the labour process in the final consumer product sector, and in the process creating a class of semi-skilled operatives, white and black, performing similar functions in the production process. Lewis has argued in a more recent article that it was amongst these 'deskilled' workers that the conditions for inter-racial solidarity were to emerge.[6] A tentative explanation, at this stage of the debate, for the close working relationship between the registered and unregistered unions in these industries must be sought in the material conditions created by the changing labour process as a result of the rise of manufacturing industry.

FOOTNOTES

1.   F. A. Johnstone, 'The IWA on the Rand: Socialist Organization among Black workers on the Rand, 1917-1918.' Paper delivered at the History Workshop, University of the Witwatersrand, February 1978.
2.   Lewis.
3.   H. A. Turner, 'The Morphology of Trade Unionism', in W. J. McCarthy, *Trade Unions* (Penguin, 1972), p. 101.
4.   M. Stein, p. 149.
5.   See 'Conac Engineering', *SALB*, Vol. 2, Nos. 9 and 10.
6.   Jon Lewis, 'Trade Unions and Changes in the Labour Process in S.A. (1925-1930)', Institute of Commonwealth Studies Seminar, 1977.

THE DECLINE AND FALL OF THE ICU — A CASE OF SELF DESTRUCTION?

PHILIP BONNER

Author's Note: I do not now think of the I.C.U. as a failure so much as a movement appropriate to a time characterised by rural impoverishment without major industrialisation. Indeed leaders like Champion, using populist strategies, scored some very real successes within the limits of what was possible — the Anti People-Dipping Campaign being a classic of its kind. Ultimately, however, they were co-ordinating a constituency of 'losers' and so were doomed to failure.

The early 1920s were years of great ferment among black communities in South Africa. Wartime industrialisation, post-war inflation, increased pressure on rural subsistence, and accelerated labour migration together disrupted African society and brought a new surge of popular action aimed at accommodating and channelling the dislocations of change. Millenarian movements sprang up in the eastern Cape, predicting airborne liberation by black Americans, and captured the imagination of thousands of Transkeians. A rash of strikes spread through industrial centres, and reached their climax in 1920, when seventy thousand African mine-workers downed tools on the Witwatersrand demanding higher pay. And new resistance was kindled among farm workers throughout the country in response to the tightening restrictions with which they were now being faced. Most important of all, and bridging this entire spectrum of reaction was the Industrial and Commercial Workers' Union of Africa. Founded in Cape Town early in 1919, the ICU spread in the mid-twenties throughout South Africa until by 1927 it could boast a membership of one hundred thousand — the largest trade union ever to have taken root in the continent of Africa.

If the 1920s opened in an atmosphere of expectancy, they closed on an entirely different note. Dislocations undoubtedly persisted, but the hope of profiting from them had all but gone. In the Transkei and Ciskei, the millenium never materialised, and its prophecy brought only suffering to nearly three hundred Israelites shot down at Bulhoek in 1921. On the Witwatersrand mine workers achieved nothing except being driven back down their mines at bayonet point by government troops. And in the rural areas conditions steadily deteriorated as a new wave of evictions got underway in the mid-twenties. As for the ICU, it proved the greatest disappointment of all. Despite a huge membership, its formal achievements were negligible. Labour conditions registered little improvement; wages remained more or less stationary; and a whole new range of discriminatory legislation was placed on the statute books. By the end of the decade, in reaction to failure, the Union began to crumble, and by 1931 it was more or less a spent force. The question this brief essay concerns itself with is why an era of such promise faded and why a movement of such potential withered away.

At a superficial level, the ultimate disintegration of the ICU can be traced to financial instability, personal conflicts, weakness of central organisation, and so on. In a sense though, this does not explain a great deal. Had these been so serious, then the ICU would never have got underway in the first place, or at any rate would not have been able to function successfully for eight years. Considerably more important were underlying weaknesses of analysis and strategy. The *strategic objectives* of the ICU it should be emphasised were clear enough: they wanted a fundamental redistribution of economic and political power. Less clear in their minds was how this should be achieved. In particular what the ICU leaders seem to have lacked was any systematic theory of how economy and society functioned in South Africa, and this in turn prevented them from evolving any adequate strategy to promote change. As a result, for the best part of a decade, they mistook protest for pressure and numbers for strength, ignoring all the while that there had to be some way for pressure to be brought to bear for it to have any effect.

The career of Clements Kadalie, General Secretary of the Union, illustrates many of these shortcomings. Though reputedly an able organiser Kadalie spent most of his time touring round the country and giving speeches. Industrial organisation was neglected; sectionalisation by industry ignored; and scarcely any effort towards union recognition was attempted. Instead Kadalie pinned his hopes on implausible political solutions. On occasions, as will be seen, this might have had a limited justification. On others, as with his flirtation with Hertzog, it was manifestly absurd. Hertzog at this time had just allied his Nationalists to the South African Labour Party, and hoped

115

by associating himself with Kadalie to gain the Cape African vote in the coming election. The Smuts Government was admittedly in bad odour in African circles for the Bulhoek massacre and other similar incidents, but there were little grounds for expecting that a party whose labour wing had coined the slogan 'Workers of the World Unite for a White South Africa' would behave much better. Still more damning is that Kadalie took absolutely no precautions to ensure that they should do. No concessions were extracted, and Kadalie seems neither to have sought nor gained any assurance on even the question of recognition. One can only conclude that Kadalie was taken in by Hertzog's honeyed words; that tiring of stalemate he fell into the trap of mistaking dialogue for progress and of assuming that any movement at all must be better than none.

In his pursuit of such pipe-dreams Kadalie resembled certain of his rural followers, who expected supernatural deliverance on purchase of an ICU card. The same facet of his personality was exhibited still more vividly in his expectations of international trade unionism. Within limits some sort of connection with world trade unionism would have been beneficial. It would have extended expertise and resources to the ICU, together with the psychological reassurance that it was not entirely alone. As the 1920s wore on however, Kadalie began to see this more as a substitute for local action than a supplement to it. In a way not altogether unfamiliar today he seems to have despaired of internal action and to have relied increasingly on pressure from outside. Recognition from international trade union organisations was applied for and affiliation to the British Trade Union Congress was sought, with the idea in each case of using their leverage to extract concessions from government and white unions at home. By 1927 when Kadalie left to set up links with Europe, this had become the pivot of ICU strategy, and the mainstay of all their hopes.

Even so, when Kadalie set sail for Europe in June 1927 the ICU appeared on the crest of a wave. Membership was soaring, branches were springing up everywhere and the organisation was fast becoming the symbol of black resistance throughout the Union. Appearances however were highly deceptive. Rather than attracting industrial workers during this period, ICU expansion was made up predominantly of labour tenants working on white farms, who were on the point of facing the rigours of new labour legislation. This notoriously unorganisable group soon proved themselves the achilles heel of the ICU. Scattered across thousands of square miles of countryside they were virtually impossible to protect, and quickly soaked up their own financial contributions and others' in legal actions against unlawful eviction. Even then these were no more than drops in an ocean. In a situation where thousands were being evicted and where mere membership of the ICU was an invitation to victimisation, the problem was too enormous to be handled. As a result the euphoria of 1927 gave way to the recriminations of 1928. Membership slumped, finances were shattered and the organisation went into sharp decline.

A similar crisis of expectations was precipitated among the Union's urban membership. Here again the problem was one of attracting membership in an apparently random fashion, and in such a way as to preclude effective industrial organisation of action. This aspect of ICU activity had been evident almost from its inception, but it was exaggerated in 1926 by the expulsion of communists from its ranks. They at least had been prepared to use the strike weapon, if often only for premature political ends. With their departure however, the very idea of striking fell into disuse. The penalties of neglect were not long in making themselves felt. When a flurry of strikes hit Durban and Johannesburg in 1927, the organisation was neither willing or able to lend support. Instead, at the insistence of Ethelreda Lewis they counselled restraint and return to work. The impact of ICU inaction proved enormous. Confidence was undermined among many workers, and the Union's credibility lost. Coinciding with its rural decline, moreover, it put new strains on the organisation which it was unable to sustain. Regional rivalries and personal tensions which had been papered over in time of growth broke open with fresh acrimony when it entered decline, and by 1930 the ICU had effectively fallen apart.

It is sometimes argued that it was Kadalie's absence in Europe in 1927, together with his decision to import the British trade unionist, Ballinger, on his return, that tilted the ICU into crisis and decline. In practice, as has been shown, the malaise went deeper than that. Although Kadalie's absence in 1927 may have deprived the organisation of firm leadership at a critical time, and although Ballinger's attempts at reorganisation may have intensified feuding within the ICU, the real problems were the long-standing ones of a lack of analysis and strategy. To say this however merely begs the broader question of why no sounder analysis or strategy developed, and for an answer to this it is necessary to look more explicitly at the character of the leadership and the constraints of the situation in which they operated. In a sense the ICU's leaders are not entirely to be blamed for their organisation's collapse. For a long time the pitfalls of loose thinking were obscured by the spectacular gains that were achieved from projecting precisely this sort of diffuse appeal. With the African National Congress confining itself largely to elite concerns, it sufficed for the ICU simply to voice mass grievances for it to become the principle vehicle of African discontent. The inherent dangers of this approach scarcely need elaboration; what mattered was not so much numbers as their relationship and ratio to the object under attack. And when that object was broadly political, the scattered following of the ICU could have little success until organised on some more effective basis to confront the state.

Even here the leadership has some defence. They could and did claim that political and economic issues were inseparable; that in the face of measures like the Pass Laws and the Industrial Conciliation Act, both had to be confronted at the same time. The obvious weakness of this line of argument was that it confused the diagnosis with the cure. Political and economic issues might be intertwined, but since the only available power base was the organised working class it was this that had to be used. The word 'organised' is of some importance here. Agricultural labourers, as we have seen, were virtually unorganisable; so too, it can be argued were those in the reserves. Clamped into a system of tribal control and insulated administratively from outside, the ICU could never easily have achieved penetration there — whatever the merits of organising migrant labour at its rural end. Nor in fact did they really try. All this left, therefore, was the urban working class; and it is in their failure to organise this group that the ICU can chiefly be criticised.

The ICU's comparative neglect of urban workers was in some measure a reflection of its leadership calibre. While they may have been correct in adopting a political strategy, they were mistaken in pursuing it prematurely, and in not developing a trade union strategy as a platform for their political goals. The reason for this negligence can be traced to their elite or petit-bourgeois background. Whereas in European trade unionism, trade union leadership had developed organically from the working class, in the ICU movement had been created and a leadership imposed more or less from the outside. From the outset, therefore, the movement was characterised by the cult of the personality, and by contradictory bourgeois aims. Both Champion, the ICU's Natal leader, and Kadalie bear this stamp. Each relied more on charisma than on organisation, and each saw the standing of the Union as being synonymous with his own. This was damaging, not only because it substituted populism for trade unionism, but because it also gave rise to a series of personal vendettas which ultimately split the organisation apart. In the case of Champion because he believed one had to be a man of property to be a man of standing, and because he saw the stature of the Union as a reflection of his own, he felt no qualms about mingling official union finances with those of his own. While this was not necessarily disastrous from the narrow financial view it was from a broader political one. Regional conflicts became personalised, and political opponents could and did level accusations of corruption for more general political ends. Once decline and financial stringency set in, disintegration almost automatically ensued.

Leadership deficiencies were therefore critical. But some nagging questions still remain. Why did a more adequate leadership never develop? Or did the ICU in fact get the leadership it deserved? Was the situation appropriate for trade unionism, or was it impossible for effective organisation and leadership to emerge? Certainly a case can be made for this last argument. Unlike today for instance only a fraction of the black working population was absorbed in the industrial working force, which left a reservoir of untapped labour in theory available to undercut union demands. Unlike today the large majority of African workers were *effectively* migratory in the sense that they could supplement urban wages with rural subsidies, and hence were not totally committed to their industrial milieu. Unlike today there were only a handful of large-scale industries to serve as bases for authentic industrial unions. Unlike today, in short, it can be argued no viable alternative to populism existed, and no other breed of leader could have emerged.

But this again seems to paint the picture too blackly. In 1921, for instance, the black and coloured work force in urban areas numbered 837 000, a growing proportion of which was becoming stabilised. For much of the following decade, moreover, economic growth was sufficiently steady to mop up the excess of labour supply and largely erase the threat of competition from any reserve army of unemployed. Lastly, among black labour generally there had developed a sense of worker consciousness, of which the post-war strikes were but the more visible form. The potential for some sort of trade unionism, therefore, clearly existed. Whether it was enough to sustain much more than the ICU, is of course, a different matter. In the opinion of this writer it was, though the implications of greater success may have been politically ambiguous; others will disagree even with that. For the moment it seems it must remain an open question.

To conclude, what was the legacy of the ICU? Obviously to the extent that it disintegrated it was one of failure. But that failure was not as complete as is often assumed. Local leaders and linkages did not simply vanish, but remained ready to be taken up when new organisations emerged. Similarly, worker consciousness, though battered, was also hardened and prepared for action of a more disciplined form. In a sense the very memory of the ICU was to prove instructive, an encouragement and a warning to all who followed on.

FOOTNOTES

1. C. R. Diamond, 'African Labour Problems on the South African Gold Mines with special reference to the strikes of 1916', M.A Thesis, University of Cape Town, 1969.
2. C. Kadalie, *My Life and the ICU.*
3. S. W. Johns III 'The Birth of Non-White Trade Unions in South Africa', *(Race,* October 1967). 'Trade Union — Political Pressure Group or Mass Movement the ICWU of Africa' in R. I. Rotberg and A. Mazrui, eds., *Protest and Power in Black Africa* (1970).
4. E. Roux, *Time Longer Than Rope* (Univ. of Wisconsin Press, 1974).
5. Simons and Simons, *Class and Colour in South Africa — 1850-1950* (Penguin Books, 1971).
6. H. H. Smith: 'The Development of Labour Organisation in East London — 1900-1948' (M. A. Thesis, Rhodes University, 1949).
7. P. Wickins: 'The Industrial and Commercial Workers' Union'. (Ph.D. thesis, University of Cape Town, 1973) 'General Labour Movement in Cape Town 1918-1920' (*S.A.J.E.* 1972).
10. H. Slater, 'Proletarianization in Natal — The ICU' (Commonwealth Studies Seminar Papers, Univ. of London, 1970).
11. Maynard Swanson: 'Alison Wessels Champion' (unpublished paper, U.S. African Studies Association).

'THE NEW UNIONISM': INDUSTRIALISATION AND INDUSTRIAL UNIONS IN SOUTH AFRICA 1925-1930

JON LEWIS

'Unlike the old trade unions, they greet every suggestion of an identity of interest between capital and labour with scorn and ridicule. Thus we see now these new Unions taking the lead of the working-class movement generally, and more and more taking in tow the rich and proud "old" Unions.'[1]

F. Engels, 1889

Although Engels was writing on Britain in the late nineteenth century, his words capture the atmosphere of militant trade unionism which emerged amongst black and white workers in the secondary industrial sector during the second half of the 1920s.

I HISTORY

Hitherto, and since its inception in the 1880s, the labour movement in South Africa had been dominated by craft unions, with the exception of the Mine Workers' Union, which increasingly drew its membership from semi-skilled and unskilled whites. These unions, with their activities centred upon the mines, had waged an intermittent and sometimes violent struggle against the mine owners over job reservation, which culminated in the Rand Revolt of 1922. The suppression of the strike by the Smuts government dealt a shattering blow to the MWU, from which it never really recovered. Trade Union membership in South Africa fell from 108 242 to 81 861 in the aftermath of the strike.[2] The defeat also hastened the collapse of the central coordinating body, the South African Industrial Federation, which was already reeling under the increasingly authoritarian direction of its General Secretary, Archie Crawford. On the railways, members of the AEU who had struck were victimized. The general effect of the failure of the 1922 strike was to make the unions very wary of strike action.

This rejection of industrial militancy took institutional form with the passage of the Industrial Conciliation Act in 1924, and the Wage Act in 1925. These measures brought industrial relations very firmly under the law and a system of conciliation. However, these developments benefited the established unions, which were powerful enough to safeguard their interests within the Industrial Councils — those representing artisans, public sector and white collar employees.[3] Thus, the South African Typographical Union, for example, was to be a consistent champion of the policy of collaboration within the Industrial Councils.

This period also saw the beginnings of independent trade union activity amongst Africans and Coloureds, with the formation of the Industrial and Commercial Workers' Union of Africa (ICU) in 1919, under the leadership of Clements Kadalie. In his own words:

> The object of this Union was to organise those workers not catered for by the white Unions into "one big Union".[4]

By 1927, the ICU claimed a membership of 100 000. However, membership was random, scattered and unorganised, and included large numbers of labour tenants working on white farms. It has been argued that the only section of the ICU's membership which was capable of being effectively organised was the African urban working class, 'and it is in their failure to organise this group that the ICU can chiefly be criticised'.[5] Thus the ICU failed to give support to African workers during the 1927 strikes in Durban and Johannesburg.

The Report of the Native Economic Commission of 1930-32 refers constantly to a class of 'urbanised natives' who had lost all contact with the land and were wholly dependent for their existence on the wages they received.[6] These workers had been forced into the town by the breakdown of production in the reserves.[7] This must have meant that even the casual migrant worker was now more dependent upon wages. However, the Commission pointed out that the position of the 'urbanised native' worker was rendered insecure by the pressure of large numbers of rural migrants, less skilled and less efficient, and consequently cheaper as far as employers were concerned.[8] Employers preferred to employ Africans from rural areas, 'the latter being found more docile and unsophisticated'.[9] The ICU failed to take account of these differences because it was primarily concerned with building a wide front of support around the political grievances of non-whites in general. At the same time Kadalie, receiving support from the Amsterdam International and the British TUC, and increasingly under the influence of white liberals, came to reject militant trade unionism. In 1927, after expelling communist office holders from the ICU, he declared that 'strikes were wicked, useless and obsolete'.[10]

However, coincidental with the political emasculation of the 'old' unions, and the failure of the ICU, the South African economy witnessed a rapid expansion in the manufacturing sector, and this was to lay the basis for the emergence of the 'new' industrial unions.

II THE GROWTH OF SECONDARY INDUSTRY

> South Africa is in the midst of a far-reaching economic revolution, the keynote of which is the efflorescence of a great variety of secondary industries and the progressive industrialisation of large sections of the population.
> — *L. Motz (1929)*[11]

The number of manufacturing establishments in the Union increased from 3 638 in 1915-16 to 6 645 in 1929-30.[12] At the same time the total number employed in private industry rose from 101 178 to 201 180 during the same period.[13] These industries received an initial boost during the First World War when it was impossible to import certain consumer goods. Thus, for example, the furniture industry on the Reef developed in the following way: 3 firms were established in 1912, 2 in 1915, 1 in 1916 and 3 in 1917.[14] By 1929, there were 50 firms in Johannesburg alone.[15] Secondary industry further benefited from the protection policy of the Pact Government after 1924.

> The policy of protection is becoming deeply ingrained in the national consciousness, and is having decided effects in the introduction of new industries. The home market for the products of the local manufactories is assuming growing proportions, with the gradual disappearance of the old prejudice against the home made article, the improvement of the quality of the latter, and, most important, the increasing purchasing power of the population, not excluding the non-European elements.
> — *L. Motz (1929)*[16]

A change in the industrial infrastructure was bound to influence the nature of working class response. The 1935 Industrial Legislation Commission noted:

> The trend of industrial development during the past few decades has been such that it is much more convenient for employers to negotiate with one large union representing all classes of workers in their industry, rather than with a number of separate craft unions representing only sections of their workers.[17]

The Labour Force

The enlarged labour force needed for these industries was recruited from the ranks of the newly-proletarianised, both black and white, who had been forced off the land and into the towns by economic hardship, government policy, and the increasing domination of large capitalist agriculture.

The statistics for employment in private industry reveal a distinct pattern of labour recruitment in secondary industry.[18]

CENSUS	WHITES		COLOUREDS		AFRICANS		ASIATICS	
YEAR	Male	Female	Male	Female	Male	Female	Male	Female
1915-16	34 938	4 586	11 983	3 288	34 682	383	10 212	1 106
1929-30	45 168	13 234	17 975	6 791	69 216	679	8 764	502

Two trends are immediately obvious from these figures: (a) the rapid growth of white female labour, and (b) the preponderance of African males. These trends would be proportionately stronger for the Reef since the majority of Coloured and Asian workers would be employed in the Cape and Natal, respectively. It will be argued that these groups — white women, and black male factory workers — played a prominent role in the 'new unionism'.

III SKILLED AND UNSKILLED

Wage labour in South Africa has been characterised by a massive disparity between the wage levels of skilled workers and those in unskilled or semi-skilled work. This situation arose out of the specific historical circumstances of conquest and the development of the mining industry. In particular, high wages were necessary to induce skilled workers to come to South Africa, whilst continued subsistence production in the reserves allowed the mineowners to pay Africans (who constituted the majority of unskilled labour) a wage below the necessary level for the reproduction of their labour power.[19] Secondary industry could thus benefit from an already established labour market.

The Report of the Industrial Legislation Commission of 1935 drew attention to the degree of disparity in wage rates:

124

As at 31st May 1935:

INDUSTRY	AREA	SKILLED	SEMI-SKILLED	UNSKILLED
Furniture	Rand and Pretoria	2s.5d p.h. 2s.9d p.h.	8d p.h. 1s.10d. p.h.	6d. p.h.
Laundering Dyeing and Cleaning	Principal Industrial Centres	£6 p.w.	£1.5s. - £1.10s. p.w.	£1.2s.6d. p.w.
Sweet Manufacturing	Principal Centres	£6 p.w.	£3 p.w.	£1.4s. p.w.

The rates contrast sharply with ratios for other countries. For instance, the average hourly earnings of male unskilled workers as a percentage of skilled rates amounted to 75% in the U.S.A. in 1927.[20]

Mr F. A. W. Lucas, K.C., Chairman of the Wage Board, argued that this disparity between skilled and unskilled wage rates ('which might be roughly stated as the difference between £1 a day and £1 a week') led to considerable pressure for deskilling and for the downward reclassification of skilled work.

> ... the skilled worker's wage was relatively to the native's wages so high that much of the semi-skilled work which formed part of the skilled man's work was handed over to the native, generally without any increase of wages ... This process also tended to push the skilled man in some industries into entirely supervisory positions.[21]

> Chairman of the Wage Board (1928)

The tendency towards job fragmentation in order to take advantage of cheap labour was also noted by the Native Economic Commission:

> Work which, if the divergence between the wages of skilled men and of labourers were similar to the difference in Europe, would be done by the skilled man and thus help to keep up the number of posts for skilled men, is in South Africa, wherever possible, lopped off the skilled man's task and assigned to native labourers.[22]

This process had a number of implications for the various sections of the labour force employed in secondary industry.

(a) African Workers

In the first place it meant that many African workers who were categorized as labourers in fact carried out semi-skilled work. This implies the development of an increasingly stable African working class, which in turn had implications for trade union organisation. Thus Roux writes:

> It was found that the African workers in the so-called "secondary" industries were easiest to organise. Though often classed as unskilled, they are really quite skilled and it is not easy to replace them at short notice. They are usually location residents and have their wives and children with them, though they may not have severed completely their ties with the countryside. They constitute the nearest approach to a Bantu proletariat in South Africa. In contrast to the more shifting and semi-peasant miners, building labourers and railway construction workers here today and gone tomorrow, always preoccupied with cows and land, these urban workers were comparatively quick to grasp the idea of trade union organisation. [23]

The Native Economic Commission found evidence of a blurring of skill classification on the basis of colour.

> There is a slow but increasing infiltration of more advanced Natives into the non-manual occupations. [24]

There is also evidence that a small number of Africans were performing highly skilled work. [25]

(b) Unskilled White Workers

This group probably suffered most from the wide disparity in wage rates, since their standards were set by the highly paid skilled whites. Government commissions during the period were well aware of the situation, and the problems it caused in finding jobs for 'poor whites'. One of the reports submitted by the Economic and Wage Commission (1925) argued that:

> With the present volume of production the existing wages of Europeans are possible only if Europeans are restricted to a limited number of supervisory and more skilled posts. Work which is not of this character cannot be paid similar rates. While in any industry the rates of skilled to unskilled labour at any time is influenced by the stage of technical development which the industry has reached, a high standard of rates for skilled work encourages the employers to organise production on the basis of a small ratio of skilled to general labour. For the two reasons stated the great mass of wage earners — native, coloured and *white* — are restricted to work calling for no special skill or capacity for initiative, and rates of pay for general unskilled labour remain low.' [26]

In other words there were not enough non-manual and skilled jobs to absorb the entire white work force. This situation was not improved by the continuing fragmentation of what skilled jobs there were. However, in addition, white unskilled labour was hindered from assuming semi-skilled work, which had been newly created by secondary industry. The Native Economic Commission concluded:

> Owing to his virtual exclusion from unskilled work (by reason of his being uneconomic at "civilised" rates of pay — author) the European has not been

able to find his way into certain higher classes of work. Through employment in labourer's work many labourers acquire the skill necessary for various kinds of semi-skilled work. Thus the European, being excluded from labourer's work, has been prevented from becoming qualified for such semi-skilled work, while Natives, through working as labourers have become qualified for it. This handicap on the European has been aggravated by the fact that Natives when they are so qualified and actually do such semi-skilled work seldom get a wage higher than that which is customary for labourers work.'[27]

Whilst the Pact Government provided jobs directly for 'poor whites' on the railways and in the post office, the Industrial Councils and the Wage Board were expected to maintain a 'civilised' standard of wages for unskilled whites in industry. The Chairman of the Wage Board argued that part of his job was to 'fix steps in the wage gap for semi-skilled work',[28] and that this would provide jobs for unqualified whites (as well as providing an incentive for Africans). However, this intervention by the state was strongly resisted by employers. As regards the Industrial Conciliation Act, employers were able to circumvent its provisions by merely dismissing white workers and substituting blacks.[29] (In 1930 the Industrial Conciliation Act was amended to allow wage agreements to lay down wage rates for workers not defined as 'employees' in the original Act, i.e., for 'pass carrying natives').

Furthermore, the records of the Trade Union Congress (SATUC) are full of complaints from unions, such as the Garment Workers' or the Furniture Workers', to the effect that employers refused to honour industrial council agreements and wage determinations, consistently underpaying workers and ignoring agreements on the rates of qualified to unqualified labour to be employed. It is not surprising, therefore, that the early struggles of the 'new' industrial unions were around these issues. (It will be shown below how industrial legislation related to the African Unions.)

Manufacturing industry was still in its early stages during the 1920s, and large-scale factory production was not yet dominant.[22] In order to accumulate capital employers were forced to keep wages as low as possible. In certain industries this was achieved by employing female labour and juveniles. This also warded off political pressure by providing jobs for 'poor whites'.

(i) *White female labour* was concentrated in certain industries. For example, in tailoring and clothing the number of white women employed increased from 1 687 to 3 238 between 1925/6 and 1929/30. The number employed in sweetmaking increased over the same period from 583 to 1 063.[31] A female work force was

127

particularly welcome to employers since women were traditionally unorganised and underpaid in relation to men. In fact, the Economic and Wage Commission (1925) recommended that the Wage Board should take two-thirds of the man's rate as the standard for women's wages. The 1935 Industrial Legislation Commission endorsed this policy and showed that it had been carried out by the Wage Board.[32]

(ii) *Juveniles* — In certain industries it became standard practice to employ large numbers of workers under the age of 21, who were not entitled to the full rate of pay. A similar technique was to employ 'probationers' or 'learners', who again received less than the full rate, and (often) to sack them once they became fully qualified. The furniture industry during this period demonstrates both techniques at work.

The investigation of the Wage Board into the Furniture Manufacturing Industry for 1930 found that, in the eleven largest firms in Johannesburg there were 261 journeymen to a total of 396 apprentices and probationers. The Board concluded that 'the number of probationers is undoubtedly excessive'.[33] On the Rand as a whole, during November and December 1928, the Board found there were 596 skilled workers to 734 juveniles and apprentices.[34] The existence of large numbers of apprentices involved new problems of trade union organisation since only qualified journeymen could traditionally join the Union. Also, since apprentices were under indentured contract they could not strike.[35]

It was reported to a meeting of the NEC of SATUC in 1927 that furniture manufacturing employers were ignoring the industrial council agreement, and that matters had come to a head on 21 February when the Central Mattress Company had locked out all men who were entitled to a rise under the agreement.[36] At the 1927 Annual Conference of SATUC, Mr Merkle, speaking for the Transvaal section of the Furniture Workers Union 'complained that men receiving above the standard rates were being sacked and replaced or re-engaged at the minimum rate allowed by the Industrial Agreement.'[37] (In other words, they were being placed back on the first rung of the wages scale).

(c) Skilled White Workers

These workers were continually threatened by a process of job fragmentation and deskilling. The threat came as much from cheap white labour as cheap African labour. The 1935 commission in explaining the displacement of men by women in employment argued:

> The preferential employment of females is, as we have shown above, part and parcel of the world-wide economic development in which less scope is being offered in certain spheres for skilled employers and more and more for machine minders, semi-skilled labour and unskilled labour.[38]

The same process was transforming apprenticeship into a cheap labour device. In his report to the 1930 Conference of SATUC, A. M. Merkle makes the point.

> The question arises again, is systematic apprenticeships a practical and satisfactory method today, remembering that the young worker is bound by contract from 5 to 6 years to an occupation wherein mass production and repetition work has replaced technique and skill?[39]

During the 1930s the Furniture Workers were to lead an agitation for the amendment of the Apprenticeship Act, a move which was strongly opposed by the old craft unions, such as the AEU and SATU whose skills had not yet been undermined.

The vulnerability of skilled workers in secondary industry attracted them to trade unionism, and in certain cases they were to play an important although contradictory role, within the 'new' unions.

IV THE EFFECTS OF INDUSTRIAL LEGISLATION
(a) The Industrial Conciliation Act, 1924
The 1935 Commission agreed that:

> The promulgation of the Industrial Conciliation Act marked a definite revival in trade unionism. This is recorded by Gitsham and Trembath (Labour Organisation in South Africa, 1926):
>
> ... the Act has tended to foster the growth of trade unions among those workers who were previously badly organised. Several new Unions have grown up or have become stronger since the Act was passed, for example in the Confectionery, Furniture and Leather Industries. In fact, employers have often encouraged workers to organise so that proper representatives may be appointed on industrial councils.[40]

The point is that in order to benefit from the provisions of the Industrial Conciliation Act, it was necessary to organise along industrial lines, since agreements were negotiated for the industry as a whole. This avoided the situation which many of the older unions faced of having to negotiate through joint trade union bodies, often weakened by division of interests between the individual unions. It is interesting that the S.A. Industrial Union (successor to S.A.I.F. and organised on the 'one big union' principle) was refused registration precisely because it claimed to represent all workers, and could not represent any one industry in particular.[41]

(b) The Wage Act 1925

Black workers (who were 'pass bearing natives') did not fall under the definition of 'employee' laid down in the Industrial Conciliation Act, and were therefore excluded from its provisions. However, the Wage Board, under the chairmanship of F. A. W. Lucas 'held that the Wage Act made no distinction between employees on the ground of race or colour. It gives as it reasons the fact that in many undertakings natives and non-natives were doing the same class and kind of work, and in some instances were working side by side in the same occupation.' [42] White workers had hoped this would work in their interests on the basis that if wages were set high enough employers would prefer to employ whites rather than blacks, at the same wage. In fact, this only occurred to a limited extent, and in an address given by the Wage Board Chairman it was stated that:

> The number of natives employed in some industries had been to some extent reduced as a first result of wage regulation, but the position of those remaining in the industry had generally been improved. The reduction meant that those who had been retained were being trained to become more efficient workers.[43]

Furthermore, Roux argued that the introduction of the Wage Board had certain important implications for the organisation of trade unions amongst Africans:

> Before deciding what minimum wages were to be fixed for different occupations, the Wage Board held meetings in the different industrial centres. Representatives of the employers and of the workers were asked to lay whatever information they wished before the Board. The new Unions took advantage of this machinery, which gave Bantu workers for the first time, the opportunity of bringing their grievances officially to the notice of the authorities.[44]

Once the wage determination had been made, trade union organisation was necessary to make sure that employers actually paid the full rates.

A contributory cause of the decline of the African Unions after 1930 may have been the restrictive amendments to the regulation of the Wages Act, which were introduced in 1929.

> Under the first regulations made under the Wage Act it was possible for the Wage Board to consider an application for an investigation from any unorganised body of Natives who could show that they were authorised to make that application. However, in 1929 the regulations were amended and they now require persons supporting the application to sign it themselves, which in practice makes it impossible for any large body of Natives to make a successful application within the terms of the Act and the regulations, and since the

130

promulgation of the amended regulations no application from Natives has been received by the Board.[45]

(c) The Role of the State

A discussion of industrial legislation prompts the question as to the role of the State. Kaplan has argued that the establishment of the Pact government in 1924 marked a decisive victory for 'national capital', in alliance with the white working class, over mining capital.[46] I would tentatively suggest that this thesis is borne out in the field of industrial legislation. The ICA did no more than draw the ring, within which the registered unions (largely white) and employers (representing 'national' manufacturing capital) could fight it out without resorting to strike action. The Wage Act, it could be argued, did more to raise the level of wages. But often minimum wages were set as low as £1 p.w., and employers who disobeyed a wage determination were treated quite leniently by the courts. Most important of all, this legislation did not challenge the ability of the employers to make full use of cheap labour, at the expense of white workers. In fact only in the mining industry was legislation passed to enshrine a colour bar, and fixed ratio of white workers. Farming (representing 'national' agricultural capital) was not touched by this legislation. (It is however true that in return for tariff protection manufacturing industry was expected to maintain a certain ratio of 'civilised' to 'uncivilised' labour. Even so it could be argued that tariff protection, and not the manufacturers themselves, was financing 'civilised' wages).

The policy of the Pact Government towards white labour was to safeguard white workers already entrenched in the mining industry, and to solve the problem of unemployed, unskilled whites at its own expense (by ensuring jobs on the railways, post office and in the municipalities) rather than by penalising the newly emerging manufacturing sector. Furthermore, the jobs provided for 'poor whites' would have been partly financed out of taxation paid by the mining companies.

V THE 'NEW UNIONS' IN ACTION

(a) The South African Trade Union Council

Although it had no colour bar, SATUC was almost completely composed of all-white unions. It originated with the convening of a special congress of trade union representatives by the Minister of Labour, Col. Creswell, in March 1925. Even the name first chosen for the organisation — the S.A. Association of Employees' Organisa-

131

tions' (changed at the 1926 Conference) — was suggestive of compliance and collaboration. However, the first congress duly shocked its sponsors by electing a communist, W. H. Andrews, to the position of secretary, which post he held throughout the period under review. From the first the influence of the Left — which increasingly coincided with the 'new' industrial unions — was established.

In the first place, the constitution of 1925, although allowing for card votes on policy, provided that 'all elections of persons shall be by ballot of the delegates present.'[48]

This allowed small and newly formed unions to exert pressure at the Conference. Also, many of the old unions refrained from joining SATUC, or like SATU and SAMWU withdrew their membership. Commentators at the time, and since, have ascribed this to alleged left-wing control and the absence of a colour bar.[49] However, this had the result of allowing those unions which remained greater freedom of action, released from the dead hand of trade union conservatism, which now characterised the older union. As the 'new' unions increased in size, so their influence within SATUC grew. Between 1926 and 1930 the GWU (formerly the Witwatersrand Tailor's Association) increased its affiliated membership from 300 to 900 (although actual membership by this time would have been considerably more), and the Furniture Workers' Union increased from 240 to 800 over the same period. Also, by the 1930 Conference many new unions had been formed and become affiliated.

The support of Bill Andrews for the formation of industrial unions should be stressed. During the war he had worked in Sheffield with J. T. Murphy, an engineering worker, and a leader of the shop stewards' movement and of the struggle for Industrial Unionism.[50] Andrews was undoubtedly influenced by this experience.[51] If Trembath and Gitsham's book on Labour Organisation (published in 1926) is at all representative of trade union thinking at the time, then it would seem that the theory of industrial unionism was in the ascendency:

> ... it is safe to say that the vision of the future is the organisation of all the workers on industrial lines, with some controlling council for the whole of South Africa.[52]

> Specialisation and the interlocking of trades tend to make the old craft division obsolete. The trustification of Industry has also tended to eliminate the single employer. We find therefore, that Trade Unions are becoming now-a-days either Industrial Unions or Amalgamated Unions, covering workers in the numerous more or less related sections of any occupation.[53]

The theory of 'Industrial Unionism' was influential in the organisation of the Building Workers' Industrial Union (1916) and the National Union of Railway and Harbour Services (1916). However, neither union was able to overcome craft and sectional differences within its respective industry. By 1926 there were eight unions operating in the building industry, and nine on the railway.[54]

Perhaps the most important function of SATUC at this time was to lend its influence and personnel towards the organisation of new unions. These unions included: the Furniture Workers 1925,[55] the Sweetmakers Union 1925,[56] the Boot and Shoemaker Union 1925,[57] the Reef Native Trade Assistance Union (1926)[58] (this was organised by Solly Sachs), the Canvas and Rope Workers Union 1927,[59] the Transvaal Leather Workers Union 1929[60] (organised by A. M. Merkel after the collapse of the Transvaal Branch of the National Leather Workers Union. In 1926 the National Union had a membership of 3 000.)[61]

One of the most striking features of the SATUC period was the attempt, for the first time, to organise women workers (almost exclusively whites, in the Transvaal at least) during this period. The leading figure was Fanny Klenerman, who attended the first conference in 1925 on behalf of the newly-formed Women Workers' General Union (WWU), and demanded that Congress give support to her organisation. The WWU was instrumental in the organisation of the Sweetmakers' Union, and later organised cafe employees in the face of intimidation and attempts by the employers to establish a 'company union'.[62] A Waitresses Union was eventually established, although this was short-lived. The WWU also aided women workers in the distributive trades, and consistently championed woman's interests in the male-dominated TUC. The point is made by an incident when Fanny Klenerman, as secretary of the Waitresses Union, wrote to ask NEC of SATUC to request the Minister of Labour to appoint a woman to each of the four subsidiary Boards of the Wage Board. The meaning not being clear to the men on the NEC, it was agreed 'that the letter be sent back for further explanation'.[63] The militancy of the 'new unionism' is exemplified in the methods adopted by the WWU:

> The WWU is increasing its strength and influence and is adopting the method of lunch hour meetings outside the various shops, works and factories in order to bring home to the women workers the need for organisation and the fact that there is a union catering for them and willing to take up their cause.[64]

(b) The Federation of Non-European Trade Unions

The first African industrial unions began to appear early in 1927, largely due to the initiative of communist party members like Weinbren and Thebidi.[66] These first unions included the Native

133

Laundry Workers' Union, the Native Bakers' Union, the Native Clothing Workers Union and the Native Mattress and Furniture Workers Union,[66] usually growing parallel with a sympathetic registered union.

It would be interesting to know to what extent these unions, which were active in the Johannesburg area, developed out of the earlier ICU. Certainly most of the leadership had held office in the ICU until Kadalie's purge against C.P. members. Also, the Johannesburg branch of the ICU, representing exactly those urban industrial workers which the ICU had failed to organise, seems to have been sympathetic to the expelled communists. At a branch meeting, immediately after the expulsions, a resolution was passed demanding that the matter of the expulsions be referred to the national conference of the ICU. This was achieved despite Kadalie's efforts from the Chair to have the motion over-ruled.[67] Two weeks later 500 members of the Johannesburg branch voted solidly to elect Johannes Nkosi, a C.P. member, to the branch executive.[68]

The South African Federation of Non-European Trade Unions was formed on March 25th 1928, at a meeting of over 150 delegates representing 10 000 workers from the African Laundry Workers, Motor Drivers and Garage Workers, Bakers, Clothing Workers, and Engineering Unions.[69] The Federation appointed Weinbren, Kotane and La Guma as president, vice-president and general secretary. The choice of La Guma was particularly significant. A leading theorist in the C.P. at this time, he championed the 'Black Republic' slogan and rejected Bunting's policy of continued reliance on the white working class.[70] In fact, the formation of an independent black trade union movement marks a break with the C.P.'s earlier stress on non-racial working class organisation. The number of African unions continued to increase during 1928 and 1929, with the formation of the African Dairy Workers' Unions, the Native Motor Drivers' Union,[71] the Amalgamated Food and Drink Workers' Union,[72] the Steel Workers' Union, the Cold Storage Union, the Cotton and Rope Workers' Union, the Soap and Chemical Workers' Union.[73] By mid-1928 it is estimated that membership had reached 15 000.[74]

The late '20s was a period of considerable industrial militancy amongst African workers. In 1927, 4 418 'non-whites' went on strike (as compared with 740 whites), whilst for 1928 the figures were 5 074 and 710 respectively.[75] The pattern seems to have been one of strikes in response to the victimisation of trade unionists; and strikes designed to enforce payment of the legal wage rates laid down by the Wage

Board. In May 1928 African workers brought Leonardo's Laundry to a standstill, after the victimisation of one of the employees. Although forced back to work by the police, the strikers secured his reinstatement.[76] During the same month the Native Clothing Workers' Union successfully coordinated a one-day strike in 3 Johannesburg factories to demand full payment for Good Friday.[77] On September 25th, 1928, 170 African, Indian and Coloured workers at the Transvaal Mattress Company struck to enforce the implementation of a Wage Board determination.

> Before nightfall the employers had capitulated and advised the Mattress and Furniture Workers' Union (non-European) that the demands of the workers would be fulfilled.[78]

In October African Furniture workers in the Louis and Metz factory struck successfully for payment for overtime.[79]

One of the failings of the ICU had been its inability to distinguish between trade union activity and political protest. Although the FNETU was certainly not non-political — in fact, in 1929 it affiliated to the Red International of Labour Unions[80] — it remained strictly a trade union body. The strikes which were undertaken by the African unions arose over wages or out of grievances in the work place. Also, the stated aims of the FNETU were limited to dealing with working conditions: the demand for a 48 hour week, and equal pay for equal work.[81]

The use of lightning strikes over immediate issues indicates effective shop-floor initiative, and the considerable success of this tactic demonstrates the bargaining power of the workers and the fact that they could not easily be dismissed by the employer. The militancy of African workers is demonstrated by the strike at Donner's Laundry in October 1929. The strike, which was 100% solid, was called over the issue of intolerable working conditions and the failure to implement Wage Board determinations. 'The boss offered to reinstate all but two on conditions demanded by the union, but these terms were rejected and the strikers took their passes and subsequently obtained employment in other laundries.'[82]

This latter statement indicates that African Unions were working in a favourable employment situation. Conversely it is argued that the Depression led to the collapse of the FNETU and African trade unionism in 1931.[83] It is probably also true that this decline was hastened by the internal conflicts in the C.P. and the ultra-left policies pursued under Wolton and Bach. In the same way that the ICU had tied its fortunes to the careers of a few individuals, so the Federation was too closely linked to the C.P. to survive the internal conflicts of the latter.

(c) The 'old' and the 'new' : the origins of the Garment Workers' Union

A history of the early GWU (the strongest union to emerge from this period) and its predecessor, the WTA, demonstrates many of the arguments which this essay has tried to put forward. The WTA had been dominated by master craftsmen deeply rooted in the British craft tradition.[84] During the early '20s most still worked in small tailoring shops, and in fact at that time the WTA still included 'middlemen' in its membership (tailors who took work from the merchant tailors to sub-contract to others).[85] The membership of the union changed dramatically with the expansion of factory production. In December 1925, a meeting of factory workers was held to elect a committee for the Factory Section of the unions.[86] During 1926, Dan Colrain became union organiser. Within 4 months the membership of the Factory Section was increased by 300, with 90% organisation of factory workers on the Rand.[87] By 1928, when Sachs became Secretary of the GWU, the membership was 1 750, of whom 2/3 were in the Factory Section, and 3/4 were women workers.[88]

It is interesting to observe the changing response of the WTA to perceived threats from other sections of workers. In 1924 the union called for the replacement of 'Kaffir pressers' by Whites.[89] The same point was made, together with an alleged threat of Asiatics to White standards, in evidence to the Cape Town Conference on unemployment called by the Secretary for Labour.[90] In August 1926, attention was drawn to the fact that firms were increasingly employing girl machinists to do the work of trousermakers, and it was agreed that attempts be made by the Industrial Council to stop this trend.[91] However, later that month the union's constitution was altered to admit non-Europeans,[92] (this meant Indians and Coloureds, since Africans were not eligible to join a registered trade union) — presumably on the basis that 'if you can't beat them, join them'. Also, from 1928 Sachs gave moral and often tangible support to the Clothing Workers' Union under Gana Makabeni.[93] The threat of undercutting and job-fragmentation, which accompanied large-scale machine production, forced the WTA to open its ranks to an increasingly semi-skilled workforce. However, friction between the two sections remained. At a general meeting held in 1932, the old membership complained of the heavy expenditure occasioned by strike action and legal expenses. One speaker commented, in connection with the 1931

136

general strike that, 'the old leaders would have prevented it'.[94] The tailors section finally seceded in 1934 to form a separate union.

IV THE SIGNIFICANCE OF THE 'NEW UNIONISM'

Firstly, it is important to place in perspective the movement I have described above. The majority of White unions did not affiliate to SATUC, and were not associated with the developments of this period.[95] Furthermore, most of the activities I have described took place mainly on the Rand (but then this was the area of most intense industrialisation). However there is evidence of a more broadly-based trade union response to secondary industrialisation. Similar unions — for example, a Garment Workers Union — were formed in the Cape. In Natal, by 1928 Indian Workers had organised unions in the printing, furniture, garment, leather, tobacco, liquor and catering trades.'[96] Also in the Cape, the remnants of the ICU formed into the Industrial and Commercial Workers' Federation, comprising African and Coloured unions.[97]

In dealing with the 'new unionism' as an 'inter-racial' phenomenon, this essay has tried to suggest that within one section of the working class — namely those employed in secondary industry — there was considerable overlap of functions within the labour process between different racial groups. It is further suggested that, at the economic level, the class determination of this section of the working class was not affected by racial categories, and that, therefore, a basis for inter-racial class alliance existed. (In secondary industry at least, White workers remained productive, and had not yet come to perform the 'global role of capital'). Contemporary communists certainly believed this to be the case,[99] and the incidence of joint strike action by black and white workers seemed to substantiate this view.

In May 1928, 400 white workers (75% women) from Germiston's 3 clothing factories struck over the victimisation of 3 workers. The Native Clothing Workers' Union, which was 100% strong in Germiston, offered to bring its members out in support. Some 120 African workers struck in solidarity. As a result of the strike the 3 dismissed workers were reinstated.[100] However, only a week or two later, the white workers failed to assist black workers in a similar dispute, involving the dismissal of a black. In this case the Chairman and Secretary of the Clothing Workers' Union, Gana Makabeni and Thebidi, and four others were charged under the Riotous Assemblies Act, whilst 75 of the strikers were charged under the Masters' and Servants' Law, and each sentenced to 10 days imprisonment, or a fine

137

of £1.[101] There were other examples of inter-racial solidarity. In 1928, the African workers at the Ideal Laundry struck in support of a white woman employee who had been victimised.[102] In 1929, a mutual defence pact was agreed between the African Furniture Workers' Union and the white union. The pact was observed by African workers in October, but in November during a strike of 200 African and Coloured mattress makers, the white workers scabbed. The left-wing leadership of the white union contemplated resigning in disgust over the incident.[103]

Despite the backwardness of white workers, there is evidence of genuine inter-racial solidarity. This showed itself in terms of trade union organisation when the garment, leather, furniture and canvas unions dropped their colour-bar against Coloureds and Indians.[104] It might be argued that this was in order to absorb the threat which they represented to the position of white workers in these industries. Even so, those who were admitted certainly benefited from membership of the trade union. Furthermore, the GWU and the Furniture Workers' Union[105] held joint meetings with their African parallels, whilst the European and African laundry workers unions actually both affiliated to a joint executive committee.[106] Although mixed trade unions (i.e. admitting Coloureds) had existed for many years in the Cape, these activities marked a major breakthrough on the Rand, and it might be argued that this contributed towards the beginnings of a more 'enlightened' racial policy on the part of the TUC. In 1929 SATUC recommended to its affiliated unions 'the enrolment of all employees in their respective unions, irrespective of race or colour . . . or, alternatively, that a policy of parallel branches in the unions be adopted.'[107]

The 'new unions' revived the technique of industrial militancy, which had lain dormant since 1922. Evidence of the militancy of the new unions has already been given. The GWU, for instance, led over 100 strikes, 2 of which brought the entire industry to a standstill, between 1928 and 1932. Although the union was later to make full use of conciliation machinery, Sachs maintained that the strike weapon should never be given up.[108]

Enough has been said already to demonstrate the significance of the 'new unionism'. But it might be argued that in the last analysis, the movement was a failure. The women's unions were short-lived. The African unions virtually all collapsed within a few years. The continued growth of the GWU, the Furniture Workers' and Leatherworkers' unions provides much clearer evidence of continuity and success.

These unions were to provide the backbone of the Left within the trade union movement. However, even the African unions did not completely disappear — Makabeni's Clothing Union survived, the Laundry Workers' Union was later revived by Max Gordon — whilst attempts to recruit women workers, in such industries as sweet-making and tobacco were revived. In fact the Waitresses' Union continued to exist as a subsection of the Witwatersrand Liquor and Catering Trade Union.[109] Furthermore, the NEC of SATUC continued to represent the interests of sweetworkers to the Wage Board after the demise of their union.[110] The latter union was later revived by Mr E. V. Spark with the help of SATUC.[111]

Most important, during these years there emerged a group of trade union organisers whose influence continued to be felt for two decades. This group included names such as Sachs, Weinbren, Merkel and Kalk, from the white trade union movement; La Guma, who helped organise unions in the Cape during the 1930s,[112] Moses Kotane and Gana Makabeni, both workers, who were destined to play a leading role in the revival of African trade unionism during the late 1930s and the war years. The impact of the 'new unionism' is best demonstrated at the Cape Conference held jointly by the Cape Federation of Labour Unions and SATUC in 1930, which resulted in the formation of the Trades and Labour Council, specifically on a non-racial basis. The new unions were beginning to change the balance of forces within the labour movement.

FOOTNOTES

1. Engels, letter to Sorge, 7 December 1889, and 'Preface to the 1892 English edition of *The Condition of the Working Class*', p.19, quoted R. Hyman, *Marxism and the Sociology of Trade Unionism*, (Pluto, 1971) p.9.
2. *Union Statistics for Fifty Years* (Pretoria 1960) G-18.
3. J. Lever, 'Labour and Capital in South Africa: The Passage of the Industrial Conciliation Act, 1924'. See this volume, section 2.
4. C. Kadalie: 'The Relation Between White and Black Workers in South Africa' (pamphlet, 1927).
5. P. Bonner: 'The Decline and Fall of the ICU — A Case of Self-Destruction?' See Section 3.
6. UG22-1932 para. 529, 536.
7. UG22-1932 para. 69, 72, 338.
8. UG22-1932 para. 547, 556.
9. UG22-1932 para. 545.
10. *South African Worker* 7.1.27.
11. L. Hotz: 'The Rationalization Movement'. *The Social and Industrial Review*, Vol. VII No. 42 (5th June 1929) p.478.
12. *Union Statistics* L-3. Some attempt has been made to allow for the change in definition of 'manufacturing' introduced 1924-5.

13. *Union Statistics* G-6. Again some attempt has been made to compensate for the change in statistical base.
14. Report of the Wage Board, Vol. 1, No. 1, September 1930, p.9.
15. Ibid., p.18.
16. L. Hotz, p.478.
17. UG 37-1935, para. 368.
18. *Union Statistics*, G-7 and G-8.
19. Discussed in H. Wolpe, 'Capitalism and Cheap Labour Power in South Africa', *Economy and Society*, Vol. 1, No. 4.
20. UG 37-1935, para. 11-15.
21. Report of an Address by F.A.W. Lucas, 'The Native in Industry', *The Social and Industrial Review*, Vol. V, No. 30 (June 1928) p.428-429.
22. UG22-1932, para. 527.
23. E. Roux, *Time Longer than Rope* (Wisconsin, 1966), p.207-208.
24. UG 22-1932, para. 525.
25. UG 22-1932, Addendum by Mr Lucas, para. 309.
26. UG 14-1926, para. 147. Report of S. Mills, M. Clay and J. Martin.
27. UG 22-1932, para. 89.
28. F. A. W. Lucas, p.429.
29. Discussed in: A. Hepple, 'The African Worker in South Africa' (pamphlet), p.22. The ICA did not apply to 'pass-bearing natives'.
30. UG 41-1927. Statistics of Production for 1924-5, p.23. Classification of Factories in the Union according to the average number of persons employed during 1924-5 — Just under 50% of factory workers were employed in establishments with less than 50 hands.
31. UG 33-1931. Statistics of Production 1929-30, p.53, p.60.
32. UG 37-1935, para. 43.
33. Report of the Wage Board, Vol. 1, No. 1, September 1930, p.6 and p.5.
34. Ibid., p.16.
35. See TUCSA: Conference Minutes 1930, p.40.
36. TUCSA: NEC Minutes 1926-27, 22.2.27.
37. TUCSA: Conference Minutes 1927, p.23.
38. UG 37-1935, p.26.
39. TUCSA- Conference Minutes 1930, p.39.
40. UG 37-1935, para. 350 — Gitsham and Trembath, p.136.
41. *The S. A. Labour Gazette* (later the *Social and Industrial Review)* Vol. 1, No. 6, September 1925, p.165-170.
42. Report of an Address by F. A. W. Lucas, 'Natives and the Wages Act', the *Social and Industrial Review*, Vol. VII, No. 39 (5 March 1929) p.201.
43. Ibid., p.203.
44. E. Roux, p.208-209.
45. UG 22-1932, Addendum by Mr Lucas, para. 320.
46. D. Kaplan, 'Capitalist Development in South Africa: Class Conflict and the State', 1974 (mimeo).
47. Discussed in: UG 40-41, para. 110.
48. TUCSA: Conference Minutes 1925, p.9.
49. C. Kadalie, p.5.
    J. A. Grey Coetzee, *Industrial Relations in South Africa*, p.21.
    TUCSA: Conference Minutes 1927 — see the debate on holding discussions

with the ICU.
50. J. Hinton, *The First Shop Stewards' Movement* (London, 1973), p.173.
51. R. K. Cope, *Comrade Bill* (Stewart 1943), p.142.
52. E. Gitsham and J. F. Trembath, 1926, p.12.
53. E. Gitsham and J. F. Trembath, 1926, p.54.
54. E. Gitsham and J. F. Trembath, 1926, p.58, p.69.
55. TUCSA: NEC Minutes 19.5.25.
56. Ibid.
57. TUCSA: Monthly Reports, May 1925.
58. TUCSA: NEC Minutes 7.9.26.
59. TUCSA: Conference Minutes, NEC Report.
60. TUCSA: NEC Minutes 2.2.26.
61. Trembath and Gitsham, p.115.
62. TUCSA: NEC Minutes 16.3.26.
63. TUCSA: NEC Minutes 12.5.26.
64. TUCSA: Monthly Reports, May 1925.
65. Roux, p.207.
66. Roux, p.207 — although most of these unions are not mentioned in *The South African Worker* until early 1928. 17/2/28, 10/3/28.
67. *S.A Worker,* 31.12.26.
68. *S.A. Worker,* 14.1.27.
69. *S.A. Worker,* 30.3.28.
70. Discussed in Simons and Simons, *Class and Colour in South Africa, 1850-1950,* p.389, 394-7.
71. *S.A. Worker,* 27.7.28.
72. *S.A. Worker,* 24.10.28.
73. *S.A. Worker,* 31.1.29.
74. J, A, Grey Coetzee, p.27.
75. *Union Statistics,* G-18.
76. *S.A. Worker,* 11.5.28.
77. *S.A. Worker,* 11.5.28.
78. *S.A. Worker,* 24.10.28.
79. *S.A. Worker,* 24.10.28.
80. Discussed in: Simons and Simons, p.377.
81. B. Weinbren, 'The Inside Story of S.A. Labour'.
    Forward 21.1.44, 21.4.44, 12.5.44 (quoted in Simons, p.377).
82. *S.A. Worker,* 31.10.29.
83. J. A. Grey Coetzee, p.27.
84. Discussed in E. S. Sachs, *Garment Workers in Action* (Jhb. 1957), p.169.
85. WTA Minutes, 3.7.23.
86. WTA Minutes, 7.12.23 — The other section was for 'Bespoke Tailoring'.
87. WTA Minutes, 31.10.26.
88. E. S. Sachs, p.7.
89. WTA Minutes, 21.7.24.
90. WTA Minutes, 21.8.24.
91. WTA Minutes, 11.8.24.
92. WTA Minutes, 24.8.26.
93. E. S. Sachs, p.86-87.
94. GWU archives: Minutes of Meeting (Joint General) held at the Traders Hall on

Thursday, 18th February 1932.
95. Simons and Simons, p.370.
96. Simons and Simons, p.372.
97. Simons and Simons, p.382.
98. Discussed in H. Wolpe, 'The "White Working Class" in South Africa', *Economy and Society*, Vol. 5, No. 2.
99. *S.A. Worker*, 1.1.29. — Programme of the CPSA, adopted by the 7th Conference. However, the weakness of the C.P.'s analysis was its belief that *all* white workers were objectively part of an anti-capitalist alliance (Simons, p.396).
100. *S.A. Worker*, 25.5.28.
101. *S.A. Worker*, 22.6.28.
102. *S.A. Worker*, 22.8.28.
103. *S.A. Worker*, 30.11.29.
104. Simons and Simons, p.381.
105. *S.A. Worker*, 31.10.29.
106. *S.A. Worker*, 27.7.28.
107. Quoted in A. Hepple: 'The African Worker in S.A.' (pamphlet), p.7.
108. E. S. Sachs, p.171.
109. SATUC: NEC Minutes, 16.9.30.
110. SATUC: NEC Minutes 19.8.30.
111. SATUC: NEC Minutes 25.11.30.
112. Dave Lewis: 'Registered Trade Unions and Western Cape Workers'. See this volume, Section 5.

MAX GORDON AND AFRICAN TRADE UNIONISM ON THE WITWATERSRAND, 1935-1940

MARK STEIN

Max Gordon's death in Cape Town on Monday 16th May 1977 was noted by few besides his family and friends. Yet he was a crucial figure in the history of South Africa trade unionism.

In 1935 Gordon became the secretary of the almost defunct African Laundry Workers Union in Johannesburg. The African Laundry Workers Union was one of only two African trade unions on the Witwatersrand (the other was the South African Clothing Workers Union) to survive the Great Depression. All the other unions formed in the years 1927-1929 had collapsed.[1] The need for organisation was evident in the very low wages which were being paid to the (black) unskilled labourers.[2] By 1940 Gordon was secretary of a Joint Committee of African Trade Unions consisting of seven unions with a total membership of between 16 000 and 20 000 workers. These unions comprised at least six-sevenths of the total number of organised black workers in Johannesburg at this time.[3] Gordon's achievement provided the foundation for the massive expansion of African trade unionism which took place during the Second World War.

The great handicap for African trade unions was of course that they were excluded from the Industrial Conciliation Act (which gave white workers collective bargaining machinery, with strike action as a last resort). Gordon was involved in an illegal strike of black laundry workers in 1936, but from 1937 to 1939 he was able to build up his unions without resort to the strike weapon. He did so essentially by enforcing the minimum wages laid down in wage determinations and submitting evidence to the Wage Board when it carried out new investigations into particular industries.[4]

143

Gordon would not have got anywhere with his 'law-abiding' strategy for building up African trade unions without a great deal of cooperation from the Department of Labour. Present day officials of the Department of Labour are decidedly unsympathetic to African trade unions. No matter how law-abiding and apolitical they may strive to appear they are perceived as a political threat. Why then did the Department of Labour behave differently in Gordon's time?

In the 1920s and 1930s South Africa was in many ways a racially oppressive society. This generalisation applies particularly to the treatment of black workers on the mines and farms.[5] However the South African State was not at this time a very well co-ordinated body. The Department of Labour shared with the Department of Native Affairs jurisdiction over blacks employed in commerce and industry in the towns. In October 1929 the Secretary for Labour, C.W. Cousins, wrote privately to J. D. Rheinallt Jones about the need for a more liberal 'native policy': 'We have madly gone out of our way to unsettle and alienate a people without whose goodwill our future is dark indeed.'[6]

Three months before Cousins had received a memorandum from his Under-Secretary which advocated that:

> The attitude of this Department . . . should be to have nothing to do with questions of general native policy: but in matters affecting wages and conditions of employment etc., in industry, the Department should regard the natives exactly as it does in regard to other employees.[7]

Such attitudes survived to smooth Gordon's path in the late 1930s. This is illustrated by the 1939 negotiations for the 'non-statutory' recognition of African trade unions. The government proposed that African trade unions should thenceforth come under the Department of Native Affairs.

This was rejected on the grounds that the Department of Native Affairs had always oppressed blacks while they had received comparatively fair treatment from the Department of Labour. (A decade later the same controversy split the Industrial Legislation Commission of Inquiry, with Van Den Berg and Slabbert arguing that African trade unions should come under the Department of Native Affairs while the Chairman, Dr J. H. Botha, wanted them to remain under the Department of Labour.)

The limits on the generosity of the Department of Labour to black workers should be appreciated. Not all Labour officials held 'liberal' views. Moreover the Department had to work within a legal framework which discriminated against black workers, e.g. the exclusion of blacks from the definition of 'employee' in the Industrial Conciliation Act and the provision of the Wage Act that the Board should consider not only the cost of living of the workers but also the 'ability to pay' of an industry which led repeatedly to the Board fixing sub-subsistence wages for black labourers.)

Having established the existence of 'liberal' attitudes in the Department of Labour, it remains to explain them.

There seem to be two explanations: firstly black unions were not regarded as an immediate political threat, and secondly their existence was not incompatible with the United Party government's expressed policy of making (some) increases in unskilled wages in commerce and industry.

In 1928 the Under-Secretary for Labour recommended the recognition of black unions under the Industrial Conciliation Act on the grounds that the industrial organisation of black workers (under the guidance of officials of the Department of Labour) would create

> legitimate channels for the ventilation of grievances and the settlement of disputes by conciliatory methods similar to those approved of by the State for Europeans. By these means the activities of those communists who see in the large masses of South African natives fertile ground for revolutionary action would best be circumvented.[8]

This is of course the present-day 'liberal' standpoint, which meets with the counter-argument that at a time when white supremacy is endangered any black union organisation — no matter how inno-cent-seeming — is a potential political threat. One was inclined to conclude that Gordon was allowed to build up his unions because in the late 1930s white supremacy in South Africa still appeared unchallenged: the African National Congress and the Communist Party were both at a low ebb. Considerable suspicion was aroused in official circles by Gordon's Trotskyism. On the other hand Gordon kept his political convictions to himself and refrained from using his unions as propaganda platforms. Moreover, in his trade union work, his closest associates were not members of the tiny group of Trot-skyites in Johannesburg but white 'liberals', who wanted African trade unionism to be law-abiding and apolitical. Gordon found their aid indispensable. It was not only that W. G. Ballinger and A. D. Saffery (secretary of the S.A.I.R.R.) assisted Gordon in submitting evidence to the Wage Board. Wage Board investigations took up to two years from start to finish while it also took some weeks or even months before the Department of Labour would reimburse workers who had been underpaid. Consequently it took a long time before a sufficient number of workers had been convinced unions were a good idea. There were thus many months in which the income from subscriptions was not sufficient to pay for office expenses and Gordon's upkeep — months in which he often went hungry. Gordon would never have been able to carry on without the financial aid he received from the Bantu Welfare Trust, of which Saffery was the secretary and Rheinallt Jones (the leading white liberal figure and Saffery's colleague at the S.A.I.R.R.) was a Trustee. In 1937 Gordon received some financial aid from Ballinger, who had received a Bantu Welfare Trust grant. In January 1938 the Trust decided to give a grant of £10 per month directly to Gordon. (This continued until mid-1939 by which time Gordon's unions were financially self-sufficient.) The reasons given in the Minutes of the Bantu Welfare Trust for the grant are worthy of note.[9] The Trustees were concerned that so little money was being donated by the white public to swell the initial gift of £50 000 with which Col. James Donaldson had founded the trust. Instead of frittering the money away in small projects, it was resolved to spend large sums on two projects which were considered likely to catch the public eye and attract sizeable donations — a legal aid scheme for blacks and the organisation of African trade unions.

The authorities were no doubt aware that economic circumstances in the late 1930s made some sort of black labour unrest almost inevitable. It was officially acknowledged that the urban black population was deeply impoverished. The rapid expansion of commerce and industry was leading to relatively full employment even among unskilled labourers. This was reducing the deterrent to strike action which large scale unemployment had been during the Depression. In Durban permanent worker organisation was much slower to emerge than on the Witwatersrand, probably because the percentage of 'rural natives' in the labour force and the rate of job turnover were both much higher than on the Witwatersrand. The absence of permanent worker organisation did not however prevent a wave of strikes by blacks in Durban in 1937.[10] The Labour Department officials may have felt that it was preferable to have somebody like Gordon to organise the workers because they could negotiate with him far more easily than with an unorganised mass. In return for certain concessions, Gordon could be expected to restrain the workers for fear that action on their part would disrupt his relations with the Department of Labour. Gordon's unions must also have seemed decidedly preferable to the Communist-led unions of 1927-1929, which made no secret of their revolutionary leanings and struck frequently.[11]

Gordon's unions were assisted to obtain wage increases by the acceptance by the U.P. government of the recommendation of the 1934 Industrial Legislation Commission that unskilled wages should be raised. Part of the motive for raising unskilled wages was to provide employment for the so-called 'Poor Whites', by making it possible for them to enter unskilled work. However if the U.P. government had intended to raise only white unskilled wages it would have followed the suggestion of the Nationalist Opposition that in the amended Wage Act of 1937 the Board should be empowered to fix higher wages for whites doing the same kind of work as blacks.[12] Instead the government retained the provision of the 1925 Wage Act that wage determinations should not discriminate on lines of race or colour. In 1936 W. G. Ballinger requested the Department of Labour to fix a national minimum wage for unskilled workers. This request was refused on the grounds that some industries could only make a profit if they paid wages much lower than others could afford.[13] The Department did however promise that it would attempt to get unskilled wages raised in as many industries as possible through either Wage Board investigations or the exertion of pressure on industrial councils.

The 1937 Industrial Conciliation Act maintained the exclusion of blacks from the collective bargaining machinery. However it provided for their interests to be represented by an official of the Department of Labour. In the past industrial councils had often fixed (increased) wages only for the skilled jobs filled by white workers. The (black) labourers were left without wage regulation, at the mercy of individual employers. In the late 1930s the Minister of Labour began to insist that before he gazetted an industrial council agreement, it must fix wages for labourers. In this way the black workers in building and iron, steel and engineering (two of the largest and most important industries) had provided for them wage regulations for the first time. When the new Industrial Conciliation Act became law in December 1937, it made it for the first time possible for black workers falling under an agreement to recover arrears of wages consequent upon underpayment.[14] This change in the law no doubt encouraged Max Gordon to take the step in January 1938 of founding an African General Worker's Union catering for black workers in industries controlled by industrial councils, including building, iron and steel, restaurants and tea rooms and the motor trade. However the minimum wages fixed for black workers by industrial councils were usually very low. The industrial council system tended to promote collusion between the employers and the registered trade unions in that white workers would acquiesce in low wages for (black) unskilled workers provided they themselves got relatively high wages. The Department of Labour officials on industrial councils did not in practice achieve very much for the black workers they purported to represent. Low though minimum wages might be, they at least gave trade union organisers something to enforce but African unions in industries covered by agreements often found it difficult to recover arrears because the industrial councils themselves were responsible for enforcing the minimum wage and not the Labour Department. (In August 1939 the Department of Labour issued a circular instructing industrial councils to pay over arrear wages to claimants — both black and white — without the unnecessary delay they had hitherto often displayed.)

The obstacles to black unionism in industry dominated by industrial councils explained why Gordon's greatest successes were achieved in those industries where no strong registered trade union existed, and minimum wages were laid down by the Wages Board and enforced by officials of the Department of Labour.

Even in the 1920s the Wage Board had shown itself to be the government body most accommodating towards black workers' organisations. One example was in the 1929 Bloemfontein wage determination for unskilled labour which affected almost entirely blacks and fixed a minimum wage of 18/- per week rising to 20/- in 1930, in many cases a considerable improvement on existing rates. (The Bloemfontein Wage Board investigation arose out of an application from the ICU in 1926, which was also supported by many of the white citizens who were anxious to avoid any recurrence of the rioting which had broken out in Bloemfontein in 1925.) During 1928-1929 the Board fixed wages for the baking, laundering, furniture and clothing industries. It is not mere coincidence that the four strongest unions of the Communist-led S.A. Federation of Native Trade Unions which emerged on the Witwatersrand in 1928-1929 were in these four industries. (In the case of baking, the formation of the African union early in 1928 was reportedly intended to facilitate the enforcement of the wage determination, which was just due to be gazetted.)

The favourable attitude to African trade unions of the Chairman of the Wage Board, Frank McGregor (1936-1943), is particularly well-documented. In January 1940 McGregor made the following public statement:

The interests of Native workers are represented, often very ably, by such organisations as the Institute of Race Relations and the Friends of Africa frequently acting in conjunction with representatives of the unregistered but none the less active Native Trade Unions. These unions appear generally to be organised by interested Europeans who usually lead the case for their members at private and public sittings of the Board. It is beyond ... question that European leadership in this connection is of great value to the workers whose cause they represent; their presentation of evidence and their grasp of the issues at stake and of the ebb and flow of argument is generally more effective than is the case when presentation is in the hands of the less experienced Natives ... I hope I have said sufficient ... to emphasise the value of the organised assistance that is being afforded to unskilled workers both through their own unions and from such interested bodies as I have referred to; this aid is also of service to the Wage Board.[15]

In September 1941 McGregor wrote to Rheinallt Jones, who was a close personal friend, that within six months or so the Board would have provided a basic wage for practically all unskilled and semi-skilled in the larger industrial areas, something like 250 000 'non-Europeans' and 150 000 Europeans.

I do not claim that the minimum wages we are paying are adequate — but they are a big advance on existing wages and conditions and there will be no going back. In fact once we have completed the first round (of wage increases), efforts should be directed at a second round and it is to be hoped that productivity will justify further permanent increases ... The old type of Trade Unionist ... thinks that strike action and the class war are the best media of progress and the only food on which trade unions thrive. But I agree with you ... that no army of inspectors ... will be able effectively to enforce wage regulation — that can only be done by organisation amongst employees and employers. And that is to my mind a sufficient reason for the existence of trade unions ...[16]

The resemblance is obvious between McGregor's conception of how African trade unions should function and Max Gordon's practice.

It was because Gordon had submitted evidence to the Wage Board in the course of its investigation that he received much of the credit when the Board fixed higher wages for black workers, as in the case of Wage Determination 60 for the Baking and/or Confectionery Industry, Witwatersrand and Pretoria (gazetted in June 1938) and Wage Determination 70 for the Commercial Distributive Trade (gazetted in December 1939).

The baking determination increased the wages of labourers from 16/6 to £1.9.3. per week. This latter figure was not only one of the highest wages fixed for black labourers on the Witwatersrand at this time but also approximated to the minimum estimate of the cost of the weekly necessities of life for an urban African family.[17] The fixing by the Board of relatively high wages for blacks in these

149

industries can be attributed not only to Max Gordon's evidence but to the fact that employers in these industries appear to have been split on the issue of higher black wages (rather than united against them). Baking was one of the relatively few industries on the Witwatersrand where Africans had moved into skilled work. That half of the 150 (skilled) 'bakers' in the industry were black can be attributed to there being two types of employers in the industry. This division manifested itself in the existence of two employers associations in the industry, the 'Price Protection Association' and the 'Master Bakers' Association.' The Master Bakers' Association represented the larger and better capitalised employers, who prided themselves upon employing white labour: their 'bakers' were paid the wage laid down in the industrial council agreement. The members of the M.B.A. were being undercut by the Price Protection Association, who employed as many blacks as possible because they were not covered by any minimum wage since the industrial council agreement had not been extended to blacks. The Master Bakers urged the white public to buy only bread made by white labour, but they found to their chagrin that many whites persisted in buying bread made from 'dough mixed with kaffir sweat' because it was cheaper. The Master Bakers then tried to get the industrial council to extend the agreement to blacks. They succeeded in doing this because they had a preponderance of voting power in the council. However the agreement was declared null and void by the Supreme Court on a technicality in June 1935 and to forestall a new agreement the other employers withdrew from the industrial council, causing it to break down.[18] Since the industry was left without wage regulation, the registered union applied in September 1936 for a Wage Board investigation, which was granted. The Board fixed a minimum of £4.10.0. per week for 'bakers' and £2.0.0. per week for 'bakers' assistants'. This meant a dramatic increase in wages for blacks doing these jobs. That black 'bakers' were no longer much cheaper to employ than whites must be accounted a success for the Master Bakers' Association and a blow to the Price Protection Association. The wage determination's impact on the African union was recorded by Gordon himself. At the end of 1938 he wrote that:

> This union has increased its membership on the Reef from about 300 to nearly 600 members. It intends establishing a branch in Pretoria as the Determination for the Industry has now been extended to cover . . . Pretoria . . . For the first two or three months of the operation of the Determination, nearly every employer in the industry was underpaying his employees. The Department of Labour was instrumental in obtaining arrear wages for many of our mem-

bers ... well over £800 has already been paid out ... A full-time organiser is employed by the Union, and has been provided with a bicycle to facilitate his work.[19]

It is probably no coincidence that the other major increase recommended by the Board was also where employers were divided in their attitude to higher black wages. The smaller employers in the commercial distributive trade were much harder hit by the £6.0.0. per month for labourers recommended by the Board than were the larger employers, some of whom had already conceded increases to the African Commercial and Distributive Workers' Union. The Board indicated that if some of the smaller employers were driven out of business by the new wages they would not be missed for:

> If the relatively low profit of the small establishments is due to what may be called general overtrading, the number of establishments is probably too great for the needs of the community.[20]

The Board rejected objections from the Chamber of Mines and white farmer organisations that £6 per month for blacks in the Johannesburg commercial distributive trade would upset their labour supplies. On 22nd December 1939 Wage Determination 70 was gazetted. W. G. Ballinger describes the impact of the determination:

> The African workers gathered in Johannesburg in an open-air meeting in numbers that have not been equalled since the days when Clements Kadalie ... held mass meetings spellbound with his Demagogic oratory. It is confidently anticipated that this Determination will give a new impetus to the whole African Trade Union Movement. African industrial organisations in general are formulating plans for an extension of the Determination to other trades.[21]

As the African trade union movement grew in strength during the last years of the decade, it reiterated the demand for recognition of African trade unions under the Industrial Conciliation Act. The government was not prepared to concede African unions the rights to strike and participate in collective bargaining because it feared the political and economic consequences. This was rationalised by saying that the 'native' has not yet reached a 'sufficiently high level of development' to be granted full trade union rights. The recognition scheme with which the government did come up was openly described by the Minister of Labour as intended

> To afford the Native worker and the State some protection against the activities of unscrupulous persons who exploit Native workers' organisations for their own ends and whose subversive influences are a menace both to the European and the Native.[22]

The proposals which the government put forward in mid-1939 were for 'non-statutory' recognition. (This was in itself undesirable from the point of view of the African unions since a 'recognition' which was not incorporated in an Act of Parliament could be withdrawn at very short notice.) The government proposals stipulated that the black unions would co-operate with Divisional Inspectors of Labour in the enforcement of wage regulating instruments affecting their members. This black unions had of course been doing for some time and were anxious to continue to do. Two of the proposals were however objectionable to the representatives of the black unions. The government wanted to replace the existing practice whereby African trade unions made direct representations to the Department of Labour by having them make representations 'in the first instance' to the Native Affairs Department. The objection made to this was that the Native Affairs Department tended to 'oppress' blacks while the Department of Labour treated them with comparative fairness. (It was also pointed out that Native Affairs Department officials lacked the technical knowledge of industry possessed by the Department of Labour.) The government proposals also made provision for the withdrawal of recognition from any organisation or its officers if it or they had committed an unlawful act (such as strike). The negotiations culminated in deadlock. The government could conceivably have gone ahead with its own proposals, but it did not do so, probably because of the strong objections raised by the Chamber of Mines to even a limited recognition of African trade unions.

From the above statement by the Minister of Labour it is obvious that by 1939 the authorities were starting to regard African trade unions as a political threat. The Emergency Regulations promulgated by the government after the outbreak of War gave it wide powers to intern people suspected of subversive activities. The government promised the South African Trades and Labour Council (SATLC) that it would not take action against people engaged in legitimate union work. However in May 1940 Max Gordon was interned, and held for a year in the 'Anti-Nazi Section' of Ganspan Internment Camp.

In December 1940 Gordon was given an interview with the Chief Control Officer at which he was told the reasons for his internment. These were:
1.   That he had organised trade unions for the purpose of exploiting them and pocketing the money.
2.   That in 1936 he had organised a strike in the Laundry Trade and since constantly agitated to bring about unrest and hostility between African workers and employers.
3.   That he was a communist and had used the trade union for

152

propaganda purposes.

4. That he had intended to incite hostility between black and white by organising a mass meeting after the shooting of seventeen black mine workers at Nkana in Northern Rhodesia in 1940 and was responsible for the issuing of a very inflammatory pamphlet calling this meeting.

5. That study classes conducted in the union offices for Bookkeeping, English, Geography etc. were used as a means to inculcate communism into black workers.

The first, second and fourth charges were completely or substantially false, while — whatever the truth of the allegation made about them — the study classes mentioned in the final charge involved only four to six people. It would however appear that the government genuinely believed that Gordon was a political threat. This was in spite of the fact that, as Rheinallt Jones pointed out, Gordon had eschewed political agitation and confined himself purely to 'legitimate trade union work'.

Deprived of the promised aid and advice from Gordon in Johannesburg, the newly formed Pretoria branch of the ACDWU collapsed because its organisers were too inexperienced to handle the members' complaints properly. Even in Johannesburg the union suffered from Gordon's absence. Saffery complained that money was being squandered, that the Post Office Savings Book of one of the unions — which contained £1 000 — had vanished, that regular meetings were not being held as formerly to report back to the membership, that complaints were not being properly attended to and proper representations were not being made to the Wage Board or industrial councils. In consequence subscriptions being paid had fallen to one-third of their previous total.

While in detention camp Gordon was allowed by the authorities to communicate with Saffery by letter. He therefore tried to run the unions by remote control, using Saffery as his intermediary. It was apparently proposed that Saffery take Gordon's place at the head of the Joint Committee. However the African trade unionists whom Gordon had trained were impatient of continued white supervision. The Joint Committee split. The dairy and chemical unions, under the leadership of A. M. Thipe, seem to have remained loyal to Gordon. But the four unions which opted for all-black control included the two largest and most important organisations: the African Commercial and Distributive Workers Union and the African General Workers Union. (The other two were the African Laundry Workers Union and the African Printing Workers Union.) The leading figure to reject Gordon was Daniel Koza of the ACDWU. Ten years later Rheinallt Jones testified to Koza being 'the most competent of the Native Trade Union organisers', and this judgment is borne out by a variety of sources.[23] Jones' assessment of Koza had changed considerably over those ten years. In 1940 he had — without mentioning him by name — denounced Koza to the authorities as a dangerous and subversive influence. This was intended to frighten the government into releasing Gordon so that he could steer the unions into 'moderate and constitutional channels'! It is not very surprising that the government paid little heed to the proposal. What is perhaps more surprising is that it did not act against Koza as well, although this must be seen as part of a general toleration by the wartime U. P. government of industrial and political activists who were to be proscribed later on.

The break with Koza in 1940 was not the first time Gordon had run into opposition from 'black racism'. In mid-1938 an attempt was made to unite all the 'non-European' unions in Johannesburg into a single Co-ordinating Committee. Gordon initially participated in this attempt but withdrew after encountering opposition from J. F. Mackay of the African Furniture Workers Union and Gana Makabeni of the S.A. Clothing Workers Union. Mackay said later:

> As non-Europeans we want the help and advice of European Trade Union leaders, but if we are going to have European Officials at the head of the Non-European Trade Union Co-ordinating Committee, we will be ridiculed by all thinking non-Europeans throughout the country and also by the official European Trade Union Movement of South Africa.[24]

Gordon protested his dedication to the African trade union movement.

> He : : . stated that he could have got a job as Labour Inspector, and also a job at his profession as a chemist at Pretoria at £50 per month, but he is quite prepared to make every sacrifice for the sake of the Bantu workers.

Makabeni:

> in a heated reply to Gordon said he is pleased that Gordon has come out in his true colours, by his attitude he had definitely shown that he wants to be the 'Leader', and is not prepared to accept the wish of the majority, his whole conduct has shown that he is not sincere in his efforts to help the African workers, but is only out for self.[25]

W. G. Ballinger states that the black members of the NETUCC accused Gordon of withholding a financial statement from them. Ballinger's opinion was that there was nothing wrong with the books but Gordon was a Trotskyist and therefore not liked by the 'Stalin Communists'.[26] By throwing doubt on his financial integrity the

NETUCC hoped to get control over one of Gordon's major assets — the £10 grant from the Bantu Welfare Trust. The SATLC requested the Bantu Welfare Trust to give its grant only to the NETUCC (i.e. to withhold it from Gordon) but without success. By 1940 the NETUCC had not more than 3 000 workers in thirteen unions, which was far outstripped by the Joint Committee with between 16 000 and 20 000 workers in seven unions. During the 1939 negotiations on recognition of African trade unions, in an effort to strengthen the NETUCC and weaken Max Gordon, the SATLC proposed that recognition be extended not to all African trade unions but to the Co-ordinating Committee alone. This proposal also fell through. It is thus scarcely surprising that when Gordon was interned in May 1940 the National Executive Committee of the SATLC refused to intervene on his behalf. It professed to accept the government's assurance that Gordon's internment 'had nothing to do with legitimate trade union activities'.[27] There is moreover evidence to suggest that when Koza broke with Gordon and Saffery, he did so with encouragement and offers of support from the SATLC.[28]

Max Gordon's Trotskyism tended to cut him off somewhat from those white trade union officials who were 'Stalinist' in tendency. However his most vocal opponents in the SATLC seem to have not been Stalinists but politically conservative 'craft' unionists like T. C. Rutherford of the S.A. Typographical Union, who at the 1940 Conference bitterly attacked Gordon for 'interfering' in the printing industry by organising the African Printing Workers Union. (Rutherford expressed his preference for a 'parallel' African union which would be safely under the thumb of the registered union, and this is precisely what the SATUC set out to create a few years later.) The National Executive Committee's refusal to intercede for Gordon was paralleled by its refusal to intercede for the Stalinist Issie Wolfson when the latter was threatened with internment during 1940.

In the 1938 split Gordon had been able to keep control over the unions which he had created. But by the time of his release from internment in June 1941 there was no place left for him in the African trade union movement in Johannesburg. In January 1942 he was sent to Port Elizabeth to organise black workers there under the auspices of the Southern African Committee on Industrial Relations, a small group centreing around his old colleague Saffery. He stayed in Port Elizabeth until early April. From the point of view of trade union organisation, Gordon's visit was a great success. He founded six new unions for Coloured and African Workers. However, Madely, the

Minister of Labour, apparently accused him of having once again taken part in subversive activities. Those who had cooperated with Gordon in Port Elizabeth denied these charges and stated that Gordon had confined himself purely to legitimate trade union work. (The local Department of Labour had expressed its gratitude that the black workers were being organised because this would make possible the enforcement of existing wage regulation measures.)

However after Gordon's return from Port Elizabeth there are no more recorded references to his taking part in trade union activities and his career falls into obscurity. He may have feared re-internment if he continued his trade union work. He was probably also disillusioned at the way he had been rejected by the black trade unions in Johannesburg, unions which he had created and whose leaders he had trained. Gordon seems consequently to have escaped the repression which overtook so many trade union leaders after the Nationalist victory in 1948. At the time of his death in 1977 he was working for the Cape Town finance company, Gerber Goldschmidt and living in the suburb of Constantia.

FOOTNOTES

1.   E. Roux, *Time Longer Than Rope;* E. & W. Roux, *Rebel Pity*.
2.   T. Phillips, *The Bantu in the City,* pp.30-39.
3.   A. L. Saffery, 'African Trade Unions and the Institute', *Race Relations, 1941.*
      W. H. Andrews, *Class Struggles in South Africa.*
      The 1938 census showed that the total number of blacks employed in Johannesburg was 86 000. The Joint Committee must however have drawn some of its membership from other centres on the Witwatersrand.
4.   Then as now very considerable evasion of the minimum wage levels laid down for blacks in wage determinations and industrial council agreements was taking place. Individual workers were afraid to complain because they feared they would be victimized. However a trade union could take up the claims for arrear wages of the whole labour force at once.
5.   In the late 1930s and early 1940s mine-owners and white farmers were probably the groups most vehemently opposed to any recognition of African trade unions. This was the case because their labour was being drawn away by the higher wages and better conditions in urban employment. The existence of African trade unions was deplored because they tended to push urban African wages even further up and consequently to increase unrest among the black mine and farm labourers.
6.   C. W. Cousins to J. D. Rheinallt Jones, 23.10.29. Rheinallt Jones Papers (R.J.P.).
7.   Memorandum: 'Proposed Recognition and Attitude towards the ICU', 14.11.28., Department of Labour Records, State Archives.
8.   ibid.
9.   Bantu Welfare Trust Minutes, 10.1.38., 9.7.38., R.J.P.

10. *Report of the Department of Labour for 1937*, p.3.

11. The strikes however were not politically motivated. They were called over instances of victimisation or non-observance of the wage determinations. If the workers needed to strike to get the wage determination enforced, this implies that the Department of Labour was reluctant to assist in such enforcements (i.e. by prosecuting delinquent employers).

12. The proponents of a national minimum wage claimed that it would stimulate commerce and industry by increasing the size of the market. See R. Phillips, *The Bantu in the City*, p.63. Its opponents stated that low wages were necessary to accumulate capital, while under-consumption was a problem only of mature industrial economies like Britain or America. See *Report of the Board of Trade and Industries*, No. 282 (1945).

14. S.A.I.R.R. Records, B38(a).

15. F. McGregor, 'Minimum Wage Regulation in South Africa', *Race Relations*, 1940.

16. F. McGregor to Rheinallt Jones, 5.9.41., S.A.I.R.R. Records. He seems to be referring to both black and white trade unions.

17. R. Phillips, *The Bantu in the City*, p.38.

18. *Report to the Department of Labour for 1935*, p.73; *Sunday Times*, 16.6.35., 'Report of the Wage Board ... Baking and/or Confectionery Industry, Witwatersrand and Pretoria', No. 394 (1937) p.3.

19. 'Report to the Bantu Welfare Trust', 20.12.38. S.A.I.R.R. Records.

20. *Report of the Wage Board ... Commercial Distributive Trade* (1940), p.8.

21. 'Report of the Friends of Africa', October/December 1939, Ballinger Papers.

22. H. G. Lawrence quoted in *The Star*, 20.4.39.

23. Rheinallt Jones to H. F. Oppenheimer, 16.2.51., R. J. P. C12/20. Koza's obituary in South African Trade Union Council, *Report of the National Executive Committee for the year ended March 1960*.

24. Minutes of NETUCC Conference, 7.8.38., SATLC Records.

25. Minutes of NETUCC Conference, 14.8.38., SATLC Records.

26. W. G. Ballinger to W. Lowe, 25.7.38., Ballinger Papers.

27. W. J. de Vries (General Secretary: SATLC) to M. Gordon, SATLC Records.

28. SATLC, National Executive Committee Minutes, 10.6.40.

SECTION 4

CLASS AND AFRIKANER NATIONALISM

INTRODUCTION

Recent work has considerably refined our understanding of the nature of 'the white working class', and the structural conditions which restricted any alliance with black workers. It is argued that many white wage-earners were no longer productive workers but over time came to perform a policing function within production, and that they existed in an antagonistic relationship to black workers. At a political level this made possible the incorporation of the white working class, symbolized by the Pact government in 1924. Whilst recent writers do allow for the possibility of differentiation in the class determination of sections of the white working class, it is perhaps necessary to stress that a sizeable group of whites remained productive workers, and that this implies the continued possibilities of independent political action by a section of the 'official' labour movement and a non-racial class alliance in the work place. Lewis argued in Section 3 that these possibilities were temporarily and imperfectly realized during the years 1925 to 1930 in the New Unionism which emerged. We provide further evidence of this non-racial class alliance in this section in our focus on Afrikaner women workers in the Garment Workers' Union and particularly the leadership of Solly Sachs, secretary of that union.

However, it was this area of semi-skilled and unskilled Afrikaner workers, led by skilled English speaking trade unionists represented politically by the Labour Party, which was to form the basis of the Afrikaner Nationalist strategy. In 1936 Albert Hertzog, Nico Diedericks and Piet Meyer formed the Nasionale Raad van Trustees to break the loyalty of these Afrikaner workers. The philosophical basis of their strategy was that of Christian National trade unionism. The first duty of workers, so they argued, is to work hard in return for the right to a 'fair' wage. Workers must be disciplined and obedient. The relationship between worker and capitalist is interdependent. To quote a contemporary statement of this position: 'How different would the world be if capital and labour everywhere became allies! If each helped and served the other; if the capitalist strove to provide as many as possible of the good things in life for the worker; if the worker strove to give the capitalist the best and most abundant labour'.[3] The problem with the existing trade unions they argued, was twofold. Firstly they were 'foreign' institutions run by 'foreign' leaders, in unholy alliance with 'foreign capitalists' designed to line the pockets of both. But secondly these 'foreign Communistic' leaders imbued with the 'cancerous' ideology of class, set workers and capitalists against each other in one continuing struggle which threatened the entire social framework. Their main target was the Mine Workers' Union. It was 90% Afrikaans speaking and largely unskilled, and therefore easily threatened by black advancement. At the time it was under the control of a corrupt trade union bureaucracy. O'Meara, basing his argument on a book by Naude on Hertzog, argues that if Hertzog had not won the support of the Mine Workers' Union the Nationalists would not have won the six working class constituencies that put them into power in the 1948 general election by five seats.

Why was the Garment Workers' Union able to resist the assault of Afrikaner nationalism? Firstly, the leadership of the Mine Workers' Union was hopelessly corrupt and continually failed to respond to the grievances of its members. In this situation the Raad was able to use economic grievances in their struggle for control of the union. The Garment Workers' Union, on the other hand, had been successful in defending its members — Sachs was able to locate his appeals to national sentiment in a class context. Secondly, there were differences in the labour process between the mining industry and the garment industry. White mine workers had been transformed from a productive into a non-productive supervisory class, whereas the Garment Workers' Union, as we have argued, still constituted large numbers of productive white workers performing similar functions in the work place.

O'Meara sees an important lesson in the struggle for control in the Mine Workers' Union — i.e. the myth of an all pervasive monolithic Afrikaner nationalism — a mystic cultural unity which allegedly establishes a priori bonds between all members of the Volk, welding them into an overriding organic political and ideological unity, whatever their socio-economic position. In this myth, he says, class cleavages are irrelevant for social action as the ideological vision common to all Afrikaners, derived from Calvinistic theology, unites them into a much broader social unity. He argues that in fact it was class factors, 'sheer naked economic interest', rather than the supposedly common cultural unity which achieved the victory of the Nationalists in the Mine Workers' Union in the end. This attempt to establish a class basis for Afrikaner nationalism is in sharp contrast to much writing in that field. Moodie, for example, writing on the rise of Afrikanerdom, has stressed cultural factors as far more important than class. Using the concept of 'civil religion' he has stressed the common cultural and symbolic unity within Afrikanerdom that rose above class cleavages.[4]

FOOTNOTES

1. H. Wolpe, *Economy and Society,* Vol. 5, No. 2.
2. R. Davies, *Journal of Southern African Studies,* Vol. 3, No. 1, p. 66.
3. Quoted from *Inspan,* 5th February 1949, by Dan O'Meara in ' "Christian National" Trade Unionism in South Africa, 1934-1948,' unpublished paper given at the conference on Southern African Labour History, University of the Witwatersrand, April 1976.
4. Dunbar Moodie, 'The Rise of Afrikanerdom as an Immanent Critique of Marxist Theory of Social Class,' in P. L. Bonner, ed., *Working Papers in Southern African Studies* (African Studies Institute, 1977).

WHITE TRADE UNIONISM, POLITICAL POWER AND AFRIKANER NATIONALISM*

DAN O'MEARA

Author's Note: The general argument of this essay has been extended and developed in 'Analysing Afrikaner Nationalism : The "Christian-National" Assault on White Trade Unionism in South Africa, 1934-1948', *African Affairs* (January, 1978).

The years between the formation of a coalition of the Nationalist Party of General Hertzog and the South African Party of Smuts in 1933, and the wafer-thin electoral victory of the 'Reunited' Nationalist Party coalition in 1948, were some of the most significant in South African labour and political history.

Not only were they a period of enormous economic growth, with the final emergence of a genuine industrialised economy; not only did they witness the emergence and political victory of a more thorough going and militant Afrikaner Nationalism than the rather woolly brand practised under General Hertzog, but more fundamentally, they were also a period of intense social and political conflict at all levels over the nature of South African society and the pattern in which it should develop. During this period, as perhaps in no other, the basis of social conflict in South Africa was laid bare and the class nature of the system of exploitation and racial exclusion revealed. A strong and militant African trade union movement developed to seriously challenge the structure of exploitation and was broken only by sustained and ruthless force. While the registered trade unions did little to assist the African movement, and in most critical areas actively opposed it, white workers were still organised and mobilised

* A review of: Louis Naude, *Dr A. Hertzog, Die Nasionale Party en Die Mynwerkers* (Nasionale Raad van Trustees, Pretoria 1969).

along class rather than cultural lines. The depoliticisation of *class interests* amongst white workers and their mobilisation in *cultural terms* and the seizure of key unions in the trade union structure, was *the essential step* to secure a Nationalist victory.

Naude's History

In this context Naude's is a fascinating and important, though thoroughly cynical history. It tells of the organised and cold-blooded assault by a small clique of petty bourgeois politicians on a key group of white workers and their all-white trade union during the late Thirties and Forties: the cynical manipulation of miners' grievances against the hopelessly corrupt Mine Workers' Union for petty bourgeois ends. The attack on and takeover of the MWU had the explicit, and eventually successful, goal of breaking the solidarity and power of the organised white working class, and in particular its two key organisations, the South African Trades and Labour Council (SAT & LC) and the still powerful South African Labour Party (SALP). It put into power a class alliance which through making a few concessions to the white fraction of the working class, ended its independent political power, and set out to thoroughly suppress the interests of black workers. It entrenched the political power of elements of the petty bourgeois as a means by which they were able to transform themselves into a fully-fledged bourgeoisie; a capitalist class pure and simple.

Hertzog's Political Testament

At the same time, this book is quite blatantly Dr Albert Hertzog's political testament. Published by one of the many powerful pressure groups controlled by him (Die Nasionale Raad van Trustees) at a critical stage of the vicious conflict within the Nationalist Party just before the Herstigte split, it is clearly designed to justify his position, and in particular, his view of the class basis of the Nationalist Party. The message to an ungrateful party leadership is quite clear, and suitably decoded reads: 'Look what I did for you lot. If it wasn't for me you'd still be in opposition, so beware!' The issues it raised within the Nationalist Party have still not been settled within the Party (despite the Herstigte split) and remain important areas of conflict.

Distortions and Omissions

The book is in fact badly written, and the chapters constructed in such a way as to be deliberately misleading. For instance, Naude hints on page 106 that the withdrawal of financial support for the Hertzog organisation by the Ekonomiese Instituut of the F.A.K. in 1944, left it virtually penniless, while 8 pages later we are told that by this stage the Pieter Neethlingfonds was providing them with a steady £3,000 p.a. The time dimension is similarly distorted. The reader is offered almost no guide to even the approximate dates of important events and decisions. The author is guilty too of very serious and deliberately misleading omissions, and in a few instances of outright falsification. Two examples will suffice. Quite incredibly, given the fact that it was behind the entire operation, the Afrikaner Broederbond is mentioned only once, and then in quoting the 'Rand Daily Mail'. Secondly the corruption of the leadership of the Mine Workers' Union is repeatedly, and quite correctly, emphasised, yet the Hertzogite successor as Secretary of the MWU from 1948, Daan Ellis, is praised to the skies for his ability, strength and integrity. No mention is made of the fact that in 1952, this valiant Hervormer was found guilty of the gravest corruption and sentenced to eighteen months' hard labour. Released on a legal technicality he continued in his post till his death in 1963. Other anomalies must be mentioned. Naude attacks, often very movingly, the poverty, humiliation, deculturalisation and naked exploitation of the mineworkers' by the Chamber of Mines aided and abetted by a docile government . . .

Yet not once in 284 pages are the migrant Africans, who comprise over 90% of the mining labour force, even mentioned. Let alone their appalling working and living conditions, desperate exploitation and ruthless oppression by Chamber and government, aided and abetted by white miners. There is also a long, sick, passage (pp. 78-82) in which the author describes the glorious, innocent, and apparently quite legal enjoyment the Bloemfontein Blackshirts found in beating in the heads of the (largely Afrikaans-speaking) female members of Solly Sach's Garment Workers' Union with 'verskillende wapens'. Sachs was the red rag to the Nationalist bull in that he (as a Jew, none the less) found the secret of utilising Afrikaner cultural symbols for effective class mobilisation. That of course was the ultimate threat!

The Central Thesis

Yet, despite all this, the central thesis of the book is sound! But for the sustained attack on the trade unions by Albert Hertzog and his associates in Die Nasionale Raad van Trustees, the by then largely Afrikaans-speaking, white fraction of the working class would have continued its long tradition of support for the Labour Party. The Nationalist Party would not, for the first time ever, have won the six working class constituencies on the Rand which put it (in coalition with the Afrikaner Party) into political power with a Parliamentary majority of five on a minority vote in 1948. So despite its pathetic quality as serious history, its tendentious nature and myriad faults, this is an important book, because of both the conjuncture and class view it represents. It is full of direct and indirect clues on the role of the Broederbond in South African politics; the changing nature of that role; and the particular class concerns of the so called 'ethnic' ideology of Afrikaner Nationalism. Though notable more for what is left unsaid than said, it illuminates and raises most of the critical questions about the specific type of industrial society which developed in South Africa. Particularly issues relating to the control of the working class, white and black; the role of the state in relations between capital and labour; the development of a racially divided working class and the changes affected by Afrikaner Nationalist rule in the relationship between fractions of this class and the state.

Need for a Structural Explanation
If these important issues are to be fully grasped, it is essential that analysis transcends that of the propaganda of the actors involved and goes behind the personalities (Naude's is a personality oriented History) to seek structural explanations for the developments in white trade union politics during this critical phase in South African labour history. In this approach it is necessary to see what it was about the mining industry and the composition of its white labour force which made it the focus of the attack on trade unions.

Central Importance of Mining
Since the discovery of diamonds in the late 1860s, South Africa's social history has been dominated by the needs of, and the conflicts surrounding the mining industry, particularly gold mining. The historical and contemporary economic importance of the mining industry speaks for itself and need not concern us here. What is relevant is a brief outline of how the class structure, and particularly divisions within the working class, are largely a function of mining interest. From 1890 onwards, intense class conflict between fractions of Labour and Capital developed on the mines, centering almost exclusively on the question of cheap labour and the relationship between skilled and unskilled. Initially the skilled labour requirements of the mining industry had been met through the importation of experienced workers from the coal and tin mines of Britain. For a

167

significant part of the early period of mining, the skilled work force was composed largely of foreigners. These 'Cousin Jacks' as the British miners were commonly known, brought with them their habits of trade unionism, and sought to protect their interests by organising themselves into *craft* unions. The key to the power of craft unions lies in the fact that they, and not management, lay down the criteria for, and control admission to, the craft. Where craft unions are operating successfully, no person can enter these skilled trades without the consent of those already in them. Where the need for skilled labour is strong, this craft unionism is obviously a potent weapon in the skilled workers' arsenal. It is in their interests to keep admissions to the craft low, and the criteria rigorous, to ensure strong demand for their skills and correspondingly high wages. The apprenticeship system was generally the means by which this was effected. Thus by their nature, craft unions are elitist and exclusivist, concerned primarily to protect the position of the skilled worker from competition from other less, or unskilled workers.

Class and Race on the Mines

The often vicious and bloody conflict between capital and labour on the gold mines up to 1924 centred largely on this issue — the right of the skilled workers to control admission to their crafts and exclude less skilled workers. It is crucial to note that from the outset this exclusivism was motivated by blatantly economic, rather than racial, interests. Initially at least, the 'Cousin Jacks' directed their concern at both the major sources of cheap labour, migrant Africans, *and* the increasing numbers of Afrikaans-speakers who had been forced off the land by the devastating economic effects of the British scorched-earth policy during the Anglo-Boer War. The initial impetus for the large-scale proletarianisation of Afrikaners was, just as for Africans, conquest! Yet despite the often extreme proverty of the urban Afrikaner, there was a critical difference between the position of unskilled African and unskilled Afrikaner workers. After 1906, every white male in the Transvaal, however humble, had the vote. His interests thus became a source of political competition in which he had some say. As Afrikaners moved into the cities, those who could find employment filled low paid, unskilled or semi-skilled positions — a pattern which persisted for years. In 1939, 60.2% of all unskilled white workers were Afrikaans-speakers, as opposed to only 19.1% of artisans. The first large-scale influx of Afrikaner workers onto the mines occurred in 1907 when striking British miners were simply replaced, at lower wage rates, by unemployed Afrikaans-speaking workers. Yet these workers were at best only semi-skilled, and only a stopgap replacement. Though the British exclusivity had been broken, Afrikaans miners as a group filled the lower ranks of the occupational hierarchy on the mines. Their economic position too was precarious. The Chamber of Mines was forever seeking cheaper sources of labour, and thus these Afrikaans workers too began to act collectively to protect their position from undercutting by semi-skilled black labour. The vote was a powerful weapon in this struggle which was waged for two decades culminating in the bloody 'Rand Revolt' of 1922 on precisely this issue.

Thus the *racial* division of labour between skilled and unskilled was finally laid down by the intense *class* conflict 1890-1922. The development of the so-called 'white labour aristocracy' has been well covered by Johnstone and others[1] The point to note for the purposes of this paper is that it was the product of thirty years of bitter and always very violent class conflict between capital and labour. Between the Chamber, interested only in cutting its steep operating costs and raising often low profit margins, and skilled, semi-skilled and unskilled white workers, interested only in protecting their positions from undercutting *from whatever source*. Moreover, and this point is crucial for the understanding of Hertzog's successful assault on the Trade Union establishment, labour was led by skilled, organised, English-speaking workers. The leadership of the white trade union movement came from an exclusivistic, long-proletarianised group. On the other hand, the largely Afrikaans-speaking membership had been proletarianised by conquest and its economic effects, and despite their large numbers, were not represented in either the Trade Union or Labour Party leadership (at least till the fairly late Thirties). Yet, Afrikaans workers responded socially and politically in terms of their perceived economic interests, displaying a healthy interest in working class organisations, and appear to have voted solidly for the Labour Party. They made *no attempt* to organise themselves along cultural, 'Christian-National' lines. On the other hand, their skilled, English-speaking class fellows displayed a strong susceptibility to the imperialist message of the South African and Unionist Parties. The Labour Party's loss of 12 seats to the South African Party in the 1921 General Election was due to large desertions by the British miners to the blatantly jingoistic appeal of the S.A.P. Afrikaner workers remained loyal to the Labour Party, which in 1924 entered a 'pact' with Hertzog's Nationalists and won the election. From this date till its eventual demise in the 1958 elections, the Labour Party lost its independence, remaining closely and cosily identified with the Nationalist till 1933, and the United Party thereafter.

The PACT Government

The Pact government represented a class alliance. On the one hand the Nationalist Party represented Cape and Free State commercial farming interests, nascent Cape Afrikaner capital (Sanlam and Santam), the smaller dispossessed or severely threatened farmers of the Northern Provinces and the Afrikaans-speaking element of the urban petty bourgeoisie. On the other the Labour Party represented English speaking skilled labour and recently proletarianised Afrikaners. The groups represented in the class alliance attacked the imperialist interests of mining capital, and through the state appropriated part of its surplus (a) to allow the emergence of a national bourgeoisie based on industry and agriculture, and (b) to protect white labour in a position of privilege.[2] It took important steps to establish some form of economic independence for South Africa (protection, ISCOR etc), set up statutory entrenchment for white labour's privileges and provided subsidised employment for the newly proletarianised unskilled through the 'civilised labour policy'. The crisis of South African capitalism during the Depression and the Gold Standard crisis in particular, broke this coalition. The Fusion between Smuts' South African Party and elements of Hertzog's Nationalist Party in 1934 weaned industry, the Free State commercial farming interests and organised white labour out of the Pact coalition into an alliance with Transvaal commercial farming, and, more importantly, mining capital. Given the nature of the boom following the abandonment of the Gold Standard, the mining interests rapidly gained the upper hand in the United Party — just as the core of the national bourgeoisie who remained with Malan in the 'Purified' Nationalist Party had predicted.

The Emergence of Black Worker Militancy

The industrial and political conflict 1933-1948 did not centre on the struggle of white workers for peripheral incorporation into the system of privilege. Rather it reflected the changing structure of production — the emergence of an industrialised economy with, simultaneously, the final collapse of the Reserve economies which had provided the key to the accumulation which facilitated this industrialisation. The leadership of the white trade union movement had been incorporated into the formal structures of power with the

Pact government, and continued in this position under the United Party regime of General Hertzog. Confrontation between capital and organised white labour was thus ruled out.

Yet two important potential and real areas of labour unrest remained, centering on the two most recently proletarianised fractions of the working class: Afrikaans-speaking whites and Africans. The former are discussed below, but during this period an organised, militant black proletariat emerged to severely threaten the structure of exploitation.[3] Intense and bitter conflict developed centering on these two groups. In this struggle, whichever political party managed to *win the support* of white labour *and control* the militant African proletariat, was bound to achieve power. By 1948, the Herenigde Nationalist Party had managed the first (through gaining the support of a key group of white workers) and appeared to have policies which would achieve the second. The U.P., hopelessly divided by the conflicting interests of its class constituents, failed in both areas and narrowly lost the election.

The Struggle for the Soul of White Trade Unionism

Naude's book is Dr Hertzog's suitably edited version of the achievement of control over the strategic Mine Workers' Union. But moreover, it sheds much light on the intense struggle for the soul of white trade unionism during the Thirties and Forties. During the historic conjuncture which saw the rise and apparent fall of Fascism and the emergence of the Soviet Union as a major power, a small group of lawyers (Dr Hertzog and Danie Malan), academics (most prominently the ubiquitous Dr Diedrichs), bankers (Frikkie de Wet and J. J. Bosman of Volkskas) and cultural agitators (particularly Dr P. J. Meyer), decided to try and capture strategic trade unions for Afrikaner Nationalism. In 1936 they formed Die Nasionale Raad van Trustees. The force behind this group was the Afrikaner Broederbond, of which all were important members. Whilst not wishing to indulge in the conventional 'Sunday Times' type conspiracy theory of the Broederbond as a behooded and insidious band of fanatical conspirators running the entire country, an understanding of the role of the Broederbond is crucial. The particular rationale behind its activities and its links with emerging Afrikaner capital in the North is critical to an understanding of the political forces at work during this period.

The Formation of the Broederbond

The Broederbond had been founded in 1918 by a railway clerk and a clutch of theologians as an organisation to foster 'Afrikaner interests', and operated as a secret society after 1922. During the Twenties its operations were confined to the Northern Provinces, and it attracted support from petty bourgeois groups, particularly teachers and railway clerks. Until 1927 the Bond functioned as a semi-masonic organisation, but two events in the Twenties and Thirties were to alter its functions and lead to an expansion of its role.

After the 1926 Imperial Conference General Hertzog announced that the constitutional aims of the Nationalist Party had been largely achieved, to the great dismay of the many ardent Republicans in his Party. It would appear that the formation of a Broederbond clique within the Nationalist Party dates from this event, with the decision that Hertzog was no longer to be fully trusted, and the Bond was definitely reorganised during the late Twenties. Its major achievement was the formation in 1929 of a cultural front, the Federasie van Afrikaanse Kultuurverenigings (The FAK) which soon came to dominate Afrikaans cultural life. Yet it was the shock of Fusion which provided the real stimulus to the Broederbond's activities. Given its petty bourgeois nature, the vast majority of its 2,500 members opposed Fusion as a sell-out to imperialism. It was only after Fusion that Dr Malan joined the Broederbond, and General Hertzog claimed in a famous speech to his constituents at Smithfield that the Bond and the 'Purified' Nationalist Party were one and the same body merely operating on different social planes. The Bond was again reorganised along much more vigorous lines and began to play a critical policy-making and catalytic role in political and social life. Its three major areas of operation were: in the ideological and organisational redefinition of 'Afrikanerdom' during the Thirties;[4] the assault on the trade unions; and the establishment and promotion of Afrikaner business interests.

Class Structure of the Broederbond

The class nature of the Broederbond is the key to an understanding of its role and of 'Afrikaner Nationalism' during this and subsequent periods. For much of its existence it was a petty bourgeois organisation pure and simple. The importance of clerks, which had been crucial to its growth during the Twenties, declined during the Thirties. Though designed to cover the occupational spectrum in any area in which it operated, it was dominated by professional groups after 1933, the most important being academics (particularly those at Potchefstroom), teachers and lawyers. It was mainly an *urban movement* operating in the Northern Provinces which catered for those groups which had been moved/pushed off the land, yet did not have to sell manual labour in order to subsist. Its influence and importance among the Cape commercial farming and financial interests which remained in the 'Purified' Nationalist Party under Dr Malan was small. Indeed, Naude discusses the powerful opposition by 'a large Afrikaans Trust Company' (obviously Santam) to the provision in Pieter Neethling's will which established a trust fund to finance Die Nasionale Raad Van Trustees. Santam's Chairman, Senator W. A. Hofmeyer was an immensely powerful figure in the Nationalist Party, often at variance with Northern elements. Hofmeyer virtually founded the Cape Nationalist Party in 1915, refused its offered leadership and had been responsible for Dr Malan's appointment. During the fusion crisis, he was largely responsible for holding the Branch organisations for Malan. As the founder and chairman of Nasionale Pers, he had also established Voortrekker Pers in 1936, and was its chairman until he fell out with its Broederbond editor, Dr Verwoerd, in 1939. His relationship with the Broederbond was always stormy, reflecting the different class bases of support for the Nationalist Party in the Northern and Southern provinces. This north/south division in the Bond's influence remains largely true today.

The Organisation of Afrikaner Capital

For the Afrikaans-speaking petty bourgeoisie in the first half of the Twentieth Century, economic opportunities in the system of capitalist exploitation were limited not only by class position, but also by language. The economic system was dominated and controlled by foreign interests, and run as an appendage to the British economy. For Afrikaners who owned no land, who possessed a modicum of training which rendered them unsuitable for manual labour, and who were not prepared to assimilate to the dominant British culture, integration into the economy was difficult. The only broad avenues of available employment were the lower levels of state bureaucracy (the senior posts were long dominated by those trained under the hated Lord Milner), education, law and the church. As an organisation explicitly designed to foster the interests of the Afrikaner petty bourgeoisie, the Broederbond sought ways out of this economic impasse. In the Thirties it set about organising explicitly Afrikaans capital in the Northern Provinces (again in the Cape, with the relatively early establishment of Nasionale Pers, Santam and Sanlam, the position was somewhat different). In 1934 it established Uniewinkels, and with Albert Hertzog prominent in the proceedings, set up Volkskas as a co-operative Bank. In 1939, it organised the Ekonomiese Volkskongres which led directly to the founding of Federale Volksbeleggings (with massive aid from 'non-Broederbond' Sanlam), Die Afrikaanse Handelsinstituut, and numerous other concerns. One of the critical products of the 'Kongres' was the Reddingsdaadbond, the Broederbond's economic front designed to make the Afrikaner 'economically conscious'. The strategy established at the Volkskongres concentrated on the consolidation of Afrikaans financial capital, rather than commerce and industry, and then the gradual filtering of ownership of the means of production downwards.

If infant Afrikaner capital was to grow in the face of tremendous hostility and competition from established capital, it was faced with a number of priorities. It had to organise the Afrikaans market by persuading Afrikaners to invest in infant and not very promising ventures when much more attractive avenues were available. But there were very few Afrikaners in the North with capital to invest, and they were largely associated with the United Party. Thus the only source of capital was the savings of Afrikaans farmers and workers. If these individually small sums were to provide the large amounts of capital needed, both groups had to be mobilised extensively. The only available mobilisational device which could unite their diverse interests was that of ethnicity, their common 'Afrikaans' culture. Political power too was essential to this aim, not only because government contracts could be awarded to the 'right' people, but because of the role of government in determining economic policy and its power of appointment to the critically important advisory boards, planning councils and control boards.

The Afrikaner Workers' Savings

Thus in this Broederbond co-ordinated, petty bourgeois attempt at independent accumulation, the savings of Afrikaans speaking workers were to be a major source of finance, the basis for accumulation. Higher wages for these workers, gained at the expense of either black workers, or less likely, the English-speaking capitalists who controlled mining and private industry, provided greater potential for accumulation and could be wholeheartedly supported. There was however, one serious flaw in this scheme. Despite sustained attempts at cultural mobilisation, Afrikaans-speaking workers displayed a dangerous tendency to act in terms of class rather than cultural interest. To respond as workers — admittedly protected from and

174

therefore hostile to the aspirations of black workers, but as workers none the less — rather than as Afrikaners. The basis of this tendency was the trade union organisations, led by English-speaking artisans, and dominated by the craft unions which clearly had no interest in cultural mobilisation. Afrikaans workers thus belonged to class organisations, had their interests articulated in these terms and voted for the Labour Party. They had thus to be weaned from both. This was quite clearly the aim of the Hertzog group's assault on the unions. As Naude writes:

> In teenstelling met die meeste Westerse lande waar die werker hom georganiseerd tot die Sosialisme gewend het in sy strewe om volle erkenning van sy regte te kry, het dit hier in Suid-Afrika presies die teenoorgestelde uitwerking gehad. As sogenaamde beskermheer van die werker het die Labour Party oor 'n tydperk van jare 'n magtige faktor in die Suid-Afrikaanse politiek geword ... *Hierdie verband tussen die werker en die Labour Party moet verbreek word, want dan alleen sou die Stryd van Dr Hertzog en sy klein groepie manne enige sin en betekenis kon kry. Dit was dan die oorheersende boodskap wat van hulle uitgegaan het* ... Geleidelik het hy (die Afrikaner werker) sy rug op die Labour Party begin keer en daardeur ook die sosialistiese stelsel in Suid-Afrika vernietig (page 257-258, my emphasis).

The Spoorbond
In point of fact, the MWU was not the first Union to bear the brunt of the Broederbond attack. In 1934, H. J. Klopper, the railway official who had virtually founded the Broederbond (and was later to become Speaker of the of the House of Assembly) set up a railway workers' union, Spoorbond. Despite initial success, Spoorbond was wrecked on the rocks of craft unionism. Interestingly enough, the final death blow was dealt by Oswald Pirow, then United Party Minister of Railways and a self confessed Nazi. Given the role of the Broederbond in fostering Afrikaner capital and its relationship with worker organisations, another illuminating feature of Spoorbond was its establishment of a savings bank — Spoorbondkas — with an operating capital of £170,000, a mere three years after this trade union was founded. It was on the initiative of Spoorbondkas that the first Afrikaans building society was established, which, after a change of name, became Saambou.

Why the Mineworkers' Union?
However, this still leaves the question 'Why the Mineworkers' union?' unanswered. The strategic position of the Mining Industry has been discussed at some length. The Mine Workers' Union was a key union

within the Trades and Labour Council, potentially the largest white Union, contributing a large portion of the T & LC funds. Yet after the 1922 Strike it had split, the artisans forming their own separate craft unions. By the 1930s, of the 8 white unions in the mining industry, the MWU was the only non-craft union. Over 90% of the workers at the lower level of technical skills were Afrikaans-speaking, and therefore members, or potential members of the MWU. The depression began another exodus from the rural areas to the cities, which, together with the expansion of mining after the rise in the price of gold, saw a large increase in the number of semi- or unskilled Afrikaans-speaking whites employed on the mines. Yet once again the craft unions responded exclusivistically. The T & LC's delegates to the 1934 Volkskongres on the Poor White problem indignantly reported back to the T & LC congress that attempts were being made to solve the poor white problem by relaxing the apprenticeship system and other craft safeguards against labour dilution. Skilled workers, they insisted, were in danger of being ousted by lower paid rural migrants, white and black. The craft unions on the mines reacted in true fashion.

At this stage the leadership of the MWU had been captured by Charles Harris by dubious means. Harris quickly struck a bargain with the Chamber which protected his position, and like the infamous John Lewis, ran a thoroughly corrupt union which ignored the interests of the (largely Afrikaans-speaking) membership. Yet, throughout the twelve-year struggle for control, it was *not cultural* but *class issues* on which the membership attacked the corrupt Harris clique, and its equally corrupt successors under Broderick, after Harris had been assassinated in 1938 by a young Afrikaner miner. Because of the crucial position of the MWU within the SAT & LC, the Labour Party made the fatal, though inevitable, error of supporting the Harris clique against the bitter complaints of a very seriously aggrieved membership. The Labour Party had been founded to represent politically the class interests of white workers. Within the limitations of the South African social structure it had done so fairly and faithfully. But when it took the side of Harris in this dispute, it was seen by the membership to be supporting the Chamber of Mines (who backed Harris and Broderick), rather than their class interests. In a very real sense it *had sold out* its constituents to the bourgeoisie for a taste of political office: first in its alliance with the rural bourgeois in the Pact, then with the mining and industrial bourgeoisie of the U.P. regime. It thus gradually alienated unskilled white workers whose share of the fruits of the vicious exploitation of blacks was minimal, whose economic position was precarious, and who through the workings of South African history happened to be largely Afrikaans-speaking. The evidence suggests that electorally at least these workers continued to support the SALP until 1943. However by the late Thirties they were available for mobilisation by any group which would articulate their interests, and particularly their precarious economic circumstances.

The struggle for the MWU

It was on these legitimate grievances against the trade union and Labour Party Leadership that the Hertzog group fastened, and for twelve long years fought both the Labour Party and the State for control of the MWU. They formed first a rival trade union, the Afrikanerbond van Mynwerkers, and then, when Harris concluded a closed shop agreement with the Chamber (in return for a promise of industrial docility from the MWU), the 'Reform' movement within the MWU. Throughout its struggle for control, and despite its Afrikaner Nationalist ideology, these Hervormers were aided by English-speaking miners. Impervious to pleas for 'Christian-National' unionism, they fought for their interests which the MWU leadership clique ignored. When the Hervormers eventually won control of the MWU in 1948, their success was in no small measure due to these workers.

By 1948, Afrikaans-speaking workers in the MWU had been successfully weaned from the Labour Party and the T & LC. Their votes in six mining constituencies put the Nationalists into power. Soon after gaining control, the new MWU leadership under Daan Ellis led the Union out of the T & LC (hitherto the only co-ordinating body) to form the right-wing Koordineerende Raad. Yet despite Hertzog's success with the MWU other white trade unions with large Afrikaner membership were slow to adopt his 'Christian-National' trade unionism. It was only when left-wing trade union leaders (many of them Afrikaans-speaking) were removed from office by the State under the Suppression of Communism Act in the fifties, that the back of white trade union opposition was broken, and 'Christian-National' trade union ideology made substantial progress.[5]

There are two important lessons of the struggle for control within the MWU, one obvious from a critical reading of Naude's uncritical account, the other emphasised by him, albeit indirectly.

The Myth of an Inherent Cross-Class Afrikaner Unity

The first is the myth of an all pervasive, monolithic Afrikaner Nationalism — a mystic cultural unity which allegedly establishes a priori bonds between all members of the volk, welding them into an overriding organic political and ideological unity; whatever their socio-economic position. In this myth, class cleavages are irrelevant for social action as the ideological vision common to all Afrikaners, derived from Calvinist theology, unites them into a much broader social unity. It is obvious, but equally needs constant reiteration, that Afrikaner nationalist ideology developed historically as a *response to social change,* and is no immutable *weltanschuang.* Afrikaner Nationalism has always been articulated by a shifting class alliance, until very recently, dominated by a relatively deprived petty bourgeoisie. Indeed, the emergence of a fully fledged Afrikaans-speaking bourgeoisie has discernibly loosened the ideological hold of Afrikaner Nationalism per se. It is the petty bourgeois groups over whom the ideology still holds the strongest sway. Only after 1945 were Afrikaans-speaking workers incorporated into the Nationalist class alliance, and the petty bourgeois nationalists of Die Nasionale Raad van Trustees had to work long and extremely hard to win these workers to their cause. It was class factors, sheer naked economic interest, rather than the supposedly common cultural unity, which achieved this in the end. That the myth of Afrikaner cultural unity was, and is, at its weakest among Afrikaner workers is shown by the continuing opposition of such groups, but particularly the less technologically skilled, to elements of government policy which appear to threaten their position of privilege (eg. the 1965 refusal of the MWU rank-and-file to allow labour dilution despite the agreement between the union leadership and the Afrikaner Nationalist government). That Naude should spend 284 pages describing the twelve year struggle of the Afrikaans-speaking fraction of the petty bourgeoisie to wean just a small group of Afrikaans-speaking workers away from the Labour Party, and that it was the Hertzog group's manipulation of the day-to-day economic concerns of workers rather than the emphasis on cultural symbols which finally achieved this goal, highlights the myth of an inherent cross-class Afrikaner cultural, political and ideological unity.

The Changing Class Basis

Both the ideology of Afrikaner Nationalism and the class alliances which have articulated it, have undergone many changes since the

178

formation of the Free State Nationalist Party in 1914. And they will undergo many more, precisely because Afrikaner Nationalism was the basket which historically could hold the interests of various class fractions as they were subjected to the intense economic and social pressures associated with the development of first mining and then industrial capitalism. Whether it can continue to perform this function is debatable. The interests of the groups which composed the 1948 alliance are now clearly diverging, primarily as Afrikaner capital begins to articulate its interests as capitalists rather than as nationalists. As the continuing conflict within the Nationalist Party since 1960, but particularly after 1966 would seem to indicate, it is now doubtful whether the painfully forged cultural bonds can hold the nationalist alliance together.

Dividing the Working Class

The second point relates to the inherent tendency of South African capitalism to divide the fractions of the working class off from each other as the prime means of bourgeois political control. While this is a tactic common to all capitalist social formations, in South Africa it is facilitated by the existence of various racial categories. This is not the place to begin an analysis of racialism in South Africa, but rather to point out that through the operation of the interests of all fractions of the bourgeoisie, white and black fractions of the working class have been irreconcilably divided, to the point where the economic and social position of the former rests on the economic exploitation and political oppression of the latter.

There is much evidence (eg. the recommendations of the Van Zyl Commission and the utterances of the Afrikaanse Handelsinstituut of late) to suggest that similar tactics are in the offing to divide black workers, not only ethnically within Bantustans, but hierarchically as well. A small group of technologically skilled blacks would be bought off (at the same time allowing a small black bourgeoisie with limited political rights to emerge), leaving a vast, rightless army of operatives ripe for exploitation. This has long been the cherished tactic of certain industrial, financial and mining interests represented mainly in the Progressive Party. That Afrikaner capital is no longer a struggling infant to be protected from competition and in need of regular doses of nationalism to shore up its strength, but has grown into a vigorous and efficient adult, in search of higher productivity and new markets, adds to this possibility. For the first time in South African history, all elements of the urban bourgeoisie have a common

179

interest in higher productivity, and to achieve it are prepared to invest in higher wages for limited numbers of blacks. A united bourgeois front, independent of the demands of other white groups, can emerge.

Naude's book is the heavily biased yet fascinating story of one critical phase in the division of workers from each other in the interests of a fraction of the bourgeoisie. That phase is clearly over and, as the acrimonious departure of his major protagonist from the Nationalist Party indicates, would seem to have outlived its usefulness as the once common interests of the Afrikaner urban bourgeoisie, petty bourgeoisie and workers diverge. The crucial questions now are:

1. How will these groups respond to the demands of black labour?
2. What political alliance will they forge in response?
3. How will black labour meet the threat of division?

FOOTNOTES

1. F. A. Johnstone, 'Class Conflict and Colour Bars in the South African Mining Industry' (Institute of Commonwealth Studies, Collected Seminar Papers No. 10, 'Societies of Southern Africa in the 19th and 20th Centuries', 1970).
2. D. Kaplan, 'Economic Development and the State' (Workshop on Southern African Studies, Oxford University, September 1974).
3. D. O'Meara, 'The 1946 African Mineworkers' Strike and a Political Economy of South Africa' (Journal of Commonwealth and Comparative Politics, March 1975).
4. D. Moodie, The Rise of Afrikanerdom (University of California Press, 1975).
5. A. Hepple, Trade Unions in Travail (Johannesburg, 1954).

SOLLY SACHS AND THE GARMENT WORKERS' UNION

JON LEWIS

Solly Sachs died on Friday, 30th July, 1976, in the University College Hospital, London, at the age of 75. However, his effective work in the service of the garment workers had been brought to a premature end long before, when Sachs became one of the first to be banned under the Suppression of Communism Act, on 8th May, 1952. After the Nationalist victory of 1948 the full power of the state was used to attack Sachs and his union. Sachs fought back, at first through the courts when, for example, the Minister of the Interior compelled him to surrender his passport. After these channels had been closed to them and Sachs had been arbitrarily banned, the garment workers took to the street. A public protest meeting on the City Hall steps, Johannesburg, was called for Saturday morning 24th May. Some 15 000 protesters had already assembled when 10 000 coloured garment workers, marching abreast, reached the City Hall. However, as Sachs began to speak, the crowd was viciously attacked by the police. The protest campaign tested, and proved, the courageous solidarity of the garment workers in defence of their union, as thousands marched under such slogans as 'Klerewerkers Veg Vir Vryheid'. The lasting respect which Sachs earned from the members of the union is summed up in the words of a banner which draped the platform of one protest meeting: 'They Can Remove Him from the Union, but never from Our Hearts'.

Sachs' own personal history helps to explain the extraordinary sympathy and understanding he held for the Afrikaner women, who worked for such low wages in the clothing factories during the 1920s and 1930s. According to Senator A. Scheepers, the President of the Union, writing in 'Saamtrek', 6th August, 1976:

> Solly Sachs was born in Latvia from working parents — his mother was a garment worker and his father a leather worker. He grew up in poverty and

expressed many a time the grief he felt that his mother had to work so hard as a garment worker and still attend to her children and all other domestic chores. It was because of these circumstances that he vowed that if he could do something to make the lives of workers easier, he would do it.

Obliged to leave university in order to gain employment, Sachs nevertheless continued to study law. He worked at a concession store, later becoming Secretary of the Concession Stores and Allied Trade Union. On 14th November, 1928, Sachs accepted the position of Secretary of the Tailoring and Garment Workers' Union, in which post he served for 24 years.

GENERAL STRUCTURAL CONDITIONS

In order to assess the achievement of the GWU, it is necessary to locate its activities within the specific conditions of the emergence of the clothing industry in South Africa. In particular, it is important to investigate the structure of capital in the industry, and the nature of the labour force.

1. Capital

Secondary industrialisation and the establishment of a national manufacturing sector in South Africa was not a uniform process. In some areas, particularly steel and railways, capital was provided by the state. In the engineering, construction and chemicals sectors, mining capital and foreign capital was very important. The origins of the clothing industry, however, were indigenous, and dependent for capital on a process of primary accumulation. The large-scale factory production of the 1930s and 1940s was preceded by small workshop and 'outwork' production, run by individuals and family partnerships.

These establishments, lacking capital resources and under pressure from foreign competition, existed on low profit margins, which could only be maintained by holding down the wages of the workers. Thus the first struggles of the GWU from the late 1920s were over wages, and Sachs spent much time ensuring that employers actually paid the rates laid down in the Industrial Agreements for the industry. During this period, employers' sanctions included the keeping of a 'black list' *(Star,* 21/3/29).

Pressure on wages increased during the depression of the early 1930s, resulting in 2 major strikes in 1931 and 1932. The Union was defeated, but the employers' original demand for a 25% reduction in wages had to be reduced to 10%. The sheer economic misery of the

182

young women workers is illustrated in the biographical sketches of Hester Cornelius, Katie Viljoen and Anna Sophia Swanepoel in this section. Thus Sachs always stressed the primacy of 'bread and butter' issues in trade union work, and the very real gains achieved in this area, often through strike action, partly explain the continued loyalty and militancy of the membership. The scale of success in improving conditions is shown in a comparison of the wages of women workers in the industry between 1928 and 1952:

1928   Actual earnings of workers from *Nil* to about £2.10.0 per week. Not a single woman worker earned £3.0.0. per week.

1952   Weekly wage, qualified women workers £6.6.11. minimum. About 1 000, mostly Afrikaners, earned from £50.0.0. to £150.0.0. per month. In order to give some idea of the *real* rise in wages, it should be noted that during the period 1928-52 food prices roughly doubled *(Union Statistics for 50 years,* 1960 H-24) and house rents increased by a half (H-28). The index of retail prices for all items rose from 106.9 in 1928 to 185.9 in 1952 (H-25).

2. The Labour Force

Prior to 1939 the work force in the clothing industry was predominantly newly proletarianised, recently urbanised, female and Afrikaner. Each of these categories involved the Union in some new task or responsibility.

(a) Urbanisation

The misery and perplexity of 'poor whites' forced off the land and on to the urban labour market is amply chronicled in the Carnegie Commission Report of 1932. The trauma of proletarianisation and urbanisation is captured in a play entitled 'Die Offerande', written by the National Organizer of the GWU, Hester Cornelius, in the late 1930s. According to a synopsis given in 'Klerewerker', Julie/Augustus, 1942:

"Die Offerande" is 'n Afrikaanse werkendeklas drama wat handel oor die tradisies en lewe van die plattelandse bevolking van die 20ste eeu. Dit beskrywe die stryd van die klein boer; hoe hy spartel om sy plaas te behou en tenspyte daarvan was dit 'n mislukking en hy was verplig om uitkoms te soek op die delwery, met die vurigste hoop om eendag weer terug te keer na sy plaas. Die moeder en die seun is die slagoffers van die wrede Kapitalistiese stelsel.[1]

However, there is yet hope:

... Maar 'n nuwe uitweg, 'n boodskap van 'n vry en beter lewe, bevang die harte van die delwers. Werkers van die stede, wat verenig het in magtige Vakunies bring hierdie blye evangelie oor aan die delwers.[2]

As well as offering hope, the Union gave practical assistance to

183

members newly arrived in the town. The Union arranged accommodation, obtained cheap second-hand clothing for its members, worked with the Johannesburg and Germiston authorities to establish cheap hostels, and provided a whole social life with dances, picnics, sports days, Christmas parties and beauty contests. These 'home boy' functions which the Union performed helped to produce a very tight-knit organization. Such social occasions also had an educative function. This was particularly the case with May Day celebrations. On May Day 1939, for example, the garment workers of Germiston held a demonstration and public meeting in the morning, followed by a picnic by the side of Lake Germiston in the afternoon.

(b) Women

Unlike African societies, where the women were the last to leave for the towns, in Afrikaner rural society, it was the women who occupied the front line in the process of urbanization. Often, they supported parents who remained on the land, as well as themselves, on very meagre wages. The GWU, therefore, campaigned on issues which specifically affected the welfare of women workers: for example, confinement allowances, and the building of crêches. Furthermore, the union stressed that the members were not mere 'factory girls', but 'workers', who need not feel ashamed of their position. Managers and foremen were expected to show respect when addressing a member of the union.

(c) Afrikaners and Afrikaner Nationalism

The greatest achievement of Sachs and the GWU was in retaining the allegiance of the members to a class-based organization, in the face of the massive ideological and political onslaught waged by the nationalist movement.[3] This included sustained abuse against the 'Jew, Communist Sachs' from the nationalist press and politicians (giving rise to a succession of successful libel cases), physical attacks on meetings held by the GWU, repeated attempts to split the union on racial lines, and finally, the banning of Sachs himself.

The methods of the nationalists, in using racist ideology and manipulating Afrikaner symbols in order to destroy the union, are demonstrated in the 1944 strike in Germiston. This was led by two Nationalist workers, who objected to the employment of 6 coloured workers in the same factory. When the 2 were expelled by the union executive, the whole battery of nationalist organizations went into action against the GWU: press, Nationalist Party, F.A.K., Ossewa

184

Brandwag, and the Dutch Reformed Churches. The latter formed the Breë Kerklike Komitee which issued a pamphlet entitled 'Blanke Suid-Afrika Red Uself!!', in which they appealed for Afrikaners to:

> ondersteun die blanke fabriekswerkster en die drie Afrikaanse Kerke in hulle stryd om die behoud van die Kleurskeidslyn en die Christendom.

Some of the factors which enabled the union to survive these attacks have already been discussed: particularly the union's militant lead on the wages front. The achievement of a 'closed shop' agreement was another important factor. But whilst stressing the primacy of economic issues, Sachs always recognised the legitimate cultural aspirations of his Afrikaner members. He believed, for example, that the Labour Party had done so badly in the 1938 elections precisely because it had failed to take up a position on the Afrikaner 'National Question', and had not fought for the national rights of Afrikaners.

The policy of the GWU on 'Afrikaner Nationalism' is seen clearly in its response to the 1938 Voortrekker Centenary Celebrations. A crude socialist response might have been to condemn the whole affair as a propaganda exercise, staged by the nationalists. The Union's position, however, was that Afrikaners had a unique heritage which was worthy of celebration. Furthermore, given that the majority of union members were Afrikaners, the celebrations were something that the Union should actually participate in. In this way leadership could be kept out of the hands of the nationalists, and the impact of nationalist ideology, implicit in the celebrations, would be diffused. The GWU organized its members into 'Kappiekommandos'; issued leaflets with instructions on how to make your own 'Kappie' and Voortrekker dress; held Voortrekker Dances; and hired buses to take the members up to Pretoria for the celebrations. Thus, Afrikaner garment workers would attend the celebrations by virtue of their union membership, rather than their inclusion in the 'volk'.

SOLLY SACHS HIMSELF

Whilst it is important to recognise the general structural conditions in which the GWU operated, there can be little doubt that much of the responsibility for the achievements (and failures) of the Union lies with Solly Sachs himself. It is therefore important to attempt a very tentative analysis (in the absence of more detailed research) of Sachs' general political position, and the theoretical framework within which he worked. This will be in two sections. The first, roughly speaking, deals with Sachs' theoretical perspective, and the second describes his consequent political practice.

185

1. Class or Colour

In Sachs' view South Africa was characterized by a primary division between capitalists and workers. The working class, it is true, he saw as divided into 3 layers, based on skills, and largely co-incidental with differences in colour, with some blurring at the edges. However, Sachs believed the interests of all sections of workers were fundamentally the same, and there is no hint that the interests of white workers and black workers could actually be antagonistic.

It is largely in these terms that Sachs dealt with the problem of the 'white working class', and where exactly to locate it in South African society. Essentially it is the theoretical position held by the Communist Party in the period before it adopted the 'Native Republic' slogan, in 1928. It is not clear why Sachs was expelled from the Communist Party in 1931 (the official version being that he failed to turn up at a Communist Party May Day rally, preferring to accompany union members on a picnic), but it would be consistent with views he expressed later, to expect him to have supported the Bunting faction against the 'Native Republic' position, and hence incurred the wrath of the Communist Party leadership.

We have already noted that, until 1939, the workforce in the clothing industry was predominantly 'poor white' Afrikaner, and there was a real sense in which the interests of these workers were directly opposed to those of their employers. Sachs, it would seem, tended to generalize from this experience, and consistently argued that white workers could be won to an anti-capitalist position.

Hence, he devoted much effort to trying to save Afrikaner workers from the hands of fascism and the Nationalist Party. It is precisely in this area that Sachs' greatest achievement lies, as far as the clothing industry is concerned. However, it has already been hinted at that there were special structural considerations which made this possible.

In the first place, there did not exist the same divisions along lines of colour within the workforce, which was such a prominent feature of the mining industry, for example. In fact, until the Second World War, the workforce was overwhelmingly white, and the question of colour was not important. Furthermore, it was a new and relatively small industry. The white garment workers did not have the numerical or economic power to bargain their way into the power block. This contrasts sharply with the early success of white miners and railway workers in archieving considerable economic advance and job protection for themselves, largely at the expense of black workers. (The period of formal cooption of white workers is usually dated from the Pact victory of 1924.) It must be concluded that Sachs' hopes that the white working class could become a force for change in South Africa were wildly over-optimistic.

It is this complete mischaracterisation of the white working class which lies at the root of Sachs' 'economic determinism', which seems to have developed towards the end of the war. By this I mean Sachs' belief, held in common with many writers at the time (and ever since), that capitalism was a liberalizing force, and, that the contrived secondary industrialisation of South Africa would lead inexorably to some kind of meaningful change. He seems to have envisaged a general proletarianisation, in which black and white would all be workers together, and would come to find their common interests in opposition to the capitalist class.

However, the role of white workers within the production process had changed. Increasingly they performed a supervisory, or 'policing' function within production. Their 'productive' function declined, and they progressively came to perform the 'global function of capital', although they did not own the means of production.[4] (I am referring here to Sachs' political strategy in relation to the white working class as a whole. In the area of white garment workers, however, it would not be true to say that, as a group, they became less 'productive' over time.)

2. Economics or Politics

It has been argued that the basis of Sachs' position in the GWU was a successful, militant struggle on wages. However, Sachs tended to carry his trade union economism into the wider politics of the Left. It was on this issue — 'bread and butter' politics — that he clashed repeatedly with the Communist Party. He believed that this was the only platform which could gain the support of white workers. Only by leading (white) workers into the struggle for concrete realities and a better life could they be won over to the socialist position. Again, this kind of political strategy reflects Sachs' faith in the white working class. This faith survived the Nationalist victory of 1948, after which he continued to believe that the white working class could still be relied upon to defeat the nationalists at the ballot box.

Paradoxically, in trade union affairs Sachs always dissociated himself from union leaders who would have nothing to do with politics. In fact, one of the reasons given for establishing an official union journal — 'The Garment Worker' — in 1936, was precisely to facilitate the political education of the membership and, in particular, to combat the rising tide of racialism and fascism during the 1930s. However, crucial as this activity was to the survival of the union, the area of political discussion was largely confined to 'white politics'. The primary concern was always to unite the white working class, both in the Trade Union Movement, and at the ballot box.

This concern is clearly reflected in Sachs' party political involvement, which was based on two fundamental principles: 1. the need for a *mass* working class party, and 2. the need for *independent* working class action. The first principle lies behind his rejection of the Communist Party, and the support he gave to the Labour Party, both before and after the war. During the war he broke with the Labour Party because it contravened the second principle by going into an unconditional alliance with the United Party. In fact, his consistent stand on these two principles forced Sachs into a political wilderness during the war years. With the rest of the Left 'collaborating' with capitalist parties, Sachs was pushed into an increasingly lonely, and often highly idiosyncratic, political position. Political isolation led to the establishment of various 'independent left' groups between 1943 and 1945 largely under the direction of Sachs. These included the Independent Labour Party, the Socialist Party, and the National Labour Congress.

The important point is that all this activity remained largely within the sphere of 'white politics'. It was in these terms that the Communist Party criticised the decision of the GWU to support the Labour Party, whose 'native policy' was held to be reactionary. The Union replied to criticisms with the argument that the salvation of the non-Europeans would be realised all the sooner, when white workers had been won over to support for the Labour Party.

However, it would be wrong to give the impression that Sachs was not concerned with black workers, or that his attitude towards them was paternal. He consistently rendered financial and organizational support to the black unions formed during the war years, particularly to Makabeni's South African Clothing Workers' Union. (He was attacked for these activities in the Commission of Enquiry appointed to look into the affairs of the Union, in 1949.) Sachs' position seems to have been that white workers, involved with racist ideology, could not be expected to embrace their fellow workers of a different colour overnight, and that if anything at all was to be salvaged from the white working class this must be borne in mind. Hence he supported the idea of parallel unions, which allowed all workers in the industry, irrespective of colour, to be organized, but minimized racial tension by segregating them into a No. 1 Branch (for Europeans) and a No. 2 Branch (for Non-Europeans). However, within this structure, coloured, black and Asian workers seem to have controlled their own affairs, and were fully consulted in the activities of the union.

In 1953, the Bantu Labour (Settlement of Disputes) Act was introduced and African workers, both male and female, were no longer permitted as members of the union. A separate union for the African women (with Lucy Mvubelo as General Secretary) was immediately formed, which later amalgamated with the existing Clothing Workers' Union (African males) to form the National Union of Clothing Workers (SA).[5]

Sachs' contribution to trade unionism in South Africa should be viewed in relation to the changing nature of the working class, both black and white. His greatest achievements are marked in the response of the GWU to the proletarianisation of Afrikaner women. However, things do not remain the same. By the time of his banning, the nature of the work force, both in manufacturing generally, and in the clothing industry, had radically altered. The demand for labour, and the breakdown of influx control during the war years, had led to the proletarianisation of blacks on a massive scale. According to Wage Board investigations, the racial composition of the labour force in the clothing industry on the Witwatersrand (where the clothing industry industry was largely concentrated) changed as follows:

Year	% European	% Coloured	% Native
1936	88,7	2,0	9,3
1946	54,0	22,1	23,9
1955	32,6	29,3	38,1

Quoted: Report of the Industrial Tribunal to the Minister of Labour on Reservation of Work in the Clothing Industry in the Union of South Africa (1975) p.6.

The changing composition of the labour force, a reflection of developments in the manufacturing sector as a whole, meant there would be little future for either Sachs' style of trade unionism or his general political strategy, dependent as they were upon a particular conception of the white working class, which no longer held true. In any case, given the repressive legislation of the Nationalist Government, such a strategy was not a realistic option. Even so, during the 1930s, Sachs' strategy had proved effective, and had laid the foundations of a strong multi-racial union, which has survived to serve the garment workers to this day.[6]

POSTSCRIPT ON THE GARMENT WORKERS' UNION
The following was written in the light of Eddie Webster's article, 'Towards a Stable Truce', in Vol. 3 No. 1 of the *SALB*. The article provides a useful framework for analysing the early establishment of the GWU.

Stage 1 Recruitment
The Union had to be virtually completely rebuilt following the defeat of the 1932 general strike. Amidst victimization by employers, former union members were individually visited by union officials, in order to keep them in touch with developments. When the current wage award expired in 1933, the union decided against pressing for a full restoration of the 1932 wage level, and accepted the employers' offer of a 5% increase. This policy was adopted at a mass meeting of members, on the grounds that it was better to concentrate on rebuilding the union, than to risk everything in a premature strike. Furthermore, even a small gain demonstrated to the workers the ability of the union to represent their interests.

Stage II Winning Management Recognition
During 1934 there was a significant shift in management-union relations. The larger, more capital-intensive firms realised that uninterrupted production was dependent upon good 'labour relations', which in turn was dependent upon recognising the union. Thus the employers' association co-operated with the GWU in penalizing employers who paid less than the rates laid down in the wage determination for the industry. In this way unfair competition was prevented, and harmony within the industry was promoted.

Stage III Negotiating and Maintaining an Agreement
The GWU always made full use of any machinery or rights which existed under the law. For example, the union worked for the establishment of an Industrial Council for the Clothing Industry. This had been abandoned during the 1932 strike. Its restoration was a necessary part of the union's struggle to gain recognition. In negotiations the GWU would always back up its demands with the threat of strike action. But once an agreement had been signed, the union scrupul-

ously honoured its commitments. The stability which resulted for the industry was of obvious benefit to the employer. Thus, when in 1949 the Government refused to gazette an agreement because it contained a closed shop clause, it was the employers themselves who called most strongly for the retention of the clause.

By 1936 the GWU had achieved a 'stable truce' with employers. Without this strong base the union would not have been able to withstand the attacks which were later launched against it.

FOOTNOTES

1. *The Sacrifice* is an Afrikaans working-class drama which deals with the traditions and life of the rural population of the 20th century. It describes the conflicts of the small farmer, how he struggles to maintain his farm, but despite this, fails, and is forced to seek work on the diggings in order to survive. He remains passionately hopeful that the day will come when he can return to his farm. The mother and the son are the victims of the cruel capitalist system.
2. However, a new hope, a message of a free and better life takes hold of the hearts of the diggers. Workers of the cities who have united in powerful Trade Unions bring this glad tiding to the diggers.
3. For an analysis of nationalist subversion of the unions see D. O'Meara.
4. G. Carchedi: *Economy and Society* Vol. 4, No. 1 (1975) and N. Poulantzas: *New Left Review* 78 (1973).
5. W. H. Thomas, ed., *Labour Perspectives in South Africa* (David Phillip, Cape Town 1974), p. 127.
6. Permission from the Garment Workers' Union to work in their archives is gratefully acknowledged.

BIBLIOGRAPHY

Solly Sachs' writings include the following:

E. S., Sachs *The Anatomy of Apartheid* (Collets, London 1965).
The Choice before South Africa (Turnstile Press, London 1952).
Garment Workers in Action (The history of the garment workers of South Africa to 1952.) (Eagle Press, Johannesburg 1957), also published as *Rebel Daughters* (McGibbon and Kee, London 1957).

AFRIKANER WOMEN OF THE GARMENT UNION DURING THE THIRTIES AND FORTIES

JOHN MAWBEY

Below we publish three edited versions of autobiographical sketches by Afrikaner women members of the Garment Union. The sketches cover the period of the 1930s and 1940s and deal with three major issues: the nature and extent of their exploitation; the development of trade unionism among them; and their successful defence of their Union in the face of the onslaught by the 'reformers' of Afrikaner Nationalism.

The story of these women and the nature of their response to the changes taking place in the South African social formation during these years of rapid secondary industrialisation must be of central concern to those involved in an analysis of the development of South Africa's racially divided working class. Heavily exploited, there developed amongst these women the seeds of a trade union consciousness which went far towards transcending the racial antagonisms which South Africa's ruling classes have used so successfully to inhibit the development of working class solidarity.

The proletarianisation of Afrikaner women began, as with the Afrikaner people as a whole, as a consequence of the economic devastation of the rural areas during the Anglo Boer War. It was only after the onset of secondary industrialisation, however, that sufficient employment opportunities were created, and that substantial numbers of these women entered industry. The first such influx took place as a result of the accelerated development associated with the First World War. It was followed by further and more substantial increases at the end of the twenties and during the early thirties following the boost given to secondary industry by the protectionist policies of the Pact Government and more particularly by the increased foreign investment which followed the devaluation of the South African Pound in 1933.

Unskilled and newly arrived in an industrial milieu Afrikaner women faced crude exploitation. If wage rates for Afrikaner men had to be based on a recognition of the needs of their families as the reproducers of labour power the rates for women workers could be differently assessed. On the assumption that part of the cost of the reproduction of their labour power was met from elsewhere, their wages were calculated at a level close to that of migrant Black workers who were similarly assumed to have other resources. Thus in 1917 a Government Commission of inquiry concluded that in the clothing industry 'the payment of wages (to white, mainly women, workers) below what may be called the subsistence minimum is common.' The extent of their sufferings during the thirties is told in the sketches below.

The Garment Union of predominantly Afrikaner women developed out of the earlier Witwatersrand Tailors Association under the able leadership of Solly Sachs. The WTA was initially a union of the more highly skilled bespoken tailors and contracting tailors of the Witwatersrand. During the twenties an Industrial sector had been established in the face of the threat posed by industrial production. It was however only after the assumption of office by Solly Sachs in 1928 that a concerted effort was made to organise the Afrikaner women. The early development of the Union was characterised by sharp conflict with the employers, with two major strikes taking place in 1931 and 1932. These actions also led to conflict with the state particularly in the second case where the defiance of the Garment women was seen by the Nationalist Government of the time as threatening their chances in an impending by-election in Germiston. Minister of Justice Pirow decided on harsh measures to contain the strike and large numbers of women were arrested. Yet the Garment women were not intimidated, and during the following years they were to move even further along a path which was perceived as threatening by all classes of the South African establishment.

The trade union sympathies of the large mass of Afrikaner workers had always posed a threat to the development of Afrikaner Nationalism and it was in fact only after a sustained attack on key trade unions that the Nationalists were able to gain the electoral victory of 1948.[1] The success of the Afrikaner 'reformers' in capturing control of some unions (e.g. the Mine Workers' Union) contrasts strongly with their complete failure in the case of the Garment Union. Despite repeated assault both verbal and physical the women of the Garment Union remained committed to the trade unionism which they had forged and moved even further in the direction of the non-racial class solidarity so inimical to Afrikaner Nationalism (or for that matter to all of the dominant classes in South Africa).

At one level the reasons for their steadfast adherence to their union can be located within the structure of the Union and the nature of its leadership. A comparison with the Mine Workers' Union is instructive. The leadership of the Mine Workers' Union was hopelessly corrupt and continually failed to respond to the grievances of its members. In this situation the Reformers were able to use economic grievances in their struggle for control of the Union. The Garment Union on the other hand had been successful in defending its members and in responding to their needs. Thus the Reformers had to rely entirely on appeals to national sentiment whereas Sachs was able to locate his appeals to the national oppression of Afrikaners in a class context. There were however underlying structural causes for the direction in which the Garment Union developed. The industrial development of the thirties was not merely quantitative, but also entailed qualitative changes in the structure of industrial production. Where the Garment industry had previously been characterised by production on the basis of small-scale factory units and 'contracting out' systems it began now to be increasingly dominated by larger factories. These changes also threatened the previous labour structure of industry based on skilled and unskilled, entailing their replacement by increasing numbers of semi-skilled operatives. Faced by this process of 'deskilling', skilled workers react by attempting to entrench their privileged position while the unskilled find the development to their advantage as it strengthens their bargaining position. For the majority of the skilled workers in South Africa (or for those who had previously had their jobs defined as skilled through the imposition of job colour bars) the response was to call for further entrenchment of such colour bars. For them the threat was posed by the increasing number of African men entering industry. For the Afrikaner women of the Garment Union the threat was posed in a very different way. The formative years of the thirties were barely passed and they had only just achieved tenable conditions when in the forties the accelerated development of the war period led to an influx of African women into the industry. Being themselves at most only slightly more skilled than the new recruits the threat was particularly acute especially as employers assumed that African women did not qualify as 'employees' under the Industrial Conciliation Act and paid them much lower wages. In this situation the Garment Union's strategy was to enter into legal proceedings to procure African women rights under the Act. The I C Act specifically excluded 'Pass bearing natives' but as African women were not obliged to carry passes the Supreme Court was forced to admit in the case of Christine Okolo vs the Industrial Council for the Clothing Industry (Tvl) in 1944, that African women were entitled to the rights of workers as defined in that Act. Employers were thus forced to pay the rate for the job and the threat of undercutting was averted. At the same time the Garment Union went ahead with the organisation of African women as a section of the Union.

If in subsequent years the Nationalist Government was to take measures to exclude all Africans from the Industrial Conciliation machinery through the 1953 Bantu Labour (Settlement of Disputes) Act, forcing African women to establish a separate union, this does not detract from the solidarity displayed in this earlier period. As an example of the potential for non-racial class solidarity and a tribute to the Afrikaner women of the Garment Union we publish the following self portraits.

HESTER CORNELIUS

In 1930, at the age of twenty-two, I came to Johannsburg to look for work. I worked for one year as a table hand in a clothing factory and was then dismissed. In 1931, I tried to find another job, without success — there were hundreds of girls looking for jobs. I returned to the farm and became an ardent Nationalist, believing that the South African Party was to blame for our poverty and unemployment. Later, I returned to Johannesburg and found work. My sister Johanna and I shared a back room in Vrededorp with the two Vogel sisters. Although I was a fast worker, I was paid only 17s. 6d. a week and there was a lot of slack time in the industry.

I began to fight for my rights and the rights of my fellow-workers almost immediately I started work in a factory. The girls in the factory would come to me with all their complaints and I would take them up with the employer. As I was a good worker, I was confident he would not sack me. Then I heard about the Garment Workers' Union and, one lunch time, we went to the union office. Mr Sachs, the secretary of the union, took down all our complaints, and I felt straightaway that we could rely upon the union to help. The more I saw of the union activities, the more I realised how necessary it was for the workers to become organised.

At first I could not understand why Mr Sachs, who was a Jew, fought so hard for the Afrikaner daughters. I spoke to many Nationalists about this very good Jew, who was doing so much to help us. They attacked him bitterly and this made me lose faith in the Nationalist Party. In 1934, I was elected as a member of the executive committee of the union and learnt much more about trade unionism and about Mr Sachs. I saw how angry he used to be when employers treated workers badly, and how hard he worked to improve our conditions. I also learnt that Mr Sachs fought not only for garment workers, but for all the workers. It took a Jew to make me understand that poverty could be wiped out in sunny South Africa and that, if the workers were organised and united, they could gain higher wages and a better life.

In 1932, my sister Johanna was arrested in Germiston whilst taking an active part in the general strike in the clothing industry. My parents came for a few days and I took them to my uncle's family, who were disgusted with Johanna. One of them asked my father what he thought of his daughter going to jail. My father smiled and said she was a 'chip off the old block.'

The first strike in which I took a leading part was in 1936, in Cape Town. The garment workers of Cape Town were even worse exploited than we in the Transvaal. Our Union had sent delegates to Cape Town to organise the workers and I was one of them. The workers came out on strike in several factories and I was arrested together with about twenty others. The workers lost the strike and, even today, they are paid much lower wages than the workers in the Transvaal. Over the years, I took part in numerous strikes of garment workers of the Rand and in Port Elizabeth. In 1942, I helped the Johannesburg sweet workers in their strike for higher wages, and was again arrested together with Anna Scheepers and Dulcie Hartwell.

Over twenty years have passed since I started work in the clothing industry and, during that period, there has been a complete change in our wages, conditions of work and way of life. It was the union with its courageous, able leaders, which set us free from the hell of starvation wages and slum squalor, and no-one else. The Nationalists, the so-called friends of the Afrikaner workers, have never helped us. On the contary, they have always tried to break our union.

KATIE VILJOEN

I left school at the age of fifteen and, to help my parents, took employment in Kimberley as a dressmaker at £2 a month. I stayed with relatives who did not charge me for board and lodging, and regularly sent my parents £1 to 30s. a month. I worked in Kimberley for about three years, until 1932, without any increase in wages.

In 1932 — a year of depression — I came to Johannesburg and obtained a job with a private dressmaker in Bezuidenhout Valley at 30s. a week. Unfortunately she closed the workshop after two weeks. I boarded with a Jewish family, Suzman by name, who were extremely good to me and whom I paid £1 a week for board and lodging.

I knew a girl, Lena van Rensburg, also from Boshoff, who had already worked in the clothing industry for some time, and she found me a job in a dressmaking factory at £1 a week. The firm's motto, inscribed in white letters on black cloth, affixed to the entrance, was 'Work Like Hell and Still be Merry'. They employed about forty women and we did, in fact, work like hell, but were not particularly merry.

As I could not afford tram fares on £1 a week, I walked home from work with my friend, Lena, who, though she lived in an entirely different suburb, acted as my guide. To make sure I would not lose my way, I took a piece of white chalk with me and made various marks on the route from the factory to my lodgings. Next morning, I left the house at 5.30 a.m. as I had to walk a distance of about four miles and work started early.

For a month I walked to and from work every day, but then these long journeys became unbearable. The work was really slave-driving. We started at seven a.m. and finished at six p.m. I could not send anything home to my parents, as my total earnings just covered my board and lodging.

At the end of the first month, I went to see my friend, Lena, again, and she found me a job at Awlwear Overall factory. I started as a shirt machinist at £1 10s. a week. Most beginners started at 15s. a week, but when Lena told the manager my sad story, he agreed to raise the wage. I was very anxious to send some money to my parents, and I needed new shoes and clothes as the old ones were wearing out. I did not know the town, but I went from building to building enquiring about cheap accommodation and at last, after a great deal of walking, found a room to share with another young girl, a sweet worker, for which we had to pay 17s. 6d. a week.

My budget was made up as follows:

Rent: 17s. 6d. per week.

Saving up for new clothes: 7s. 6d. per week.

10s. a month I sent to my parents.

The balance of 2s. 6d. a week had to be sufficient for food.

Once a week I used to buy a loaf of bread for 6d., and a pound of butter at 1s. 8d. I lived on bread and butter the whole week and still had 2d. left over at the end. Deeply religious, I used to pray every night for enough strength to carry on with my work. I was a very healthy girl, strongly built, weighing a hundred and forty pounds. I kept my health, but in a short space of time my weight dropped to a hundred and seventeen pounds. My parents never knew the hardships I had to endure.

I knew nothing about trade unionism at that time, but after I had worked for a short while, Johanna Cornelius came and appealed to the workers to join the union. When she mentioned that the contribution was 6d. a week, I decided not to join. I did not know what the word 'union' menat, but I knew that if I paid 6d. to the union there would not be enough for a loaf of bread.

A month later, Mr Sachs, the general secretary, came to the factory and spoke to the workers about joining the union. I remember him telling us that, although the employers paid us our wages, it was the union that fixed the amount. About a hundred and fifty workers were employed in the factory, of whom more than half were already members of the union, and after this visit more joined. When Mr Sachs left, a girl, Maria Primavesi who was sitting next to me at the machine, said that I was a coward for not joining the union. I was too proud to admit that I could not afford to contribute 6d. a week, so I merely replied that one day she would find out the reason.

After working for three months, I received an increase of 5s. a week. I immediately went to Maria, told her why I had not joined before and became a member of the union. From that day onward, I took an active interest in the welfare of the workers of the factory where I was employed. I brought all the workers' complaints before the manager, who rather liked my courage and straightforwardness. This made me popular with the other workers, who regularly came to me with their complaints. I managed to settle many minor disputes over wages with the management and put a stop to petty underpayments altogether. I also succeeded in getting the cloakroom regularly cleaned and washed and in having tea served for all the workers.

My wages increased every three months, in accordance with the agreement which the union had made with the employers' association and, in time, life became more tolerable. When my weekly wages reached £2 10s. I could afford to rent a room for myself and to send money regularly to my parents.

In 1938 I was elected a member of the central executive committee of the union. I found the work on the committee very interesting and took an active part in union work. In the same year, the 'Reformers', led by a certain D. B. H. Grobbelaar, started their attacks on the union and on Mr Sachs. I understood at once that these people were not interested in the welfare of the workers, but were out to destroy the union, and I despised them intensely. All the workers in my factory felt the same.

In March 1938, the union had arranged a challenge meeting with Grobbelaar at the City Hall, Johannesburg, and all the workers were greatly excited. A few days before the meeting was held, I spoke to the workers and told them that we were going to march as a body to the meeting hall. We received information that a gang of Reformers was going to attack us when we left the factory. The Manager received several anonymous telephone calls, saying the mob would be waiting for Katie Viljoen, but on the afternoon of the meeting, the workers marched out of the factory and nothing happened. Ours was the only factory where the workers — three abreast — marched to the City Hall, singing home-made songs and shouting, 'Down with Grobbelaar and up with the Sachs'. When we arrived at the City Hall, we gave three cheers for Solly Sachs. The hall was crowded and an overwhelming majority of the workers showed, in no uncertain manner, their bitter hostility towards Grobbelaar and the Reformer disrupters.

Some months later, the union sent me to Port Elizabeth to organise the garment workers there. I had no previous organising experience, and fully realised that I had a tremendous job of work ahead of me, but I was determined to do my best. There were about eight hundred garment workers in Port Elizabeth and not many were members of the union. Wages and conditions were bad — much lower than in the Transvaal — and most employers were not well disposed towards the union.

Apart from having to battle against the employers for higher wages and better conditions, there was the tragic position, common in South Africa, that the workers were divided amongst themselves.

Many of them had come under the influence of the Reformer disrupters.

In 1942 the union decided, after months of negotiations, to call a strike in Port Elizabeth. The union was asking for increased wages, paid holidays and the introduction of the closed shop. The employers agreed to the first two demands but obstinately refused to accept the principle of the closed shop.

When the strike began, Mr Sachs, Hester Cornelius, Dulcie Hartwell and Anna Scheepers came from head office to help. Philip, my husband, took leave from his work at the Ford Motor Company to give assistance. We divided our forces. Hester and I and a group of pickets went at about six a.m. to Mosenthal's factory, and Anna and Dulcie went to Teikamdas.

When we arrived at Mosenthal's we found a large number of policemen and a 'pick-up' van. Groups of pickets were placed outside the four or five entrances and, at 7.45 a.m., when the factory was opened, not a single worker tried to go to his work. At 8 o'clock, however, a group of scabs who had gathered in a worker's house near the factory attempted to force their way through. They were organised and led by the Reformers. A fight ensued, and the police, as usual, protected the scabs, most of whom were by no means against the strikers, but had been misled. At about nine o'clock, the sergeant in charge of the police came up and very politely asked whether he and his men could have some of the refreshments which we were serving to the pickets. Many of the police had members of their families working in clothing factories and they themselves have always been badly underpaid. A jug of coffee and plates of sandwiches were soon brought out and the entire police force got into the pick-up van, closed the door and enjoyed the refreshments. They were certainly in no hurry to come out to attend to their duties. Indeed, the sympathy of the police and of the public of Port Elizabeth as a whole was entirely on the side of the workers. Later in the day and during the following days, whenever the strikers assembled in a hall in the centre of the city for refreshments and dancing, quite a few policemen in uniform used to come inside to enjoy a snack and a dance.

At the Teikamdas factory, things did not go well. The majority of the workers were non-European and they were terrified of losing their jobs. A large number of scabs brushed the pickets aside and poor Dulcie, who had come to Port Elizabeth to help in the strike, was knocked over the head by several scabs and found herself covered with blood. She was rushed to a doctor, had her head bandaged and went back to the factory on picket duty; during the lunch hour, when we called a mass meeting in the cente of Port Elizabeth, Dulcie, with a huge bandage over her head, addressed the audience, bearing no malice towards the misguided workers and no hatred towards any-one. Her bandages had attracted as much attention as her ringing voice.

On the third day of the strike, the employers agreed to refer the closed shop to arbitration. Mr T. Freestone, an officer of the Department of Labour, was by mutual consent appointed arbitrator.

A satisfactory agreement was reached and, as soon as the closed shop was introduced, there was complete harmony amongst the workers and between the union and the employers.

My whole family has always been staunchly Nationalist, except for my sister, Jacoba, and my brother, Johannes, who are United Party supporters with very strong Labour sympathies. Whenever I discuss politics and trade unionism with my brothers, Koos and Albert, who are both fanatical Nationalists, I can see clearly the tragedy of the workers of South Africa. Like tens of thousands of others, they have a tremendous amount of energy and capacity for hard work. As with many other Afrikaners of their generation, the terrible wrongs of the Boer War still rankle in their hearts. They have many English and Jewish friends, but in their hearts they are fanatical followers of Dr Malan. They read only the Nationalist papers, they hate non-Euro-peans and firmly believe in apartheid. To them communism means 'your sister marrying a "kaffir" '. They hate the 'Jew-Communist', Solly Sachs, and also dislike the other officials of the union, whom they regard as communists. I often argue with them and tell them: 'But look, it is Solly Sachs who has done so much for the garment workers, the majority of whom are Afrikaners. He fought for im-provements in their wages and working conditions, organised them and helped them to gain a better living standard'. The reply is that they do not believe it and that the Government has improved the workers' wages and conditions. I tell them that no government has ever helped the workers, and that Sachs and the other leaders of the union have often had to fight the government. They remain uncon-vinced and say: 'We believe what we want to believe and what we do not want to believe we will not believe'.

ANNA SOPHIA SWANEPOEL

At the beginning of 1911, I arrived in Johannesburg and obtained employment through a school friend of mine, Julia Makonik, whom I had known in Bloemfontein. She found me a job in a small workshop where she was a tailoress. I started at 10s. a week. The hours were from seven a.m. to six p.m. daily, with an hour for lunch, and seven a.m. to twelve noon on Saturdays. The workshop was terribly overcrowded and hot, with primus stoves going all day and the smell of paraffin filling the air.

For about three months, I lived with my brother and sister-in-law and did not have to pay board. Then I went to Julia's people, where I also had nothing to pay. A month later my parents arrived in Johannesburg and my father got a job as a ganger on the railways. My family rented a house and I went to live with them.

Very often, we had to take work home and sit up late at night finishing it. For this, we received no extra pay. The boss of the workshop was Mr Schiller, a highly qualified tradesman, friendly but fond of using bad language. There was no union in existence, as far as I know, and workers were entirely at the mercy of their employers. I worked for Schiller for one year and during that time, I received a rise of 2s. 6d. and, a few weeks before I left, one of 5s. making my wage 17s. 6d.

I then went to work in another tailoring workshop, where I received 25s. a week to start with and, after six months, was earning £2 a week; this was considered a particularly high wage at the time.

At the end of 1912, I married Pieter Swanepoel, a labourer-fitter on the railways. His wages were about £6 a month, but we got a free railway house and he also earned about £6 a month in his spare time from boot-making. We moved to Germiston, and my husband changed his work several times in order to better our income. In November, 1927, he died, leaving me with two children, aged eleven and fourteen. We were practically penniless and my total income was 17s. 6d. a week, which I earned as an usherette at the Apollo Theatre, Germiston. One evening, Mr Schiller, my employer of sixteen years ago, came to a show at the Apollo. He told me that, if I wanted work, I should get in touch with him at the African Clothing Factory, Germiston, where he was now employed as a foreman. I did so and, on the 23rd January, 1928, I started work there at 25s. a week, which in those days was the highest wage paid to any factory worker. We worked from 7.30 a.m. to 6 p.m., with a lunch break of one hour, and on Saturdays from 7.30 to noon. The African Clothing was the largest factory in the Transvaal and one of the largest in South Africa. There was a piecework system in existence and we had to turn out a certain amount every day. Many workers would start work before time and work through their lunch hour to make up their quota. There were no rest intervals.

I found it impossible to live with two children on my wages of approximately £6 a month. I therefore continued working as an usherette at the cinema and also took in two young girls of the factory as boarders at 10s. a week each.

When I started working for the African Clothing there was a union of garment workers in Johannesburg and I believe they had a wages agreement, but the workers of Germiston were not organised. One day, about three months after I had started work, Mr Dan Colraine, who was then secretary of the Johannesburg union, visited our factory and spoke to us during lunch hour. The majority of the workers readily agreed to organise a union and Mr Colraine handed me several membership forms. Immediately he had left, one of the girls said to me: 'Don't take the forms round. You will get the sack. A union has been started once before in the factory and the workers who helped to organise it were all sacked'.

I took no notice of the warning and, with the help of three others, got over a hundred and sixty workers to sign the forms and enrol as members of the union. At the end of the week I found a week's notice in my pay envelope, and so did the three other girls who had helped. I at once got in touch with Mr Colraine and told him about it. He came the following Monday and wanted to address the workers, but only a few gathered to hear him. All the others were afraid. He called another meeting outside the factory for the following day and this time all the workers who had enrolled as members turned up. The workers there and then decided to strike for the right to belong to a union and for the reinstatement of the four of us who had been dismissed.

The following day, all the workers turned up at the factory, but only about twenty went in to work. I automatically became the strike leader and the workers looked to me for guidance. At first the employers were bitterly hostile and said that they would sack all the strikers, but after four days an agreement was reached to reinstate all the workers, including myself. Everybody got a full week's pay, including the four days we were away, and we were brought under the Johannesburg agreement, which fixed wages for women workers at

203

£1 to start and £2 10s. after two-and-a-half years. Many of the workers received increases in wages; my own were raised to £2 a week. We also succeeded in getting a ten-minute interval in the morning and the lunch hour was properly observed. All the factory workers now joined the union and I was elected shop steward. The workers used to come to me with their complaints, which I had to take to the employer, and naturally I was not very popular with him. Most of the complaints were settled to the satisfaction of the workers, as the employers did not want to have any trouble. On one occasion, there was an argument about singing in the factory. The workers found the work monotonous and strenuous and, to break the monotony, they would start singing popular songs. Mr Sam Kalmek, one of our employers, apparently did not like the music and tried to stop it. He told me that, if I wanted to sing, I should go on the stage, where I would earn more money, and lodged a complaint against me with the industrial council for leading the singing. The Chairman of the Council told Mr Kalmek that there was no ground for complaint and that, in his own factory, he encouraged the workers to sing as it meant more production.

Trade unionism spread quickly among the workers of Germiston and, within a short time, all the garment workers were members of the union. The workers gained more and more confidence in the union when they saw that it was successful in getting them higher wages.

In 1931 the union called a general strike of all workers in Johannesburg and Germiston against the attempt by the bosses to cut our wages by twenty-five per cent. The workers loyally responded and there were no scabs.

After about three weeks, the strike was settled, neither side winning a victory. But the employers started organising immediately to break the union and to reduce wages. They did not openly attack the union, but used all sorts of tricks to get the workers away from it.

I did not return to the factory as I had been appointed organiser of the union for the Germiston branch. There were about a thousand workers in Germiston at that time and the town had become an important clothing centre.

In 1932 the employers once again tried to cut the workers' wages and the union called a general strike for the second time in August, 1932. This time, the workers were not as united as in 1931 and there were a number of strike-breakers in some of the Germiston factories. We organised pickets and did everything possible to prevent scabs from entering the factories. The pickets had to be outside the factories early in the morning, even before five a.m., as the employers were doing their utmost to bring in scabs.

The pickets did not use violence against them, but resorted to booing and singing uncomplimentary songs or pelting them with tomatoes and eggs. Later on, the bosses called in scores of police to break the strike. The police must have had instructions from Mr Pirow, who was then Minister of Justice, to handle the strikers without kid gloves and many workers were beaten up and arrested. On one occasion, one of the girl strikers standing outside one of the factories had her pockets filled with rotten eggs. One of the policemen came up to her and slapped her on the pockets, with disastrous consequences to her clothes. He then arrested her. I went up, got hold of the girl and tried to pull her away from the policeman, but suddenly I 'saw stars'. The policeman had slapped me violently across the face and, for a whole week, I proudly bore my badge of honour — a black eye.

One day, when there was a crowd of pickets standing outside one of the factories, about five or six mounted policemen rode up and told the workers to disperse. Before the workers had time to make up their minds what to do, one of the mounted policemen rode into the crowd and several of the girls were knocked down. There was a general commotion and some of the girls were severely injured. A few had to be taken to hospital and one of them suffered from an injured ankle for some years. The general treatment by the police of the girl strikers was shameful.

In the end the workers had to give in, and after about two months they returned to work with a cut of ten per cent in their wages. Many of them had lost their faith in the union, and the employers, taking advantage of the situation did everything in their power to discourage union activities. Many workers were paid off and there was a great deal of unemployment.

In 1934, I gave up the position of union organiser and went to work for a factory in Johannesburg. After about a year, I returned to work in Germiston. In 1936, I started to work for New York Clothing, where I was employed until 1951.

By 1936, the workers had forgotten their earlier defeat and the union once again began to make progress. For a year or two, I was quiet, then I started taking an active interest in union affairs again. For the last ten years, I have served on the Germiston branch committee, on the industiral council, the medical aid society and as a member of the central executive committee of the union.

In the last twenty years there has been a complete change for the better in our wages and conditions of work. My wages now are £5 4s. a week and I work a five-day week of forty hours. I get three weeks and six days paid holidays, as well as free medical attention and sick pay in case of illness. The small, overcrowded tin shanties of the earlier years have disappeared and today Germiston has a dozen large, modern factories, with cloakrooms and other amenities. But what is more important, perhaps, than any material improvements in our conditions, is the fact that we no longer feel like slaves, but like free men and women, and know that we have a strong union to depend on in time of need.

FOOTNOTES

1. For an analysis of the 'Reformer' attacks see: Dan O'Meara, 'White Trade Unionism, Political Power and Afrikaner Nationalism' *(SALB*, Vol. 1 No. 10).

For permission to publish these autobiographical sketches we are much obliged to the archives of the Garment Workers Union in Johannesburg.

SECTION 5

ORGANIZED LABOUR UNDER APARTHEID

INTRODUCTION

O'Meara has argued that the victory of 1948 by the Nationalist Party was the result of the reaction of Afrikaans workers, farmers and the petty bourgeoisie to the developments highlighted by the 1946 strike. What were these developments?

The 1940s represented a period of crisis for the State — the rapid proletarianization of Africans had led to industrial unrest culminating in the 1946 mine workers' strike[1] and an upsurge in African trade union activity. By the end of the war the Council for Non-European Trade Unions (CNETU) claimed a membership of 158,000 and 119 unions, covering more than 40% of the 390,000 Africans employed in commerce and industry. However, unrest was not confined to industry — transport boycotts and housing shortages had led to squatter movements. Some of the squatter movements, it was believed, were being manipulated by left wing political organizations.[2]

Faced by these challenges the state was divided. Commerce and industry were arguing for a more stable urban labour force, while the mining industry, with the possible exception of Anglo-American, wanted to continue migrant labour. The United Party government represented this contradictory group of mining and manufacturing interests and consequently its policy was ambivalent. This very ambivalence and indecisiveness appeared to further threaten the labour supplies of agriculture and did not soothe the fears of mining capital. Many examples could be given but we are concerned here with the field of labour. The recognition of African trade unions in the 1947 Industrial (Natives) Bill comprised part of the state's generally indecisive position in the 1940s. In 1947, the Smuts government introduced this bill which, if enacted, would have accorded some formal recognition to African unions, while providing separate arbitration for Africans and excluding them from the Industrial Council system. Strikes were outlawed. Because of opposition to the bill it was never brought before Parliament. As Lewis has argued, 'under these conditions the state was too weak to smash the organizations of the dominated classes, and, similarly, it was too weak to appease the dominated classes. So instead it offered a measure which was, of itself, incapable of destroying the organizations of the working classes, but which was similarly incapable of commanding their support. Simultaneously, within the power bloc, industry was incapable of representing its interests as the general interest of the dominant classes — the state was thus forced to offer an alternative solution which drew only lukewarm support from industry, and no support at all from other fractions within the power bloc.'[3]

The 1948 Nationalist government scrapped the Industrial Conciliation (Native) Bill, and appointed the Botha Commission to examine African trade unions. This commission acknowledged frankly that if Africans were allowed to secure parity of bargaining power, they could not be restricted indefinitely to unskilled or even semi-skilled work, but would gradually penetrate the skilled occupations. Thus it argued that nothing less than white supremacy was at stake. For the 'logical result of the proposal to include them in the category of employee was 'solidarity' of labour irrespective of race in the long run, and the complete racial and political equality of all races.' Nevertheless the commission proposed, when its recommendations were eventually made in 1951, that African trade unions should be recognized and given bargaining rights. Although stringent conditions were laid down for recognition and the right to strike was outlawed, the proposal aroused considerable governmental hostility and was turned down. By the time parliament was debating the recommendations of the commission in 1952 and 1953, conditions had changed — the state was now on the offensive and this was reflected in the nature of the (Native) Settlements of Dispute Act of 1953.

In drafting legislation, the government had to choose one of three courses: it could amend the Industrial Conciliation Act to include Africans as employees; it could set up separate legislation for African trade unions; or it could provide completely separate 'representation' for African workers in a different system. The opposition wanted the first solution, Botha wanted the second and the government chose the third. In introducing the Bill in Parliament in 1953, the Minister of Labour, Ben Schoeman, stated the government's position. 'My proposals are the following: first of all we do not prohibit Native trade unions. Consequently the question of freedom of association does not arise. They will still have the right to associate, they will have the right to form their own trade unions. We do not prohibit it. But what we do in this Bill is to create machinery which will ensure justice to Native workers, to enable them to channel their grievances and bring them to the attention of the authorities — or some alternative machinery. If that machinery is effective and successful, the Natives will have no interest in trade unions and trade unions will probably die a natural death.'[4] The final legislation set up a three-tiered system. A system of 'inplant' bargaining through works committees elected by workers constituted the first tier. A second tier of regional labour committees was to be staffed by labour officers employed by the Department of Labour. The third tier was the Central Native Labour Board. In the initial proposal no provision was made for works' committees; these were included as an amendment sponsored by the United Party Opposition and accepted by the government in return for the U.P.'s support fo the Bill. Strikes were to be outlawed in terms of the Bill.

This rejection of African trade unions, Lewis argues, was the chosen course of an 'offensive' state — i.e. a state prepared to act more decisively, particularly in response to the agricultural fraction of capital, than the United Party Government of pre-1948. He adds that the state hardened its line against the trade unions because the dominated classes had gone onto the offensive. The most dramatic example of this was the 1952 Defiance Campaign — a campaign of passive resistance against certain 'unjust laws' launched by the African National Congress, the most prominent of the black organisations. The defiance campaign was the culmination of a change in the strategy of the A.N.C., signalled by the establishment of the Youth League in 1943, the adjournment of the Native Representative Council in 1946, and the Programme of Action in 1949 (which envisaged various campaigns including strikes, 'stay-at-homes', and boycotts of segregated facilities and bodies like the N.R.C.). The fact that the CNETU linked up with this campaign provided the government with its overriding argument against recognising African trade unions, i.e. that trade unions would become 'political' if extended to Africans. However, the crucial fact that the African unions had declined over this period needs to be added to any attempt to explain the changing response of the state to African unions.[5] Against this background we can consider, in more detail, the government's policy towards organized labour and opposition to the policy in the 1950s.[6]

Government labour policy covered three main issues: racial separation of trade unions; separate representation of African workers; and job reservation. We have dealt with the emergence of

211

separate representation in 1953 in our description of the Native Settlement of Disputes Act. The works committee was intended as the 'front line' channel of communication between African workers and employers. It seems clear that neither African workers nor their employers (nor even, perhaps, the government) set any great store by them, judging from the first twenty years. For example, only 7 committees existed from 1953 to 1957, ten in 1960, nineteen in 1961 and 24 in 1965. It is surely conclusive that when the strikes broke out in Durban in 1973, this last total was unchanged.[7]

It was on the issues of racial separation of trade unions and job reservation that most of the conflict in the early '50s took place, and the Industrial Conciliation Act was the legal nub of the disputes. A new Industrial Conciliation Bill was presented in 1954 and passed after much controversy in 1956. It contained three provisions.

Firstly no further 'mixed unions' were to be registered. Should half of the white or coloured members of an existing 'mixed union' wish to break away and establish a separate union along racial lines, they could apply for registration. (It was on the strength of this permission that NUCAW broke away from the NUDW in 1966.) Secondly any mixed union which continued to exist was required to have separate branches and hold separate meetings for its white and coloured members, while its national executive could consist only of whites. Except for the white office bearers no one could attend a branch meeting other than his own. (The Minister might grant exemption, as he did for example in the case of the Garment Workers' Union.) Thirdly job reservation machinery was extended to make it possible for specified types of work to be reserved for persons of a defined racial group. Provisions were made for an industrial tribunal, one of the functions of which was to make recommendations in regard to job reservation.

What effect did the Industrial Conciliation Act have on trade unionism? It caused a major realignment. In 1953, when information about the government's planned amendments to the Industrial Conciliation Act was released, many trade unionists became concerned about the possible threat to the collective bargaining system. Two members of the Boiler Makers' Society took the lead in setting up the trade union Unity Committee. It was composed of leading members of the Trades and Labour Council, the Federation of Trade Unions, the Western Province Federation of Labour Unions and the Amalgamated Engineering Union, all serving in their individual capacities. The co-ordinating Council (the right wing co-ordinating committee, and forerunner to the S.A. Confederation of Labour) was unwilling to participate because of the attitude of the Unity Committee to mixed unions. The Council of Non-European Trade Unions was not invited.

Ensor argues in this section that over the next two years the conflict with the state centred on this act, and in particular the debate on mixed unions, was basically about the method to be used in protecting the white workers. The mixed unions (mainly located in the manufacturing industry) believed that the only guarantees of protection were a closed shop and the 'rate for the job'. The conservative wing of white trade unions, consisting largely of mine workers and state employees, relied on the state for protection. Based on these differences in approach to the common objective of protecting the white workers — the unionist strategy versus the separationist strategy — different policies were adopted. While this analysis of opposition to the government's policy towards organised labour stresses its 'white protectionist' nature, Lewis on the other hand, stresses the historic dominance of craft unions and the lack of organisation of unskilled workers. He concludes, in the final contribution to this volume, that 'there are other factors which drive a wedge between coloured workers of the Western Cape (besides race) and which have given rise to a unionised skilled workforce and an unorganised unskilled mass — interestingly, many of the unions which vehemently opposed the racial separation of unions in 1956 have not attempted to repair the rift between their members and the unorganised, but eligible, unskilled workers.'

The Unity Committee had numerous meetings with the Minister of Labour to express opposition to the Industrial Conciliation Bill. Feeling that greater solidarity was necessary, in 1954 it founded TUCSA (Trade Union Council of South Africa). To woo conservative white members they excluded African unions, but decided to establish a liaison committee to maintain contact with them. It was out of this liaison committee that FOFATUSA (Federation of Free African Trade Unions of South Africa) was to emerge in the late 1950s. FOFATUSA had close links with TUCSA, rejected any association with the Congress movement and had 'africanist' sympathies. When TUCSA opened its membership to Africans in 1962 most of the FOFATUSA unions joined that organisation. Why did TUCSA (to this degree) support African trade unions? Ensor has argued that their motive was to protect white workers by bringing Africans into the collective bargaining system, thus preventing the

213

undercutting of their wage levels. Furthermore, they argued that 'suppression would instil in workers a desire for political power'; their aim was, therefore, to pre-empt militant independent African unions.

Another main protagonist emerged from the realignment which followed the Industrial Conciliation Act. To its strategy we now turn. ✗ SACTU (South African Congress of Trade Unions) was set up in 1954 specifically to oppose TUCSA's strategy, and articulated from its inception a 'political' conception of trade unionism. Thus SACTU emerged in opposition to TUCSA and posed a threat to it because SACTU rejected control of African trade unions by registered unions, and embarked on a programme of political mobilization of the African working class by linking up with the Congress movement. Ensor concludes by arguing that while the non-recognition of African trade unions drives them into the realm of politics, this same non-recognition assures that their political activity can be effectively contained by the repressive apparatus of the state. In fact by the early 1960s much of SACTU's leadership had been banned and by 1965 it ✗ had ceased publicly to operate within S.A.

The 1950s close with a major realignment within organised labour. Among registered trade unions we see TUCSA pursuing a 'unionist' strategy favouring parallel unions as a preliminary step towards an amendment of the Industrial Conciliation Act. On the other hand, we see the emergence of the S.A. Confederation of Labour following the 'separationist' strategy and articulating the traditional call of the white worker for job protection. Among unregistered trade unions the two main protagonists, FOFATUSA and SACTU, represent two different strategies towards trade unionism in general and the African worker in particular. The former strategy is a more conventional trade union approach; the latter attempts to link up the trade union struggle with the movement for national liberation.

FOOTNOTES

1. D. O'Meara, 'The 1946 Mine Workers' Strike', *Journal of Commonwealth and Comparative Politics* (1975).
2. David Lewis, 'African Trade Unions and the South African State, 1947-1953', unpublished paper, Cape Town, p. 11.
3. Lewis, ibid., p. 27.
4. Quoted by Webster, 'Management's Counter Offensive', *SALB* Vol. 2, No. 3.
5. L. Welcher, 'African Trade Unions and the State, 1939-1943' unpublished Honours dissertation, University of the Witwatersrand (1978).
6. An analysis of labour policy in general, as distinct from the Government policy towards

organised labour, would have to include the extension of influx control and the Labour Bureau system after 1948, where the main aim was to ensure an adequate labour supply to low wage-sectors such as agriculture. See R de Villiers, 'The Johannesburg Municipality and Apartheid (1948-1961). Unpublished Honours dissertation, University of Witwatersrand (1978).

7.   Dudley Horner, 'African Labour Representation', *SALB* Vol. 2, Nos. 9 and 10.
8.   Ensor.

TUCSA'S RELATIONSHIP WITH AFRICAN TRADE UNIONS — AN ATTEMPT AT CONTROL 1954-1962

LINDA ENSOR

The Policy of Tucsa

Why did TUCSA support the recognition of African trade unions? TUCSA's policy towards African trade unions was an extension of the separation between the economic and political struggles embodied in mixed trade unions. White skilled workers allied themselves economically with the Coloured and Indian skilled and semi-skilled workers, while politically they supported the maintenance of 'white' domination. Mixed trade unionism was never used to struggle for the political rights of Coloured and Indian workers — instead it contained the struggle. This same policy was applied in relation to African trade unions — incorporation in the economic struggle would contain the political struggle by institutionalising conflict.

> Trade unions should be willing to guide the Native along the path of responsible trade unionism without endangering their own standards of leadership. . . . Suppression will instil in workers the desire for political power to alleviate their lot. That is a possibility which we cannot contemplate without grave misgivings if the European people wish to remain in Africa.[1]
>
> Our function must be to prevent their exploitation for cheap labour purposes and the frustration of their ambitions for a better working life. If we continue to withhold trade union organisation to improve themselves, they will turn to political action to overcome their frustration.[2]

That is, by incorporating trade unions into institutions of collective bargaining, the growth of a militant independent black trade union movement could be pre-empted. The method of protection embodied in mixed trade unions, namely the incorporation of Indian and Coloured workers to prevent conflict and competition, was the basis for the assumption that the institutionalisation of conflict was

216

superior to repression as a means of containing the political struggle.
This assumption necessitated that TUCSA adopt a strategy of control over this institutionalisation, to deal with the economic threat posed by *economically* militant and independent African trade unions.

> The Unity Committee[3] point of view is that if we recognise the right of Africans to establish trade unions, then we are immediately accepting responsibility, and we should exercise the responsibility in terms of the Constitution. We must either take the line that we are totally opposed to organising Africans, or the line that we must be in a position to assist them if they desire — otherwise we will be held responsible as a registered trade union movement for having agreed only in principle to Africans having their own unions.[4]

Interpreting the use of moral terms such as 'responsibility', 'assistance' and 'principles', as rationalisations for the interest in control it is clear that the differences between the State refusing to recognise, and TUCSA supporting the recognition of, African trade unions were differences in methods with the common aim of reproducing the racially exclusive political structures which guaranteed the economic position of white workers. The interest in the political and economic domination of the African working class was articulated in a strategy of raising African wages. Political discontent must be diffused by economic prosperity.

> We also unhesitatingly state that the Government should immediately legislate for a minimum wage applicable to all workers including Africans. Abundant evidence is already available as to what constitutes the present poverty datum line and long term investigations are necessary in order to arrive at the minimum wage required to lift the population out of the slough of desperate need and hunger. This above all would remove what we believe to be one of the main basic causes of unrest and dissatisfaction, especially among Africans. We believe that in the present situation (after Sharpeville — I. E) the raising of wages of African workers is one which demands the most urgent attention of the State.[5]

Raising African wages was also motivated by economic interests. Firstly the wages of skilled and semi-skilled workers are determined relative to those of unskilled workers, so that a rise in the wages of the latter would provide the unions with a bargaining weapon to increase the wages of the former — that is, the maintenance of wage differentials. Secondly, the interest in African wages was motivated by an interest in maintaining the rate for the job, which in turn gave rise to an interest in determining African wages. TUCSA's objection to the Bantu Labour (Settlement of Disputes) Act of 1953 was that one of its provisions was that a Wage Order governing wages and conditions of Africans automatically replaced those established by the Industrial

Council Agreements governing workers in a registered trade union in respect of the same occupations as those engaged in by Africans. This was regarded as a violation of the collective bargaining rights of registered trade unions which by allowing undercutting of wages would prove economically disastrous for Whites, Coloureds and Indians.[6] Thus to retain control meant submitting representations to the Wage Board, which TUCSA frequently did. Another provision of the Act was that certain areas could be excluded from the jurisdiction of the determination. This created acute problems for workers in the clothing industry. The Tomlinson Commission Report recommended the decentralisation of the clothing industry to the border areas. In the absence of a national minimum wage, factories moved to the low wage border areas to cut labour costs, thus threatening the level of wages and employment of workers in the urban areas. Thirdly, the interest in increasing African wages arose out of an underconsumptionist model of recession employed by TUCSA. An increase in African wages would enlarge the internal market, generate economic growth and thus result in an improvement for all workers.

The interest in controlling African trade unions, however, conflicted with another interest of mixed trade unions to incorporate predominantly white artisan trade unions into a coordinating body. In 1954, TUCSA was constituted on a basis of a compromise between these interests. That is, it excluded African trade unions but incorporated liaison with them as a clause of its constitution. The form of control adopted was liaison with an African body of trade unions which could 'consult' the TUCSA executive committee on matters affecting African workers. Rutherford, the first President of TUCSA, made several statements in which he emphasised that African unions had not been abandoned as TUCSA intended to serve their interests.[7] He also said that liaison was necessary not for the sake of unity but to ensure that African unions were organised 'responsibly'.

SACTU — The Subversion of Attempts at Control

This grand plan proposed by TUCSA was rejected by those unions, registered and unregistered, who opposed the exclusion of African trade unions from TUCSA, and by the independent CNETU.[8] In 1954 TUCSA made great attempts to canvass support amongst African trade union leaders for the idea and 'in order to gain such support the bait of "substantial financial support" (was) offered.' Maeka, President of CNETU, stated that African trade unions would not be satisfied with an inferior 'advisory board' status in the trade union movement, while the editorial in *Textile Unity* commented that 'not one free and independent African trade union will accept this childish attempt to dress the "wolf" of apartheid in "sheep's" clothing of parallel lines.'

Before continuing to discuss the relationship between SACTU and this liaison committee, it is necessary to digress to discuss the alternative strategies pursued by African trade unions in the period.

SACTU's strategy was one of 'political trade unionism' which Feit[9] defines as the harnessing of the workers' demands for economic amelioration to a political cause. The president of SACTU of the Fifties, expounded on its goals thus:

> SACTU recognised that the organising of this great mass of (African) workers was linked inextricably with their struggle for political rights and liberation from all oppressive laws. Every attempt by the (African) workers to organise themselves was hampered by general legislation affecting their right of movement, domicile and political representation. Every effort for higher wages, better working conditions or reinstatement of unjustly dismissed fellow workers was immediately met by the full force of the State.[9]

On the basis of this policy it joined the Congress Alliance, mobilising workers in support of its campaigns against the pass laws, white elections, for a national minimum wage, etc.

FOFATUSA's (Federation of Free African Trade Unions of South Africa) policy on the other hand was one of no politics in trade unions. Trade unions were solely for the purpose of achieving economic gains for the workers. What was the structural basis for these different strategies, and what were the determining factors which resulted in their being adopted? The argument presented here is that from the Fifties African trade unions could only be economically effective if subordinate to the registered trade unions, and that, if this subordination is rejected, the only alternative is an involvement in the political struggle.

Given the legal non-recognition of African trade unions, the intransigence of employers against cooperating with them, and the intervention of the State when strikes are employed to demand recognition, the only way of influencing employers to win concessions, is by means of the influence of the registered trade unions. The industrial councils in most industries determine wages for African workers, and by acting as a pressure on the registered union, the African union can win real, though limited economic gains for its members; for example, wage increases, deductions for benefit

219

schemes, union access to factories, employer cooperation in dealing with complaints etc. Without this influence, it is difficult for the African union to win economic gains, membership declines as a result of dissatisfaction and disillusionment, and the union is unable to maintain itself financially. The alternative is to engage in political action aimed at overthrowing the State. TUCSA realised that this is what it had to offer African trade unions, as opposed to SACTU.

I am arguing that there is an element of room, a defined area which allows certain economic demands made by African workers to be met without threatening the position of white workers. The State often claims that African trade unions are embryonic organisations for political mobilisation, that is that they are an attempt to create an economic basis for working class organisations which will in future be used for political purposes. If this were the case such a strategy would not prove successful because the requirements for a future political role, namely independence from registered trade unions, will inhibit the development of a strong power base, and thus make impossible a future political role. In any case, *any* involvement in politics will immediately mean the termination of economic functions.

The strongest African trade unions, in terms of membership, financial soundness and limited economic gains won, are those which exist in close cooperation with the registered union. However, they are subordinate in that their economic demands have to be reconciled with those of the registered union, and in that the price for this cooperation is a non-involvement in the political struggle which would threaten the interests of white workers, and the relationship of cooperation with employers. So, for example, the executives of the five African trade unions which joined TUCSA's liaison committee decided:

> that as these five unions are bound by industrial council agreements, and as the demand for better wages had nothing to do with the forthcoming General Election, that the members of these unions should ignore the appeal for the 'Stay-at-home' protest. An appeal was also made to employers to treat sympathetically those workers who may fail to report to work through intimidation.[10]

They felt that they should honour the agreement with employers, and that wage demands could only be achieved by responsible trade unions negotiating through 'proper' channels.

The State's policy of not recognising African unions denies them the ability to establish a consolidated power base from which to

220

engage in the political struggle. Thus while their non-recognition drives them into the realm of politics, this same non-recognition ensures that their political activity can be effectively contained by the repressive apparatus of the State. TUCSA's policy, on the other hand, is one of institutionalising conflict.

Given the political interests of the white working class and the capitalist class, the trade union strategies of performing trade union functions in cooperation with registered trade unions and employers, and of engaging in a political struggle are mutually exclusive. Those cases where this was not so, that is where registered unions joined SACTU (the Food and Canning Workers' Union, the Textile Workers' Industrial Union and the Laundering Cleaning and Dyeing Workers' Union) are unique in that the registered union represented Coloured and Indian workers, and because these workers were employed in labour-intensive industries as semi-skilled operatives, and thus did not have the same economic interest in an alliance with white workers as those Coloured and Indian workers in mixed unions. These workers, by allying themselves with skilled white workers, could use their superior bargaining strength to further their interests. It is also noteworthy that the best established unions in SACTU were those which retained close links with the registered union.

Thus while State policy towards African trade unions together with the political interests of white workers and employers determined the kinds of strategy possible, and their mutually exclusive nature, the course that was actually adopted depended on the historical relationship with the registered trade unions, and with the national liberation movement. All those unions in the liaison committee and, later, FOFATUSA, were parallel unions of registered unions. The refusal to become politically engaged was the price of their pursuing trade union functions in cooperation with employers and the registered union. This subordination was necessary to win limited economic gains. SACTU, on the other hand, was established because of a rejection of the subordinate position offered to African trade unions in the trade union movement.

For this analysis to be acceptable it is minimally necessary that it can account for the growth of an independent, militant African trade union movement in the Forties. By 1945 CNETU claimed 119 affiliates with a total membership of 158 000. Trade union pressure had resulted in significant wage increases, and for the only time in South African history, the wage gap between white and black workers diminished. It is also the only time that a strong, independent African

221

trade union movement made significant economic gains. These gains were made possible by the growth of secondary industry during this period, as well as by the labour shortages. One of the most obvious reasons is that these unions had a right to demand Wage Board investigations in their industries, whereas after 1955 this obligation on the Wage Board was removed from the provisions of the Wage Act, thus depriving African trade unions of an independent access to the determination of African wages. In 1953, the Bantu Labour (Settlement of Disputes) Act provided for the appointment of white Bantu labour officers to act as intermediaries between African workers and their employers, and to represent the interests of African workers on the Wage Board. Thus the State attempted to establish industrial conciliation machinery which specifically excluded any participation by African trade unions. This is, of course, an insufficient explanation as it ignores the change in State policies and the reason behind these after 1948. Though relevant, this is beyond the scope of this essay. What is relevant is that in the Fifties, unlike the Forties, African trade unions were dependent on registered trade unions for an access to the institutions determining African wages.

The Relationship between TUCSA and SACTU

SACTU was established as an alternative to the subordinate position which TUCSA offered African trade unions in the trade union movement. The early Fifties had witnessed a docility on the part of the registered trade unions to State attacks on African trade unions. Leaders were banned, the State enacted the Bantu Labour (Settlement of Disputes) Act which excluded African trade unions from institutions determining African wages. In addition, a militant African national liberation movement was growing which provided an ideology of racial equality. The exclusion of African trade unions from TUCSA, the failure of registered trade unions to actively oppose the State, and the collaboration between the so-called 'left' trade unions in the TLC with the 'right' Federation of Trade Unions and the Mineworkers' Union demonstrated the conflict of interests between white workers and African workers. The myth of a non-racial working class solidarity was revealed as such.

During 1954, when the Unity Committee was conducting its protests against the Industrial Conciliation Act, all cooperation with CNETU was rejected. The exclusion of African trade unions from the campaign to resist the Industrial Conciliation Act, and the moderate nature of the protests made, were attacked by both CNETU and those trade unions with the TLC which opposed this exclusion.

> We are concerned that in order to preserve the existence of free and independent trade unions, united and rigorous action on the part of all organised labour is needed, irrespective of the colour or origin of the workers.

CNETU organised a conference of African unions in opposition to the Unity Conference in May 1954, in order to devise means of effectively resisting the proposed Act. A Workers' Action Council was established in the belief that only united action could prevent the Nationalist Government from destroying the trade unions.

> The formation of the Workers' Action Council had become imperative because the Unity Committee was not prepared to fight for the preservation of trade union rights for all workers, or for an amendment of the Industrial Conciliation Act to allow for the recognition of African workers as employees in terms of the Act.

It was consciously conceived of as a weapon to defeat the Nationalist Government whose policies were seen as destroying the trade unions. The registered trade unions were seen as expediently compromising principles to serve their own interests by collaborating with the right wing.

In March 1955, a conference of 33 unions, consisting of 14 unions who had opposed the exclusion of African unions from TUCSA and 19 affiliated to CNETU, formed SACTU. Thus SACTU emerged in opposition to TUCSA and posed a threat to it because SACTU rejected control of African trade unions by registered unions, and embarked on a programme of the political mobilisation of the African working class.

SACTU perceived TUCSA as being in support of the State and not representative of the interests of African workers. However, despite the ideological attacks on TUCSA at international forums, and despite the conflict over the allegiances of African trade unions, both individual unions in SACTU and SACTU itself made repeated requests for TUCSA's assistance in using its influence in various matters. (This supports the analysis outlined above.) The Trade Union Coordinating Committee established by the unions from TUCSA, in order to prepare a constitution for a new coordinating body (SACTU), outlined what was to be an aspect of SACTU's policy towards TUCSA:

> The desire of the committee is complete unity in the trade union movement, and it will endeavour to cooperate with any other body, which though differing on constitutional principles, is pledged to the same end. There is a great measure of

223

common interest between the trade unions associated with this movement and those participating in the work of the Trade Union Council, and it is sincerely hoped that close cooperation will be achieved on matters which affect all sections.

The conflict between the two trade union strategies of the period was not only embodied in FOFATUSA and SACTU respectively, but also within SACTU's strategy itself. That they were mutually exclusive is demonstrated by TUCSA's refusal to cooperate with SACTU. The following instances are cited to give an indication of its attitude.

In 1957, the local committee of SACTU approached the Western Province Area Division of TUCSA for a joint meeting to discuss a statement by the Minister of Labour that he had instructed the Industrial Tribunal to investigate all industries in the Cape affecting skilled and semi-skilled workers with a view to job reservation. The TUCSA National Executive Committee (NEC) instructed the area division that 'we are not prepared to meet the Congress of Trade Unions.'[11]

In 1956 SACTU invited TUCSA to be co-convenors of a conference to discuss the Industrial Conciliation Act. TUCSA refused. It also refused the invitation by the National Union of Distributive Workers to address its 1957 Annual Conference as SACTU had also been invited. It refused SACTU's appeal for support for the Treason Trials Defence Fund, and in response to an appeal for support in a protest against the bannings of Leon Levy (President of SACTU) and Leslie Massina (General Secretary), it was decided that 'as these persons continuously opposed the TUCSA, no response be made to their appeal to assist them.'[12]

In the Report of Proceedings of the 1956 Annual Conference, the NEC reported on the widespread police raids on the houses of individuals and organisations including trade unions, and on the policy decision of the management committee of TUCSA 'that it would only take up such cases if *affiliated* unions of which such persons are members or officials so request.'[13]

On economic issues, SACTU attempted to solicit TUCSA's support for the £1 a day campaign; again no response. In 1957 the General Secretary reported that a number of African trade union officials had been to see her to obtain some assistance in making representations to the Wage Board in its investigations into the employment of unskilled labour in the Witwatersrand and Pretoria areas. It was decided 'that such assistance could only be given where they have no connection with the Congress of Trade Unions.'[14]

Finally, in 1962, SACTU, admitting the necessity for cooperation with registered trade unions which negotiated wages for African workers, requested TUCSA 'to ask your unions to submit demands at all times for a *minimum* wage of not less than R2,00 per day in all industries.'[15]

These are merely a few examples of the many occasions where SACTU requested assistance or cooperation from TUCSA, which were merely noted without discussion or replies.

Not quite the same attitude was adopted to registered trade unions within SACTU and to the National Union of Distributive Workers which, although not affiliated to either SACTU or TUCSA, retained close links with both. Here the problem was one of competition between the coordinating bodies to retain and attract unions to affiliate, thus adding to its strength. For example, the Food and Canning Workers' Union made frequent requests for TUCSA's assistance. In 1958 it asked TUCSA, via its representatives on the Unemployment Insurance Fund, to support its application for the reinclusion of certain areas under the jurisdiction of the Fund. Because of its representation on public bodies and its greater strength, TUCSA had more influence than SACTU. When discussing these requests, the position held by some NEC members was that:

> We should advise them that we cannot deal with the matters that they continually write to us about, since they are not affiliates of the Council and, although we are naturally interested in the workers as a whole, our first obligation is to our affiliates.

The position of the General Secretary however prevailed that 'we would rather have them write to us than to another federation on these matters.'[16]

The attempt was made to entice the registered unions in SACTU into TUCSA by offering the kind of assistance that SACTU was unable to offer. The same attempt was made in relation to the National Union of Distributive Workers, which remained unaffiliated until the early Sixties when it joined TUCSA.

Another aspect of this conflict was a conflict over the Coloured and Indian workers in mixed trade unions. TUCSA's fear was that they would be enticed out of mixed unions to join SACTU. While no evidence exists for this actually occurring, an ideological battle between SACTU and TUCSA was sufficient to stir the fears of the latter, especially since the provisions of the Industrial Conciliation Act, which required the separation of mixed trade unions into racial

225

branches under the control of white executives, was bound to cause resentment amongst Coloured and Indian workers. That there was a real conflict is demonstrated by the fact that a meeting was held during the 1959 Annual Conference of TUCSA, of Coloured and Indian trade unionists to discuss establishing a separate coordinating body.[17] When the TLC was dissolved, those unions opposing the decision warned that in future the white workers would do to Coloureds and Indians what had been done to African workers — their interests would be expediently abandoned. The Food and Canning Workers' Union publicly attacked TUCSA for wanting to dominate Coloured and Indian workers by supporting white executives in mixed unions.[18] In reply to a letter from the National Union of Distributive Workers urging TUCSA to accept SACTU's invitation to co-sponsor a conference on the Industrial Conciliation Act, the General Secretary replied:

> I have to advise you that my NEC is of the opinion that no good purpose could be served by taking the steps suggested by your Union, particularly in view of SACTU's policy regarding the Apartheid provisions of the Act. A number of public statements by prominent members of SACTU indicate that SACTU favours breaking away of Coloured workers from their mixed trade unions.[19]

SACTU's rejection of a subordinate position for African trade unions in the trade union movement was extended to incorporate a rejection of the subordination of Coloured and Indian workers in mixed trade unions. Given the vital importance of mixed unions in the protection of the interests of white workers, urging Coloured and Indian workers out of these unions struck at the core of the interests represented by TUCSA.

> We now have a paradoxical situation of the Government and the left wing elements sponsoring complete apartheid in the trade union movement. I presume the left wing elements hope to prove that the white worker is dependent on the non-white worker for a reasonable standard of living. Actually of course the two groups of workers, white and non-white, are completely interdependent and fostering competition between them by means of apartheid in trade unions can only result in both of them paying the penalty of a reduced standard of living in the end.
>   I strongly urge the non-white workers not to be misled by people who have always one object in regard to everything they tackle — an ideological object. The only salvation of all workers lies in complete unity and loyalty to each other.[20]

With respect to African trade unions, TUCSA's interest in their control resulted in its attempts to attract them away from SACTU and in its attempt to appear as the sole representative of African workers.

SACTU and the Liaison Committee

SACTU correctly perceived the nature of TUCSA's liaison committee for African trade unions:

> Recently SACTU had had to face a new threat — from the Trade Union Council. The TUC had ignored every approach from SACTU for cooperation on immediate issues. It bars African unions from membership. Yet, in order to woo African unions away from SACTU, it has now decided that, though it will not admit African unions through the front door, it will let them through the kitchen door to the so-called "Liaison Committee". We wonder what sort of African trade unionists are those which will prefer membership of the "Kitchen door Liaison Committee" to the free and equal membership of SACTU?[21]

When TUCSA was informed of the formation of SACTU, it was decided that contact be made immediately with CNETU before the inaugural conference of SACTU to prove 'that TUCSA was honest in its desire for liaison'.[22] It became an urgent matter to establish the Liaison Committee in opposition to SACTU. It was agreed that a sub-committee be formed to establish it and that affiliated unions be requested to encourage African unions in their industries to participate.[23] Accordingly, the General Secretary wrote to the area divisions and to individual unions urging them to encourage African unions to participate in the Liaison Committee, as opposed to SACTU. A letter to the Mechanics Union's Joint Executive noting the existence of a Metal Workers' Union in Cape Town which was not affiliated to SACTU, and of a Transvaal Iron, Steel and Metal Workers' Union, which was an affiliate, suggests:

> that with the assistance of your affiliates it could be possible to exercise sufficient influence to obtain the cooperation of African workers in the Metal trade so that their trade union will eventually participate in the Liaison Committee with this Council in preference to remaining affiliates of the Congress of Trade Unions.
>
> There can surely be no doubt that the African unions in your industries would welcome assistance from your unions, in preference to the assistance of persons who have no knowledge or experience of your industries and some of whom are more concerned with purely political issues than with establishing trade unions capable of protecting their members on a proper trade unions basis, and following a policy which would help to protect the established standards of your members.[24]

Once again it is clear that 'assistance' was a means of subordinating African trade unions, preventing their involvement in political action, and how this control served the interests of white workers.

The first meeting of the Liaison Committee was held on the 8th August 1956, at which the issue of permanent participation in the Committee was postponed since some of the unions present were still

227

affiliated to SACTU and had to discuss the matter with their executives. They expressed, however, a desire for liaison and disappointment in SACTU's failure to perform the functions of a trade union coordinating body. The following unions agreed to participate: the African Motor Industry Workers' Union, the African Tobacco Workers' Union, and, later, when it had disaffiliated from SACTU, the Garment Workers' Union of African Women — all unions with close cooperation with registered trade unions. It did not meet very often between 1956 and 1959, and little was done by TUCSA to assist in the organisation of African workers. The main intention behind its formation was to split the African trade union movement, and to allow TUCSA to claim internationally that it was representative of African workers.

In 1959, the unions in the Liaison Committee established FOFATUSA with the assistance of TUCSA and the ICFTU. It had collapsed by 1965 as a result of TUCSA's decision in 1962 to allow African trade unions to affiliate.

The Conflict over the Representation of African Workers

The conflict over representation was one which had economic, ideological, and political foundations, and involved the question of who was to claim to represent the interests of African workers who were not unionised. The economic and political interests in participating in the determination of African wages have been outlined above. Ideologically it was necessary to appear to represent the interests of African workers, to render acceptable the attempt to exercise control. Insofar as TUCSA was able to achieve real economic benefits for African workers, the ideological appearance had some reality.

On numerous occasions the NEC stressed that TUCSA should be seen to be taking the initiative in regard to the interests of African workers, and that this be extensively publicised both in South Africa and abroad. To justify the control of job advancement and wage increases of African workers, it was necessary that TUCSA be seen as the representative of their interests. This of course conflicted with SACTU's claims. So, for example, having refused to support SACTU's national minimum wage campaign which began in 1957, TUCSA itself embarked on a similar campaign in 1958, and in 1960 noted with approval SACTU's support for *its* policy.

Another way in which this operated was the intervention of TUCSA unions in strikes involving African workers whom they would claim to represent. One interesting example where this resulted in a conflict with SACTU was the strike at Langeberg Kooperasie Beperk, an Afrikaner capitalised company in the food industry in Port Elizabeth. The State declared the food and canning industry an essential industry on 25th September 1959, which meant that strikes were prohibited. On the 12th October, the President of the African Food and Canning Workers' Union, Elizabeth Mafeking, was served with a banishment order, after which she fled to Basutoland.[25] Simultaneously, the period of the Conciliation Board Agreement between the Food and Canning Workers' Union and the Langeberg Kooperasie Beperk came to an end, and the company decided to reduce wages from agreement rates to wage determination rates which meant a reduction of at least 8s for the majority of workers. On the 7th December the workers came out on strike in protest against the pay reduction despite the prohibition of strikes in the industry. The company returned to the agreement rates on the 13th February 1960.

The President of TUCSA sent a telegram of protest to the Managing Director and the Minister of Labour. The Eastern Province Area Division also intervened though its precise role is not clear. SACTU officials told them 'to mind their own business'.[26] Unlike other instances when SACTU had sought TUCSA's assistance, TUCSA's policy in this case was that since it was a matter of reduction of wages, it was TUCSA's concern, no matter what the affiliation of the union involved.

The dispute continued because SACTU threatened to sue TUCSA for defamation if it did not publicly apologise for including in its Report of Proceedings of the 1961 Conference a report from the Eastern Province Area Division, which stated under the title 'Intervention of SACTU':

> One of the major problems that faces this Area Division is that whenever there is an industrial dispute the S.A. Congress of Trade Unions rushes to the press and gives the impression that they have the support of the bulk of the workers. In many cases this is far from the truth. The Congress usually succeeds in clouding the issue and misleading the workers, bringing politics into industrial disputes. Cases in point are the strike in the Food and Canning Industry and the dispute in the Transport Services for Africans to New Brighton. In both cases, the workers were encouraged to strike but were left in the lurch in the end with the result that outside bodies had to act as mediators to bring the parties together.

Apologies were duly made by TUCSA.

Conclusion

Given the structural limitations imposed on the success of SACTU's strategy, given TUCSA's and the registered unions' refusal to cooperate, SACTU was not able to achieve any substantial concrete gains. By 1965 it had disintegrated as a result of bannings and police intervention. It did, however, apart from other possible undetectable achievements, force TUCSA to jettison its interest in an alliance with the right wing and pursue its policy of attempting to control African trade unions more vigorously.

FOOTNOTES

1. *Sunday Times,* 29/5/55, statement by TUCSA.
2. *The Star,* 30/5/55, statement by Rutherford, President of TUCSA.
3. In 1953, when information about the government's planned amendments to the Industrial Conciliation Act was released, many trade unionists were concerned about the possible threat to the collective bargaining system. Two members of the Boilermakers' Society took the lead in setting up a trade union *Unity Committee.* It was composed of leading members of the Trades and Labour Council, the Federation of Labour Unions and Amalgamated Engineering Union, all serving in their individual capacities. The Co-ordinating Council (right wing) was unwilling to participate because of the attitude of the rest to mixed unions. The Council of Non-European trade unions was not invited.

    I would argue that this conflict with the Government over this Act, and particularly the attack on the mixed trade unions, was over the method of protecting the white worker. The mixed trade unions believed that the only guarantee for ensuring protection was by means of a closed shop and the rate for the job. They were largely in manufacturing industry.

    The conservative wing of white trade unionism consisted largely of mine-workers and state employees, and they relied for forms of protection solely on the state. Based on these differences between forms of protection, different policies towards African trade unions were adopted. So the divergences between the so-called 'right' and 'left' of the registered trade union movement were based on different policies towards the protection of white workers.
4. Unity Committee Minutes.
5. Letter from TUCSA to the Minister of Labour, 29/3/60.
6. Minutes of NEC meeting 14/11/57.
7. *Rand Daily Mail,* 6/10/54.
8. Council of Non-European Trade Unions consisting of 19 unions in 1954.
9. E. Feit *The South African Congress of Trade Unions,* p.2.
10. *Garment Worker,* 18/4/58.
11. Minutes of 5th NEC Meeting, 6/9/57.
12. Minutes of NEC Meeting, 18/2/57.
13. 1956 Annual Conference Minutes, p.39.
14. Minutes of NEC Meeting, 9/12/57.
15. Letter from SACTU to TUCSA, 18/1/62.

16.   Minutes of NEC Meeting, 8/12/58.
17.   NEC Minutes 9/12/57.
18.   Mentioned in correspondence 1954/55.
19.   Correspondence 1956.
20.   1958 Annual Conference Minutes, Presidential Address.
21.   Quoted in letter from the General Secretary to President, 1/3/57.
22.   Minutes of NEC Meeting, 12/54.
23.   Minutes of NEC Meeting, 5/12/55.
24.   Correspondence, 1956/57.
25.   These details are mentioned because TUCSA held that 'the series of coincidences which followed the declaration of the industry as essential are so peculiar as to make it difficult to avoid the conclusion that those coincidences are not unconnected with the declaration itself.' (1960 Annual Conference Minutes, NEC Report.)
26.   Correspondence 19/2/60.

REGISTERED TRADE UNIONS AND WESTERN CAPE WORKERS

DAVE LEWIS

The marked lack of analysis of registered trade unions in contemporary literature in South Africa, whilst generally regrettable, is of particular political significance in the case of the Western Cape. The failure to take account of registered unions is ultimately explicable in terms of the dominance of a particular ideology. There is, in other words, a cetain 'conventional wisdom' (i.e. ideology) surrounding registered unions which characterises these unions in terms of an all too simple identification with 'white workers'. The exceptional characteristics of the Western Cape and Natal (where a number of 'coloured' and Indian workers are members of registered unions) are usually noted but only as a deviation from the empirically defined norm. Those who attempt to analyse the 'self-evident' identification between registered unions and white workers predictably resort to a variety of ideological assertions usually revolving around notions of 'white governments' with their *electoral dependence* upon and *racial empathy* with 'white workers'.[1] It follows then that the supposedly exceptional features of the Cape's trade union structure will often be explained with reference to the 'relatively liberal Cape tradition'.

Now this paper certainly does not attempt to deny the operation of ideology — in fact in certain of the key issues raised in this paper (for example, the 1956 legislation segregating the registered 'mixed' unions) the importance of ideological factors comes to the fore.[2] But, simultaneously, we must also emphasise the *skill composition* of the workforce and the changing *labour process,* and particularly, we must situate the trade union movement within the *pertinent political arena,* if we are to understand correctly the question of worker organisation in the Western Cape.

The following section of the paper looks briefly at the pertinent facets of the 'industrial conciliation' legislation, particularly those prescribing the conditions for membership of registered trade unions; I then attempt to describe the skill composition of the unions' membership; finally, I attempt, somewhat tentatively, to understand the dominance of skilled workers in, or rather, the relative neglect of unskilled workers by, the registered unions.

WORKING CLASS ORGANISATION IN THE WESTERN CAPE

a) The Legislative Framework

The legislative framework governing the important aspects of trade union activity in South Africa is familiar to most readers. I will however briefly summarise some of the major provisions dealing with the pre-conditions for membership of registered unions.

The position in respect of African workers is clear — from the first the legislation was geared towards excluding African workers from membership of registered unions. Various loopholes in succeeding Industrial Conciliation Acts permitted some African membership but the 1956 Industrial Conciliation Act, by defining 'employee' as '. . . any person (other than a native) . . .' ensured a total prohibition of African membership in the registered unions. There were no provisions explicitly governing the membership of 'coloured' and Indian workers — they were defined as employees in terms of the Act and could and did belong to the same registered unions as white workers.[3] Thus, for present purposes, we must pay close attention to the provisions of the 1956 Act in so far as it prohibited the registration of any new 'mixed' unions, i.e. unions in which the members of more than one racial group were represented. This is, of course, of particular importance in the Western Cape where a large proportion of the 'coloured' workforce is employed and where the decision to separate the registered 'mixed' unions met with widespread opposition. We will briefly examine the lengthy debate surrounding the separation of the registered unions. However, what is important to bear in mind is that, whilst separation of the unions may or may not have affected the economic bargaining position of both white and 'coloured' trade union members (and one certainly assumes that this division *would* have detrimentally affected their bargaining strength), it had no discernible effect on the mass of unorganised 'coloured' workers. In other words, whilst the racial definitions imposed by the 1956 Act may have created a divide within the ranks of the already organised, largely skilled workers, they did not affect the relationship between 'coloured' skilled, semi-skilled and unskilled workers. Thus broad ideological factors, in this particular case, the racist definitions of the Industrial Conciliation Act, certainly divide the ranks of the working class but they are not the only or necessarily the most important divisions. The technical division of labour itself is responsible for economic, ideological and political divisions within the working class ranks, and when we attempt to understand the marked lack of organisation of eligible unskilled 'coloured' workers we will have to look beyond the legislative imposition of racial categories.

To return, however, to the 1956 Act. Section 4[6] provides that

> After the commencement of the act no trade union shall be registered under this section
> (a) in respect of both white persons and coloured persons; or
> (b) if membership of such union is open to both white persons and coloured persons.[4]

Existing 'mixed' unions were not compelled to deregister although the legislation, by a variety of means, attempted to facilitate and 'encourage' the process of separation — particularly the Act prohibited multi-racial union meetings and stipulated that in the case of a mixed union the executive had to be all-white. The Minister was empowered to grant exemptions from these provisions.

The state's reasoning behind the separation of the 'mixed' unions is to be found in the report of the 1951 Industrial Legislation Commission whose recommendations in respect of the racial composition of trade unions were, without significant exception, incorporated in the 1956 Act. It is interesting to note that most of the evidence presented to the Commission rejected division of the unions. The evidence presented to the Commission revealed three major arguments in favour of retaining mixed unions:

1. The Western Province Federation of Labour Unions and the Trades and Labour Council, representing between them the great majority of the older craft dominated unions and hence including many of the unionised 'coloured' workers in their ranks, were strongly opposed to separation. They asserted that separate unions, by breaking the cohesion of the artisans, would facilitate wage undercutting and hence endanger the economic position of their members. The Commission rejected this argument and held that in 'mixed' unions the skilled workers' position would be threatened by the

standards of the 'majority'. The Commissioners referred particularly to the case of the clothing industry, and it is possible, in this instance to sustain their argument. However, their argument is sustained *not* because the union in the clothing industry is dominated by 'coloured' workers but rather because it is dominated by unskilled and semi-skilled workers who would undoubtedly favour acceleration of the process of job dilution. In other words, in a single union of clothing workers the demands of the majority of unskilled and semi-skilled workers might threaten the immediate economic interests of the skilled workers. If racial separation is at all capable of allaying this threat it will succeed in so far as the skilled workers are white. The Commission's argument is not convincing but when it is bolstered by the rate for the job and job reservation it probably offers the artisan, both 'coloured' and white, the same degree of protection as that envisaged by the unions. The sectional interests of the craft dominated unions are clearly revealed by the nature of their objections to separation of the unions.

2. Both organised (registered) labour and capital, but particularly the latter, stressed the added difficulty of negotiating with more than one union and contended that separation of the unions would endanger the Industrial Council system. The Commission, quite correctly, dismissed this argument — they pointed out that it was common practice for more than one union to be represented at an Industrial Council sitting, adding that any difficulties which might arise could be overcome by the formation of co-ordianting committees of the trade unions concerned.

3. The third argument revolved around the notion of 'freedom of association' and its protagonists — inter alia, the Trades and Labour Council and many individual unions — argued that the envisaged separation seriously threatened this 'fundamental right'. The Commission countered this argument by referring to a variety of 'red peril' fears and in fact asserted that unqualified freedom of association in a multi-racial society is conducive to workers' solidarity only in terms of a 'Marxian-Communistic' philosophy. The Commission also provided some totally spurious evidence purporting to prove that white and 'coloured' workers had no desire to associate in 'mixed' unions and that any willingness to do so was prompted by the alleged 'leftist-leanings' of the majority of the leaders of the 'mixed' unions. We should not, however, be tempted to dismiss the red bogy as mere sophistry — during the thirties and forties the Communist Party and other 'left-wing' groups and indivi-

duals were particularly active in some of the Western Cape unions. It is highly likely that this 'leftist' activity prompted the state to separate the unions, hence dividing working class organisations under 'leftist' influence.

Thus, in summary, in 1924 the Industrial Conciliation Act formally introduced a division into working class ranks by excluding the great bulk of the largely unskilled African workforce from the ambit of the Act. Thus registered unions — particularly those in secondary industry, largely comprised skilled white and 'coloured' workers and specifically excluded the largely unskilled African workers. In practice the unions did, and still do, exclude the 'coloured' unskilled workers — they were unions defined principally by the skilled rather than the racial composition of their membership. In 1956 a division was introduced into the ranks of the registered unions by prohibiting the registration of 'mixed' unions and encouraging the separation of those already in existence. The 'coloured' workers were *not* 'deregistered'; a step which would have placed them in the same position vis à vis unions as African workers, they were rather distinguished from white workers.

Certainly the divisions introduced into trade union ranks by the 1956 Act constituted a gross interference with 'freedom of association'. As such, it undoubtedly constituted an attack upon the workers' ability to unite cohesively and the opposition of progressive forces to this reactionary measure is to be commended. But if we are to explain divisions within working class ranks in the Western Cape we must go further. It is not enough to argue that the racist characteristics of the dominant ideology have been successfully employed to divide the working class, for, in fact, a corollary of the argument would assert that the now separate 'coloured' unions would inevitably and quite 'naturally' seek to incorporate *all* 'coloured' workers in their ranks — in other words, if ideological factors emphasising race are sufficient to divide a multi-racial workforce, then by the same token they should suffice to unite all workers of the same race. That the latter is manifestly not the case in the Western Cape serves to indicate that a more penetrating enquiry is necessary — it in fact indicates quite clearly that if one argues that racist ideology alone divides 'coloured' and white workers, then one is guilty of accepting a variant form of the same ideology. As one might justifiably argue that if the Trades and Labour Council and the Western Province Federation of Labour Unions had been genuinely concerned with 'freedom of association' and 'worker solidarity' they would have devoted some of their attention to more serious divisions within working class ranks. Concern with the lack of organisation of unskilled 'coloured' workers and the relationship of 'coloured' and African workers is noticeably absent from their various pamphlets, memoranda, minutes of evidence, etc., decrying, in the name of 'freedom of association', the devision of the 'mixed' unions. We must therefore look at the other, neglected, factors dividing the working class into unionised skilled workers and unorganised unskilled workers.

b) Trade Union Membership

The argument advanced in this section of the paper will be familiar to most readers and, although never rigorously verified, generally accepted on an *a priori* basis. I will argue that the registered unions, both the racially exclusive unions and the 'mixed' unions, are dominated by skilled workers — that they have always been dominated by skilled workers and that, with notable exceptions, these essentially functional criteria still determine the composition of union membership to this day.

Our concern, is, of course, entirely with the manufacturing and construction sectors which, in output and employment terms, dominate the Western Cape economy. A breakdown of the Western Cape and national manufacturing sectors reveals that, in terms of their contribution to national employment and output, four industries are of primary importance in the Western Cape: food, beverages and tobacco; textiles and clothing; paper and printing; leather. Between 1960 and 1970 all of these sectors maintained and at times increased their share of national output and employment. In terms of the Western Cape economy food and beverages and clothing and textiles dominate — in 1967/68 food and beverages' share of the Western Cape's total output and employment stood at 18,6% and 28,8% respectively and textile and clothing contributed 32,3% and 21,1% of the Western Cape's output and employment totals. On the other hand the contribution of the Western Cape in the heavy industrial sector is markedly weak.

Racially disaggregated regional employment statistics are highly unreliable — nevertheless census data indicate the historically dominant position of the 'coloured' worker in the industries of the Western Cape. Firstly, unlike other regions of the country, the 'coloured' artisan is an important component of the total artisan workforce in the Western Cape — this is particularly true of the construction sector and the furniture industry. Furthermore the dominant position of the 'coloured' worker in the Western Cape workforce is not of recent origin — Trapido provides evidence of their importance as early as 1905; Simons cites the importance of skilled 'coloured' workers in the Cape as one of the fundamental distinctions between the Cape and the rest of the country; Leslie provides statistics indicating that by 1930, 90% of the unionised painters, plasterers and furniture workers were 'coloured', the great majority being artisans. In the bricklaying and carpentry trades 50% and 40% respectively of the unionised workforce were 'coloured' as were 60% of the unionised leather workers. Secondly, again unlike the rest of the country, the 'coloured' workers dominate the semi-skilled and unskilled workforce of the Western Cape's dominant industries, viz. clothing/textiles and food/beverages. The dominant position of the 'coloured' workforce — artisan, semi-skilled and unskilled — in the dominant industries in the Western Cape is the important factor accounting for the relatively liberal outlook of many of the unions in the Western Cape.

What implications does the racial composition of the Western Cape have for union policy and practice? Unfortunately regional data on trade union membership are not available. Nevertheless we are able to assume that the majority of unionised 'coloured' workers will be employed in the Western Cape although Indian union members will largely be employed in Natal — the number of unionised Indian workers has increased rapidly over the past twenty years, but they still comprise somewhat less than one-third of all unionised 'coloured' and Indian workers. Thus although the union membership figures are only available on a national basis, the Western Cape is undoubtedly sufficiently representative of the total unionised 'coloured' workforce to permit broad generalisation in respect of union policy and practice.

It is not possible to assess accurately the effect which the 1956 legislation has had on registered trade union membership. Although the legislation has probably not had much effect on total union membership or, for that matter, on the racial composition of the total unionised workforce, it has undoubtedly affected the racial composition of a great many individual unions. Most of the 'mixed' unions are either predominantly white or predominantly 'coloured' — there are not many that are representative of a large number of workers of both races. An important factor accounting for this tendency is the Minister's power to grant exemptions from the provisions of the 1956 Act, i.e. where the union is numerically dominated by 'coloured' members the Minister may permit the election of 'coloured' members to the executive or he may permit joint (i.e. multiracial) union meetings to be held. Thus many of the unions which are only nominally 'mixed' have remained so because they have been exempted from some of the provisions of the Act. There are, of course, exceptional cases where unions representing a large number of both white and 'coloured' members have elected to remain 'mixed'; the Boilermakers' Union being the best example. Nevertheless the provisions of the Act have 'encouraged' many of the larger unions to separate — the decision of the National Union of Distributive Workers (NUDW) to split into the white NUDW and the 'coloured' National Union of Commercial and Allied Workers (NUCAW) is a clear example of successful legal pressure. The views of some of the co-ordinating bodies will have also prompted separation in certain cases — the Confederation of Labour does not accept affiliation of 'mixed' unions — SACTU encouraged its unions to separate in the belief that 'coloured' workers would achieve more in separate unions in which they would be entitled to executive membership. It is important to note that SACTU attempted, unsuccessfully, to encourage the formation of unregistered unions representative of all races, particularly 'coloured' and African workers; in 1954 the first TUCSA president, Rutherford, referred to the threatened separation of the unions as '. . . the most serious threat of all to the Movement'. The following year Rutherford indicated that while his organisation was prepared to accept legislation requiring segregated branches and meetings, they were not prepared to accept many of the important provisions of the proposed legislation, particularly the registration of breakaway unions and the appropriation of part of the original union funds by the breakaway union. Basically TUCSA was concerned with maintaining the cohesion of the artisan dominated unions and, to this day, includes the majority of 'mixed' and 'coloured' unions within its ranks.

Nevertheless the point remains that, 'mixed' or 'separate', the unions continue to be dominated by the skilled fragment of the workforce, or, in particular unions, by the operative or semi-skilled component — they do not incorporate the bulk of the working class. Now this is obviously true on a national level — Africans are not permitted to form or join registered trade unions and thus the bulk of the unskilled labour force is automatically excluded from registered unions. However, even given the lack of organisation of African workers, the existing registered 'mixed' and 'coloured' unions in the Western Cape do not appear to have made significant inroads into the semi-skilled and, certainly, unskilled workforce, a great proportion of which is 'coloured' and therefore eligible for union membership.

Table 1 indicates a steady increase in the numbers unionised. The unionised white workers has increased steadily although the number of unionised 'coloured' workers has increased at a noticeably faster rate — column 4 of the table shows the steady increase in the 'coloured' component of the total unionised workforce. This increase in the numbers unionised and, particularly, the change in the racial composition of the unionised workforce can, in part, be explained by occupational mobility. In the words of one prominent unionist, 'the workers have moved up into the unions, the unions have not moved down into the workforce'. Changes in the labour process will certainly have led to the displacement of part of the artisan workforce and, to a smaller extent, part of the unskilled component, simultaneously accentuating the role of the semi-skilled operative. It is reasonable to assume that a number of skilled workers have, in some degree, moved into a supervisory position and, as such, have moved out of the union, and that a number of unskilled 'coloured' workers have moved into the operative and other semi-skilled positions and, hence, have possibly moved into the union, thus explaining the more rapid rate of growth of the unionised 'coloured' workers. In particular industries this appears to have been exactly the case — in the distributive trade, for example, the white union, the NUDW, has weakened whilst the 'coloured' union, the NUCAW, has grown rapidly and the explanation offered is exactly that suggested above.

Because of the lack of comparative and regional data it will be difficult to prove rigorously that changes in union membership have been caused by the growth of the Western Cape industries and the accompanying changes in the labour process — in the construction industry in 1968 the Manpower Report of the Department of Labour classified 15 360 'coloured' workers as artisans and in the same year total 'coloured' unionisation in the industry was approximately 10 700. By 1973 'coloured' artisans in the building trades numbered 25 187 and total union membership numbered 16 844, the respective growth rates between 1968 and 1973 being approximately 63% and 58%; in 1973 in the furniture trade 'coloured' artisans numbered 3 452, the number of operatives and semi-skilled workers approximately 8 550 and total 'coloured' union membership numbered approximately 8 500. Comparable union membership and employment statistics are not generally available but it appears obvious that the 'mixed' and 'coloured' unions concentrate for the large part on the skilled, and, in selected instances, semi-skilled workers, and the unskilled workers remain unorganised. The craft or artisan dominated unions in the Western Cape, — for example the South African Woodworkers Union and the Western Province Building Workers Union — generally operate in industries where the 'coloured component of the workforce has been prominent, if not dominant, both in the industry as a whole and in the artisan workforce, for a significant period of time. There are not legal barriers preventing, for example, the Western Province Building Workers Union from organising the large number of unskilled 'coloured' labourers working in the building industry — many of the established 'coloured' and 'mixed' unions emerged as craft unions and they have retained this skilled orientation to the present day.

In the metal and machinery and motor industries there are relatively few 'coloured' artisans — 5 000 'coloured' and 124 000 white artisans — although there are approximately 36 000 'coloured' operative and semi-skilled workers. 'Coloured' unionisation in these industries constitutes a small part of total 'coloured' employment and once again appears to incorporate the artisans and a small part of the semi-skilled workforce. In the leather industry 'coloured' operative and other semi-skilled workers dominate and union membership in relation to total semi-skilled employment is significant.

The Cape Town Municipal Workers Association is, in some sense, an exceptional case. It is a well established union of 'coloured' workers. It has approximately 9 500 members, skilled, semi-skilled and unskilled, although the latter two categories of workers are clearly dominant. A closed-shop agreement is in force in respect of all council employees in Cape Town.

It is difficult to assess the situation prevailing in the Western Cape's dominant industries. Both food/beverages and clothing/textiles are not craft dominated industries although the proportion of unskilled labourers is likely to be greater in respect of the former than the latter. The Garment Workers Union of the Western Province, which is also party to a closed-shop agreement, is the largest union in the country with a total membership of 35 406 members, 34 713 of whom are 'coloured' workers. The union obviously includes a large number of semi-skilled and unskilled workers in its ranks. However, the position of this union is unclear — I shall comment briefly on the Garment

241

Workers' Union in my concluding remarks. Suffice it to say that press reports indicate that a significant element of the rank and file of the union is extremely dissatisfied with the union leadership. Nationally, approximately 84% of the 'coloured' garment workers are unionised. Only about 25% of the textile workers in the country are unionised although it appears that the Western Cape is the backbone of the Textile Workers' Industrial Union. Union organisation in the food and beverages industry is extremely weak. Approximately 30% of the 'coloured' workers in the national food industry are organised and the proportion unionised in the beverages industry is negligible.

Thus it would appear that where the number of 'coloured' artisans is dominant in relation to total artisan employment in the industry the 'mixed' or 'coloured' unions are narrowly craft dominated and a large number of eligible unskilled 'coloured' workers are excluded from the unions — the construction unions exemplify this state of affairs; where the 'coloured' workers are dominant in the semi-skilled and operative categories, the unions, apparently the National Union of Leather Workers and the Garment Workers' Union are examples, have organised the semi-skilled workers but, I must stress, only where the 'coloured' component of the artisan workforce is not significant. Finally, where the industry is dominated by unskilled 'coloured' workers the unions tend to be extremely weak — the food and beverages industry offers a clear example. Apparently the only exception to this pattern is the Cape Town Municipal Workers' Association which represents a large number of artisans, semi-skilled and unskilled workers.

Summary and Conclusions

Unreliable data notwithstanding, it appears that the registered union ranks are dominated by skilled, and, in select instances, semi-skilled workers, despite the presence of a large number of eligible unskilled workers. The slight changes that have occurred appear to have been determined by a changing labour process (rather than by any change in union policy) and with some artisans and other skilled workers moving into supervisory positions (and hence moving out of the union) and unskilled workers moving into 'acceptable' semi-skilled positions. There is, however, considerable doubt as to the significance of this movement — certainly the number of unionised workers as a proportion of the total white and 'coloured' workforce has declined and it is unlikely that the reverse process has occurred in any particular sector of the economy. The 1956 legislation separating

242

the unions has had the effect of introducing an essentially ideological division into the ranks of the unionised 'coloured' and white workers. Whilst the lack of a common organisation has certainly concretised this ideology and impaired the unionised workers' ability to confront the employers, it has not prompted the registered unions to salvage their lost solidarity by looking to the unskilled and semi-skilled workers.

These conclusions obviously beg an important question: we have to ask ourselves why the unions have riveted their attention upon the most skilled fragment of the workforce, why they have chosen to exclude the eligible unskilled workers from their ranks? I can do little more than offer several tentative suggestions.

One possible explanation — though decidedly historicist — has, in fact, been outlined above. The 'mixed' and 'coloured' unions in the Western Cape have been dominated by skilled craftsmen since at least the turn of the century — 'coloured' workers were thus admitted to the unions because they were firmly established in most of the important trades. The relative liberalism of most of the Cape unionists and white wage-earners is thus not to be explained by the climate of the fair Cape but rather by the expedient grasping of particular crucial opportunities. Craft unions will only open their ranks to semi-skilled workers when the job of artisan has been irreversibly diluted or fragmented and this has undoubtedly occurred in a number of cases. But in terms of the prevalent economistic 'craft-type' perspective there is no *a priori* reason for opening their ranks to unskilled workers — it is obviously far simpler to organise relatively stable employed skilled workers than to organise lowly paid, often unemployed labourers. And undoubtedly the simplest way of resolving any economically grounded conflict which might arise between skilled and unskilled workers is to keep the conflict out of the union.

Furthermore, the domination of craft or skilled unions reinforces itself. For example, if the skilled unions are dominant it is obvious that the co-ordinating bodies will be dominated by the immediate economic interests of the skilled workers. Thus when bus fares were raised recently in Cape Town it appears that several of the skilled unions were able to arrive at an amicable agreement with management whereby their real earnings were unaffected — when the leader of a predominantly semi-skilled and unskilled union publicly objected to the increase in bus fares he provoked opposition from the leadership of one of the co-ordinating bodies on the grounds that the interests of skilled workers had been satisfactorily accomodated by management at the same time that the bus fares had been increased. The co-ordinating bodies' overt support of the dominant skilled unions thus increases the difficulties faced by the unskilled unions in attempting to secure the economic demands of their members.

Secondly, if we are to understand correctly the priorities and policies of the registered unions we have to situate them within the political struggles of the time — struggles between the state and the various political organisations actively co-operating with the unions; conflicts between the various political organisations supposedly sympathetic to the interests of the broad mass of workers; struggles within the power bloc, between the dominant classes. I will attempt to deal briefly with only one facet of the political struggle, the conflict between the state and the political organisations active in the trade union movement. This does not attempt to deny the critical importance of divergences within the power bloc and within the organisations politically active in the Cape (particularly in the forties and fifties) but analysis of these conflicts must remain the subject of further research.

In some sense, the question of the conflict between the state and the political groups or individual members of political groups alleged to be co-operating with the unions is clear, and the government's views are crystallised in the action taken against trade unionists immediately after the passing of the Suppression of Communism Act. Horrell records that

> In January 1956 the Minister told the House of Assembly that, by then, the names of 75 trade union officials had been placed on the liquidators' lists . . . Of these 56 had been ordered to resign from their union. Since then, hundreds of other trade unionists who were never members of the Communist Party have been banned on the ground that the Minister considered them to be furthering the aims of Communism as broadly defined in the Act. These persons are precluded from continuing union activities. (pp 14-15)

It is generally assumed that action taken by the state against these organisations and individuals reflects antagonism towards any attempt to assist in the organisation of African workers. Although this may be the case, it is equally true to say that such action has severely retarded the development of unions of which unskilled 'coloured' workers were members. Clearly the Communist Party itself played an extremely active part in the organisation of unskilled workers — both African and 'coloured' — in the Western Cape. They together with other organisations, like the Coloured Unemployment League, were involved in trade union activity in the depression of the thirties and their pioneering activity in this period produced a healthy crop of unions of unskilled workers in later years. Communist trade unionists like Ray Alexander, Gomas, La Guma and others were instrumental in the formation of many unions including the S.A. Railway and Harbour Workers' Union with incorporated approximately 1 500 unskilled stevedores and railway workers. In later years Ray Alexander's Food and Canning Workers' Union flourished in the Western Cape and, in general, the Communist Party, assisted by the African Federation of Trade Unions, engaged in considerable activity amongst unskilled workers in the Western Cape. These organisations and individuals were subjected to considerable harassment, leaders were imprisoned and later banned in terms of the Suppression of Communism Act. The unions in which these individuals and organisations were active were, by and large, isolated from the mainstream of trade union activity in the Western Cape and were subjected to severe criticism by the established unions and co-ordinating bodies, most notably by the leaders of the Cape Federation. In the mid-fifties some of these unions affiliated to SACTU which included in its ranks unregistered African unions and several 'coloured' and African workers. SACTU officials and member unions suffered acute harassment — it is claimed that official hostility towards SACTU coupled with the open antagonism of many of the established unions and co-ordinating bodies enabled employ ers to ride roughshod over many of the member unions' minimum economic demands.

Thus the action of the state, if not explicitly directed at the organisation of 'coloured' workers, has certainly had the effect of retarding the development of organisations of unskilled workers — both African and 'coloured' in the Western Cape. I do not, of course, suggest that these two factors, the historical dominance of craft unions and the repressive action of the state — of themselves account for the lack of organisation of unskilled workers, but they are of critical importance. One registered union in the Western Cape has successfully organised the mass of semi-skilled and unskilled 'coloured' workers within its sphere of authority, the Garment Workers' Union. It is not without significance that in the early years of the GWU's life a massive confrontation between the then progressive forces from the Transvaal Union (led by Solly Sachs) on the one hand, and the then entrenched Cape leadership on the other, resulted in victory for the latter. Nor is it without significance that this supposedly powerful union appears to be torn by a conflict between

245

elements of the rank and file and the union bureaucracy — the union has not attracted the hostility of the state, but nor has it attracted the support of an articulate element of its rank and file.

Thus, in conclusion, we have seen that the 1956 legislation, separating the 'mixed' unions, whilst a flagrant violation of 'freedom of association', only directly affects the position of the skilled workers. It probably reduces their bargaining power and, in a more general sense, undoubtedly assists in bolstering the racist ideology separating whites and 'coloureds'.

There are other factors which drive a wedge between the 'coloured' workers of the Western Cape and which have given rise to a unionised skilled workforce and an unorganised unskilled mass — interestingly, many of the unions which vehemently opposed the racial separation of the unions in 1956 have not attempted to repair the rift between their members and the unorganised, but eligible, unskilled workers. But, without doubt, the critical division in the Western Cape is that existing *within* the ranks of the semi-skilled and unskilled workforce — I refer, of course, to the division between 'coloured' and African workers. Organisation of unskilled workers in the Western Cape must ultimately incorporate both 'coloured' and African workers.

In the past the difficulties have proved enormous — racist ideology certainly operates as an important wedge, and, moreover, as Alexander and Simons have pointed out, 'Coloured, Indians and Africans have a common interest . . . But their statuses are unequal. Coloured and Indians, but not Africans, *may* form and join registered unions and take part in collective bargaining under statute. As long as the registration of a union confers a real or imagined advantage on its members, it is unlikely that Coloured and Indian workers will adopt the course open to any union of not seeking registration.' (p. 25.)

FOOTNOTES

Most of the research for this article was completed in the first half of 1975.

1.　　A refreshing departure from this sort of ideological stress is to be found in Rob Davies' excellent work. See, for example, his article entitled 'The Class Character of South Africa's Industrial Conciliation Legislation', Section 2.

2.　　In fact, it might be argued that in any discussion where the 'coloured' people constitute an important object of the analysis, ideological factors, by definition, come to the fore.

3.　　There was, of course, nothing to prevent any union restricting its membership to a particular racial group. Also membership qualifications are not only racially defined — the Act also stipulates that a union has to be registered in respect of a particular occupation or industry. This effectively prevents the registration of a general workers union.

4. For the purpose of the Act 'coloured' is defined to include 'coloured' and Indian workers.

Table 1

Number of Unions and Membership by Race — 1950-1974.

Number of Members

Year	No. of Unions	All Races (1)	White (2)	Coloured & Asiatic (3)	(3) as % of (1) (4)
1950	168	355 362	284 076	71 286	20,1
1951	166	365 117	288 536	76 581	21,0
1952	170	376 800	296 906	79 894	21,2
1953	169	376 890	295 825	81 065	21,5
1954	165	377 159	291 355	84 804	22,5
1955	166	394 008	304 107	89 901	22,7
1956	171	406 971	312 566	94 405	23,2
1957	182	414 580	313 184	101 396	24,5
1958	183	420 101	319 085	101 016	24,
1959	172	429 669	328 188	101 481	23,6
1960	166	440 473	332 623	107 837	24,5
1961	172	444 727	333 295	111 432	25,1
1962	171	449 940	335 271	114 713	25,5
1963	172	466 686	344 652	122 034	26,1
1964	171	489 392	355 219	134 173	27,4
1965	168	512 618	367 714	144 910	28,3
1966	168	523 383	375 229	148 154	28,3
1967	169	542 763	386 438	156 325	28,8
1968	171	554 352	392 719	161 633	29,2
1974	174	618 694	411 952	206 742	33,4

Compiled from the following sources:

Bureau of Statistics:
Special Report No. 236 — Financial Years 1957-58; 1958-59.
Special Report No. 263 — Financial Years 1959-60; 1960-61; 1961-62.
Special Report No. 277 — Financial Years 1961-62; 1962-63; 1963-64.
Report No. 292 — Financial Years 1962-63; 1963-64; 1964-65.
Report No. 01-56-01 — Financial Years 1963-64; 1964-65; 1965-66.
Report No. 01-56-06 — Financial Years 1964-65; 1965-66; 1966-67.

D. Horner, *Registered Trade Unions in South Africa,* 1974.

Selected Bibliography

R. L. Alexander H. J. and Simons, *Job Reservation and the Trade Union* (Enterprise, 1959).

M. Horrell, *South Africa's Workers: their organisations and patterns of employment* (SAIRR 1969).

R. Leslie, 'Coloured Labour and Trade Unionism in Cape Town', *The Journal of the Economic Society of South Africa* Vol. III (2) (1930).

S. Trapido, 'White Conflict and Non-White Participation in the Politics of the Cape of Good Hope, 1853-1910' (unpublished Ph.D., London, 1970).

H. J. Simons, 'The Coloured Worker and Trade Unionism', *Race Relations,* Vol. 9(1) (1942).

Official Reports: Commission of Enquiry Regarding the Cape Coloured Population of the Union UG 54-1937.

Industrial Legislation Commission UG 62-1951.